Crime On-line

Crime On-line

Correlates, Causes, and Context

Edited by

Thomas J. Holt

MICHIGAN STATE UNIVERSITY

CAROLINA ACADEMIC PRESS

Durham, North Carolina

Library of Congress Cataloging-in-Publication Data

Crime on-line : correlates, causes, and context / [edited by] Thomas J. Holt.
    p. cm.
  Includes bibliographical references and index.
  ISBN 978-1-59460-781-3 (alk. paper)
  1. Computer crimes. I. Holt, Thomas J., 1978-
  HV6773.C763 2010
  364.16'8--dc22

                    2010032009

CAROLINA ACADEMIC PRESS
700 Kent Street
Durham, North Carolina 27701
Telephone (919) 489-7486
Fax (919) 493-5668
www.cap-press.com

Printed in the United States of America

Contents

Tables and Figures

Tables

Figures

Acknowledgments

I am grateful to the many individuals whose assistance and contributions to this edited work facilitated its creation, value, and applicability. First, many thanks to the chapter authors whose contributions compose the intellectual core of this work, as well as the reviewers for their invaluable comments. As the empirical investigation of cybercrime gains greater prominence in the social sciences, my hope is that this work will provide guidance and insights to the discipline. Additionally, thanks to the publishing team at Carolina Academic Press, especially Beth Hall for her assistance throughout the creation and submission of this manuscript. Finally, I would like to thank my family and friends, especially Bruce, Ginger, Melissa, Mike, Karen, Adam, and Justin for all of their support throughout this process. The time spent during the holidays and breaks working on this text were challenging, and I appreciate their patience, love, and concern.

Crime On-line

1

Crime On-line: Correlates, Causes, and Context

Thomas J. Holt

In 2005, a small band of hackers intercepted the wireless transmission of customer financial information from two Marshalls department stores in Miami, Florida. Hooking in to this flow of information enabled the hackers to find and access a large database of consumer credit card accounts and other sensitive financial information (Goodin 2007; Roberts 2007). Two years later, the international parent company of Marshalls, TJX, revealed that this breach led to the loss of 45 million consumer credit card records (Roberts 2007). By September 2007, new estimates indicated that more than 94 million accounts were actually stolen, causing approximately $1 billion dollars in damages (Goodin 2007). Court filings indicated that victims of the breach were identified in 13 countries, and consumers in the United States, Canada, and Puerto Rico filed class action law suits that were eventually settled out of court (Brenner 2007). Recently, 11 individuals in the United States, Ukraine, and China have been charged or indicted in this case with counts of fraud, identity theft, and computer intrusion (Vamosi 2008). Two hackers from this group have appeared in federal court related to these charges, and face 20 year sentences and over $1 million dollars in fines (Vamosi 2008).

Such an event is surprising due to the global scope and magnitude of loss, but it is just one of many criminal incidents that occur as a consequence of computer technology and the Internet. News reports have increased worldwide discussing the tremendous impact of computer attacks against businesses and personal web users alike (Furnell 2002; Taylor, Fritsch, Liederbach, and Holt 2010). Press coverage of viruses and malicious software indicate the risks that many computer users face from computer based attacks (Brenner 2008; Wall 2007). There is also growing evidence hacker groups are coming together to create such formal organizations, as with pro-Islamic hacker groups in the Middle East (Brenner 2008; Mena Business Reports 2002). The totality of these issues emphasized the need to understand how modern society can cope with the threats posed by the ubiquity of technology.

In fact, access to computers and high speed Internet connectivity have dramatically changed the way people communicate and do business around the world with far reaching consequences that affect all facets of modern life (Jewkes and Sharpe 2003). Most every critical financial, government, medical, business, and private entity is connected through the global interconnected computer networks which constitute the Internet. As a result, a massive amount of information and resources can be leveraged to benefit consumers and citizens. Businesses depend on the Internet to draw in commerce and make information available on demand. The banking and financial industries have implemented new technology enabling customers to gain electronic access to their funds and manage accounts. Home computers allow individuals to use this technology around the clock with home-based, high-speed dedicated Internet access regardless of their familiarity and skill with computers.

Though the growth and penetration of computer technology has many benefits, it has also spawned a range of deviant and criminal behaviors with unique challenges to law enforcement and the legal system (Wall 1998, 2001; Yar 2005). As noted in the TJX example, the prevalence of networked computers and databases enables individuals to come into contact with a massive number of potential victims with little effort. In fact, one of the common forms of fraud perpetrated on-line is Nigerian email schemes where individuals claim to be foreign princes or bankers who need assistance in moving large sums of money (Holt and Graves 2007; Newman and Clarke 2003; Wall 2004). They request information from the e-mail recipients so that they can reuse the information for identity theft or bank fraud. Criminals can send out millions of e-mails in a short amount of time to identify and solicit potential victims for fraud schemes (Grabosky et al. 2001; Holt and Graves 2007; Newman and Clarke 2003). By casting a wide net of email messages, the offenders increase the likelihood of finding a victim that will respond (Buchanan and Grant 2001; Wall 2004). Thus, email and other computer-mediated communication methods are ideal for fraudsters because even if a small percentage of individuals respond, they can still obtain a significant amount of money or information (see Holt and Graves 2007; Newman and Clarke 2003).

Virtual environments are also an ideal mechanism for attacks against nation states and large groups with minimal investments of time and money (Brenner 2008; Denning 2001). Recent political events in Estonia and Russia provide an excellent opportunity to explore this phenomenon. Specifically, a conflict developed between Russian and Estonian factions in April 2006 when the Estonian government removed a Russian war monument from a memorial garden (Brenner 2008; Jaffe 2006; Landler and Markoff 2008). Russian citizens in Estonia and elsewhere were enraged by this action, leading to protests and violence in the streets of both Estonia and Russia. Computer-based attacks quickly ensued against government and private resources in both nations by computer hackers and citizens (Brenner 2008; Jaffe 2006). This conflict became so large in scope that hackers were able to shut down critical components of Estonia's financial and government networks causing significant economic harm to citizens and industry alike (Brenner 2008; Landler and Markoff 2008).

In addition, computer technology affords criminals a significant degree of anonymity. Individuals can create fictitious user profiles to hide their real identities, as with hackers who create screen names or "handles" that protect their actual identity while engaging in hacking (Jordan and Taylor 1998, 765). Similarly, individuals can use a variety of technology to mask their physical location. For example, individuals who pirate music and media often utilize a technology called torrents as a means to reduce their likelihood of detection (see Holt and Copes 2010). Torrent programs enable individuals to download bits of a larger file, such as a complete album or discography for a musical group or motion picture, from multiple computers making it difficult to trace the original location where the file was found or who actually maintains the media (Holt and Copes 2010).

In light of the significant threat posed by computer and cybercrimes, there is a strong need to identify and understand the nature of on-line criminality, as well as the causes and correlates of cybercrime. Thus, this chapter will provide an overview of computer and cybercrimes, including the complexities of defining these problems and measuring the prevalence and incidence of offenses. A framework to understand and examine cybercrime is also discussed in detail to give some insight into the diverse threats on-line. A brief exploration on the applicability of criminological theories of crime is also provided. Finally, the chapter concludes by outlining the chapters of this book and their contribution.

Defining and Measuring Cybercrime

In order to understand cybercrime, one must first understand the nature of the Internet, on-line environments, and crime. The emergence and ubiquity in computer technology has led criminological scholarship to engage in some debate over this issue. Specifically, Grabosky (2001) argued that crime in cyberspace is "old wine in new bottles," in that traditional forms of offending are enabled through new tools. For example, criminals can very easily engage in identity theft through *low tech* methods, such as stealing personal information from mailboxes or during the commission of a robbery or burglary (Allison, Schuck and Lersch 2005). Offenders may also use *high tech* methods via computers and/or the internet to obtain personal information that is seemingly unprotected by the victim (Holt and Graves 2007; Newman and Clarke 2003). Computer technology simply provides another medium by which such information can be obtained from potential victims (Grabosky 2001).

Wall (1998), however, argued that the structure and power of virtual environments can be perceived as an issue of "new wine, but no bottles" (Wall 1998, 202). Specifically, the global reach of the Internet enables a scale of connectivity unparalleled in history. People can now form virtual communities that span the globe with speed and efficiency that were previously not possible. Individuals with sexual interests that are considered outside of societal norms quickly adapted to on-line environments, where they may operate in relative anonymity without fear of shame or social stigma (Rosenmann and Safir 2006). Technology also acts as a force multiplier, in that computing power and automation allow an individual, or "single agent" to engage in crimes that would have previously involved multiple partners (Pease 2001, 24; Wall 2007). This has forced a shift in the social organization of thieving by decreasing the need for conspirators and divisions of labor, and is leading to a "new 'improved' underworld" where criminals can obtain all manner of resources and engage in crimes (Mann and Sutton 1998, 225; Holt and Lampke 2010). Thus, our traditional models of policing and law must be restructured to adequately deal with the challenges posed by this new environment.

To that end, there is some debate over the terms used to describe crimes involving computers in some fashion. The terms "cybercrime" and "computer crime" have become nearly synonymous, although there is a difference between these two events. Cybercrime refers to crimes "in which the perpetrator uses special knowledge of cyberspace," while computer crimes occur because "the perpetrator uses special knowledge about computer technology" (Furnell 2002, 21; Wall 2001). Despite the differences in these two events, the terms cybercrime and computer crime are frequently treated as interchangeable in popular media and academic literature (Furnell 2002). This work will use the term cybercrime due to the large number of offenses that can occur in on-line environments and the overwhelming number of computers that are connected to the Internet.

It is important to note, however, that these schemes are rather vague and are not the only definitions used by the law enforcement community. The Federal Bureau of Investigation, for example, does not use the classification cybercrime, only *computer crime*, "where the computer is the victim" (Stephenson 2000, 167). The U.S. Department of Justice uses a similarly open definition: "any violation of criminal law that involved the knowledge of computer technology for its perpetration, investigation, or prosecution" (Conly 1989, 6). These terms are both rather broad and obscure. The U.K. police, however, use a more specific typology that distinguishes between "computer-assisted crimes" and "computer-focused crimes" (Furnell 2002, 22). "Computer-assisted crimes" involve computers in a supporting role in the commission of a crime, although the activity could be performed without computer assistance, while incidents called "computer-focused crimes" are a direct result of computer technology such as hacking and viruses (Furnell 2002, 22). This typology presents a clearer explication than other current definitions, and illustrates the wide variety of terms used to classify computer crimes.

One of the most comprehensive definitions applied to computer-based crimes was used by the National Institute of Justice (Stambaugh et al. 2001) in their seminal study on the capacity of state and local law enforcement to handle cybercrime. Before conducting this study, the researchers recognized the complex issues surrounding the measurement and definition of computer-based offenses. Thus, they worked in collaboration with state and local agencies to develop a definition of "electronic crime" that refers to:

> fraud, theft, forgery, child pornography or exploitation, stalking, traditional white-collar crimes, privacy violations, illegal drug transactions, espionage, computer intrusions, or any other offenses that occur in an electronic environment for the purpose of economic gain or with the intent to destroy or otherwise inflict harm on another person or institution (Stambaugh et al. 2001, 2).

A similarly broad definition of cyberterrorism was developed, recognizing any "premeditated, politically motivated attack against information systems, computer programs and data ... to disrupt the political, social, or physical infrastructure of the target" (Stambaugh et al. 2001, 2). The wide range of offenses included in these definitions was meant to provide some standard to assess computer-based crime, though it is unclear how much the definition permeates agency and academic definitions of cybercrime.

Some researchers have utilized a different method to define cybercrimes through comparisons of the laws made by various countries to identify criminal activity in cyberspace. As legislation against cybercrimes has increased dramatically over the past ten years, some agreement has developed regarding what acts are considered illegal on-line. For instance, the Global Cyber Law Survey of fifty countries, including nations in Africa, the Americas, Asia, Europe, the Middle East, and Oceania, found 70 percent of countries with laws against computer crimes had identified seven specific acts as prohibited (Putnam and Elliott 2001, 37). These acts, considered consensus crimes (based on the agreement in many countries that these activities are criminal), include: unauthorized access, computer-mediated espionage, privacy violations with personal data acquisition or use, damage or theft of computer hardware or software, illicit tampering with files or data, computer or network sabotage including denial-of-service attacks and worms, and the use of information systems to commit fraud, forgery, and "traditional crimes" (Putnam and Elliott 2001, 38).

While comparative law analyses provide a helpful starting point for research, it is important to note that few nations actually define what cybercrimes are, only what behaviors constitute them. Most industrialized countries, which are heavily dependent on computers and information networks, are the most likely to have laws against computer crimes. Emerging industrial nations are less likely to have developed such legislation, creating safe havens where cyber criminals can operate with minimal risk of extradition (Brenner 2008; Putnam and Elliott 2001). This disparity in codified law adds to the difficulty of defining cybercrimes transnationally.

The lack of a clear or universal definition for cybercrime is also related to the significant undercounting of cybercrimes (see Holt 2003; Taylor et al. 2010). Part of this is due to user difficulty in recognizing when cybercrimes occur. Failing computer systems and hardware can mimic criminal acts or the results of criminal activities, obfuscating the situation (Symantec 2003; Stephenson 2000). In fact, almost 25 percent of personal computers around the world that use a variety of security solutions have malicious software, such as a virus, loaded into their memory (PandaLabs 2007). Thus, many individuals are victimized despite the presence and use of antivirus software and other protective programs to defend their system against the random nature of damaging computer attacks.

There are also a range of attacks that can occur in the workplace that may go unreported to law enforcement. Many in the general public believe intrusion attempts come largely from hackers outside of computer networks (Furnell 2002). For example, one estimate of losses due to external penetration attempts suggests US companies experienced approximately $8 million dollars of damage in 2006 (Computer Security Survey 2007). This relatively small figure may not reflect all attacks that occur since businesses and financial institutions may lose face by reporting compromised systems (see also Holt 2003; Furnell 2002; Nasheri 2005). As a consequence, the true number and losses attributed to external penetration is unknown, but considered to be relatively significant and substantial (Newman and Clarke 2003).

Research involving case studies of insider attacks suggest that hackers may operate within secure environments as trusted system administrators or security professionals (Cappelli, et al. 2006; Dhillon and Moores 2001; Shaw et al. 1998). The actions employees take to misuse or misappropriate resources may go unnoticed, particularly by individuals with administrative privileges (Cappelli et al. 2006; Dhillon and Moores 2001). Insiders may also surreptitiously steal information or place backdoors in programs that can be accessed to cause damage in case they are fired or mistreated (see Cappelli et al. 2006; Shaw et al. 1998). The attacks individuals engage in can be relatively simple in nature and exploit known flaws in internal systems, though some sophisticated intrusions have been documented (see Cappelli et al. 2006). In these situations, office politics and management may enable cover-ups to occur that can increase the likelihood of non-reporting (see Shaw et al. 1998).

Confusion over where to file reports or complaints also leads to undercounting. As cybercrimes can cross state, territorial, and continental boundaries, jurisdictional issues can arise. In the U.S., for example, the involvement of local or federal law enforcement is dependent upon the crime and the extent of monetary damage to the victim. Unfortunately, many local police departments do not have the tools needed to enforce laws against cybercrime, including knowledge, forensic equipment, and personnel, decreasing the potential for resolution of these crimes (Speer 2000, 267; Stambaugh et al. 2001). Also, if an incident report must be passed from one agency to another after being filed, the likelihood of resolution is further reduced. When expanded to the international level, where both the perpetrator and victim are in different nations, these problems are even greater in magnitude. Questions develop as to who is responsible for the investigation along with other issues that can negatively affect a case, such as "the number of nations involved, the presence or absence of extreme urgency, the existence of consent and the extent to which the data sought is protected by firewalls, passwords, or encryption" (Putnam and Elliott 2001, 62). These complications make undercounting a considerable problem, particularly at the international level when coupled with the absence of computer crime laws in some countries.

An even greater obstacle facing researchers is identifying actual statistical measures for cybercrimes. Relatively few countries produce quality data on these offenses, regardless of their level of industrialization. For example, only two members of the G-8, an organization of economic world powers including the U.S., Canada, France, Germany, Japan, Italy, Russia, and the U.K., produce centralized official cybercrime statistics: the U.K. and Japan. Despite its role as a world superpower, the United States does not provide much data on computer crimes from a centralized outlet (Holt 2003; Goodman 2001).

Such information is notably absent from the FBI's Uniform Crime Report and is just beginning to appear in the National Incident Based Reporting System (see Taylor et al. 2010). As a consequence, there is a significant dark figure of cybercrime that requires further examination in the U.S. and abroad.

Cybercrime Framework

Though there is a paucity of statistics on cybercrime, a growing body of criminological and sociological research has improved our understanding of the forms of cybercrime that exist. One of the most well referenced and constructed frameworks to understand cybercrimes is Wall's (2001) four category typology of computer crime to identify the wide range of behaviors encompassed by computer based crimes.

Cyber-trespass

The first category is cyber-trespass, encompassing the crossing of invisible, yet salient boundaries of ownership on-line. The most notable cybercriminals engaging in acts of trespass are computer hackers due to their desire to penetrate computer systems that they do not own (Furnell 2002; Jordan and Taylor 1998). One of the more comprehensive research definitions identifies hackers as those individuals with a profound interest in computers and technology that have used their knowledge to access computer systems for malicious or ethical purposes alike (see Holt 2007; Schell, Dodge and Moutsatsos 2002). The need for the inclusion of ethical applications lies in the fact that the phrase hacker was originally used as a term of respect for programmers in the 1950s and 60s who had significant computer skill (Jordan and Taylor 1998; Levy 1984; Holt 2007). Modern hackers are, however, commonly tied to costly criminal breaches of computer networks and system boundaries. For example, U.S. businesses lost $7 million dollars due to unauthorized access in 2007 alone (Computer Security Institute 2007).

Hackers are also responsible for malicious software programs, or malware, that automate a variety of attacks and break into computer systems (Furnell 2002). Malware typically includes computer viruses, worms, and Trojan horse programs that alter functions within computer programs and files. These programs can disrupt e-mail and network operations, access private files, delete or corrupt files, and generally damage computer software and hardware (Taylor et al. 2010). In addition, some forms of malicious software can enable identity theft, fraud, and the loss of personal information (Britz 2004; Taylor et al. 2010).

Thus, malware infection poses a significant threat to Internet users around the globe.

The dissemination of viruses across computer networks can be costly due in part to the time spent removing the programs as well as losses in personal productivity and system functions (Symantec Corporation 2003; Taylor et al. 2010). This is reflected in the dollar losses associated with malware infection, as U.S. companies lost approximately $15 million due to viruses in 2006 alone (Computer Security Institute 2007). Because of the interconnected nature of computer systems today, an infected system in one country can spread malicious software across the globe and cause even greater damage. The Melissa virus, for example, caused an estimated $80 million in damages around the globe (Taylor et al. 2010). Thus, cyber-trespass offenses are a significant concern for home users, businesses, and governments alike.

Cyber-deception/Theft

The second and related category within Wall's (2001) typology is cyber-deception and theft. This form of cybercrime includes all the various criminal acquisitions that may occur on-line, particularly for thefts due to trespass. The increased use of on-line banking and shopping sites also allows consumers to transmit sensitive personal and financial information over the Internet (James 2005; Newman and Clarke 2003). This information can, however, be surreptitiously obtained by criminals through different methods such as phishing (James 2005; Wall 2007). In a phishing attack, consumers are tricked into transmitting financial information into fraudulent websites where the information is housed for later fraud (see James 2005; Wall 2007). These crimes are particularly costly for both the individual victim and financial institutions alike, as the Gartner Group estimates that phishing victims in the U.S. lost $3 billion dollars in 2007 alone (Rogers 2007).

In addition, there is an emerging marketplace on-line where computer criminals sell and buy information (Franklin et al. 2007; Honeynet Research Alliance 2003; Thomas and Martin 2006). Specifically, Internet Relay Chat, or IRC, channels and web forums operate where hackers sell significant volumes of data obtained through phishing, database compromises, and other means. Individuals in these sites sell credit card and bank accounts, pin numbers, and supporting customer information obtained from victims around the world in lots of tens or hundreds of accounts (Franklin et al. 2007; Holt and Lampke 2010; Honeynet Research Alliance 2003; Thomas and Martin 2006). Some also sell their services as hackers, and offer cash out services to obtain physical money from electronic accounts (Holt and Lampke 2010). As a consequence, criminals who frequent these markets can quickly and efficiently engage in credit card fraud and identity theft without any technical knowledge or skill (Franklin et al. 2007; Holt and Lampke 2010; Honeynet Research Alliance 2003; Thomas and Martin 2006). In addition, these markets can lead individuals to be victimized multiple times without their knowledge.

Beyond theft due to computer intrusions, there are several different types of fraud that are perpetrated on-line, including electronic auction or retail-based fraud schemes, stock scams, and work-at-home plans (Grabosky and Smith 2001; Newman and Clarke 2003). One of the most prevalent and most costly forms of Internet fraud are advance fee e-mail schemes (Internet Crime Complaint Center 2009; Holt and Graves 2007; Wall 2004). These messages are often referred to as "Nigerian" or "419" scams because the e-mails often come from individuals who claim to reside in a foreign country such as Nigeria or other African nations (Buchanan and Grant 2001; Holt and Graves 2007). The sender claims to need assistance transferring a large sum of money out of their country. In return, the sender will share a portion of the sum with the individual who aids them (Holt and Graves 2007). Victims of this type of fraud often lose thousands of dollars on average, and may be too embarrassed to report their experiences to law enforcement because of the often obviously false nature of the message they responded to (Buchanan and Grant 2001; Newman and Clarke 2003; Wall 2004).

Another high profile form of cyber-theft is digital piracy, or the illegal copying of digital media such as computer software, digital sound recordings, and digital video recordings without the explicit permission of the copyright holder (Gopal et al. 2004). Such files can be easily downloaded from one of many internet file sharing services or web sites and commonly do not stem from a single user. IDATE (2003) has suggested that illegal file sharing accounts for over four times the amount of official sales of sound recordings worldwide. The same report suggested that peer-to-peer (p2p) file sharing accounts for between fifty and ninety percent of all broadband internet traffic in any given day, depending on the time of day.

The financial losses estimated to result from digital piracy are staggering and participation levels in this illegal activity are commonplace, particularly among college students (Hinduja 2001; 2003; Ingram and Hinduja 2008; Morris and Higgins 2009; Rob and Waldfogel 2006; Zentner 2006). For example, the Motion Picture Association of America (MPAA) reported fiscal losses upwards of $6 billion in 2005 from movie piracy in the U.S. alone. Over forty percent of these reported losses were argued to be a result of university students in the U.S. (MPAA 2007). In addition, Siwek (2007) reported that the U.S. sound recording industry loses over twelve billion dollars annually due to piracy, and another $422 million each year in tax revenue that would have been generated via corporate and personal income taxes (Siwek 2007). Taken as a whole, cyber-deception and theft encompass a wide range of activities, each with significant economic impact.

Cyber-porn and Obscenity

The third category within Wall's (2001) typology includes cyber-porn and obscenity. Sexually expressive or explicit materials are readily available across the World Wide Web, though they may not be illegal in certain areas (DiMarco 2003; Wall 2001). As a consequence, on-line pornography has become an extremely lucrative and thriving business (Edelman 2009; Lane 2000). In fact, the pornography industry is intimately tied to the adoption and popularity of various forms of media, particularly VHS and DVD media, webcams, digital photography, and streaming web content (Lane 2000). The Internet has dramatically affected the way that pornographic content is distributed, customers are targeted, and amateur stars are made. For example, estimates from the AVN Media Network, an adult entertainment trade publication, suggest that online adult entertainment in the U.S. reached $2.8 billion in revenue in 2006 alone (AVN Media Network 2008).

The development of the Internet and computer mediated communications has also fostered the growth of a wide range of communities supportive of deviant sexual behaviors. Sexual minorities can identify a wide range of resources, such as newsgroups, web forums, and list serves where individuals can exchange all sorts of information almost instantaneously (DiMarco 2003). On-line spaces also allow individuals to find others who share their interests, creating supportive communities where individuals feel "they are part of a group, from which validation can be drawn, and sexual scripts exchanged" (Rosenmann and Safir 2006, 77). As a consequence, subcultures have developed in cyberspace around myriad acts of sexual deviance (DiMarco 2003; Quinn and Forsyth 2005). For example, the phenomenon of bugchasing has been identified where HIV negative individuals seek HIV positive sex partners (Tewksbury 2003), as well as money slavery where individuals give money to individuals in the hopes of receiving sadistic treatment via e-mail or some other electronic medium (Durkin 2007).

The illegal sex trade has also moved to on-line spaces, such as web sites and forums specifically designed for johns to discuss prostitution in cities around the globe (see Holt and Blevins 2007; Hughes 2003; Sharpe and Earle 2003; Soothill and Sanders 2005). Recent research suggests that the clients of prostitutes use the Internet to share information about their real world experiences with all types of sex workers (Holt and Blevins 2007; Hughes 2003; Sharpe and Earle 2003). Johns reveal their motivations for paying for sex, as well as detailed accounts of their interactions with prostitutes, escorts, and other sex-workers. In addition, johns use these methods to describe and warn others about the presence of law enforcement or particularly active community groups in a given area (see Holt, Blevins and Kuhns 2008). As a result, these on-line forums can provide insight into the nature of displacement and the methods johns use to obviate the wide range of targeted law enforcement strategies to reduce levels of street prostitution (see Scott and Dedel 2006).

One of the most publicly recognized and feared forms of cybercrime within this framework of cyber-porn and obscenity is pedophilia, where individuals seek out sexual or emotional relationships with children (Jenkins 2001). Re-cent media attention has focused on the behavior of pedophiles, creating a sort of panic around the number of sexual predators on-line (Berson 2003; McKenna and Bargh 2000). Despite this increased attention, criminological research has provided significant insight into the ways pedophiles use the In-ternet as a means to facilitate criminal behavior (Durkin 1996, 1997; Durkin and Bryant 1999; Jenkins 2001; Quayle and Taylor 2002). For example, the In-ternet is a vehicle for the identification, trade, and distribution of pornographic and sexual materials, including comic books, stories, pictures, and films (Durkin 1997; Jenkins 2001; Fontana-Rosa 2001; Quayle and Taylor 2002). In addi-tion, computer-mediated communications provide a wealth of potential vic-tims that can be groomed for sexual contact off-line (see Wolak, Finkelhor and Mitchell 2003; Wolak, Mitchell and Finelhor 2004).

The Internet also provides a mechanism for pedophiles to identify and talk with others through usergroups, web forums, and chatrooms (Durkin 1996, 1997; Durkin and Bryant 1999). These sites provide a way for pedophiles to come together to validate their sexual interests, share information about their habits, and find support for their behaviors (Durkin and Bryant 1999; Jenkins 2001). Exchanges between individuals provide information on the ways individuals be-come interested in relationships with children, and how to justify these be-haviors (Durkin and Byrant 1999). For example, on-line communities often use the term "child love" to refer to their attractions, rather than the more derogatory and stigmatizing word pedophile (Durkin 1997; Jenkins 2001).

Cyber-violence

The final form of crime within Wall's (2001) typology is cyber-violence, representing the distribution of a variety of injurious, hurtful, or dangerous materials on-line. For example, individuals have begun to use the Internet as a means to harass or bully others (Bocij 2004; Finn 2004; Holt and Bossler 2009). Harassment can take various forms, such as threatening or sexual messages delivered to an individual privately via e-mail, instant messaging services, or cell phone (see Bocij 2004). The emergence and popularity of social networking websites like Facebook, however, allow individuals to post threatening or hurtful content in public settings for any and everyone to see (see Hinduja and Patchin 2009). The victims of such harassing communications respond in a variety of ways; some view these messages to be nothing more than a nuisance, while others experience significant physical or emotional stress, including depressive symptoms and suicidal ideation (Finkelhor et al. 2000; Finn 2004; Hinduja and Patchin 2009). Estimates of on-line harassment and stalking appear to be on the rise, particularly among adolescent and young adult populations due in part to frequent Internet use (Bocij 2004; Finkelhor et al. 2000; Finn 2004; Hinduja and Patchin 2009; Holt and Bossler 2009). For example, a recent national examination of young Internet users found that six percent of the sample experienced some form of harassment while on-line (Finkelhor et al. 2000). In addition, evidence suggests that having peers who engage in cybercrime increases an individual's risk of harassment (Hinduja and Patchin 2009; Holt and Bossler 2009). Thus, the risk of on-line violence may share similar correlates with real world violence (Holt and Bossler 2009).

The Internet has also become an important resource for political and social movements of all types. Mainstream and alternative political and social movements have grown to depend on the Internet to broadcast their ideologies across the world. Groups have employed a range of tactics depending on the severity of the perceived injustice or wrong that have been performed (see Jordan and Taylor 2004). Often, these virtual efforts develop in tandem with real world protests and demonstrations (see Cere 2003; Jordan and Taylor 2004). For example, the native peoples, called Zapatistas, in Chiapas, Mexico used the Internet to post information and mobilize supporters to their cause against governmental repression (Cere 2003).

Politically-driven groups have also employed hacking techniques to engage in more serious strikes against governments and political organizations (see Furnell 2002). These actions are sometimes called "hacktivism," as the hack or attack is used to promote an activist agenda or express an opinion (Furnell 2002, 44). Their actions may, however, violate the law and produce fear or concern among the general population (Jordan and Taylor 2004). For example, members of a hacktivist group called the Electronic Disturbance Theater developed an attack tool called FloodNet that overloaded web servers and kept others from being able to access their services. This is called a Denial of Service attack, as it keeps people from accessing web content and services. Flood-Net was used against the U.S. Pentagon, as well as other government and business targets as a means of protest against their activities and policies (Shell et al. 2002; Cere 2003).

The most extreme forms of on-line political actions involve individuals using hacking techniques to attack networks, systems, or data under the name of a particular social or political agenda (Furnell 2002, 44). Entrenched and stable organized terrorist groups like Sri Lanka's Tamil Tigers have engaged in acts of cyber-terrorism to disrupt or damage Sri Lankan government computer networks (Denning 2001, 269). Similarly, evidence has been found indicating that Al-Qaida cells amassed hacking tools and equipment to perform cyber-attacks against government resources around the world (Taylor et al. 2010). Thus, there are significant risks and threats from cyber terror and politically motivated crimes on-line.

Criminological Theories of Cybercrime

Given the diverse range of deviance that can occur as a consequence of computers and technology, a growing body of criminological research explores the applicability of traditional theories of crime to offenses in this new environment. One of the most well-known and established criminological theories is Ron Akers' (1998) social learning theory. This framework argues that crime is a learned behavior stemming from the interaction of four factors: deviant associations, definitions, imitation, and differential reinforcement. Specifically, individuals associate with various deviant and non-deviant individuals in the course of their daily life. Those who more closely and frequently associate with deviants are exposed to definitions that support the violation of the law and justify or rationalize criminal behavior. The presence of deviant associations and definitions that favor breaking the law increase an individual's likelihood of imitating the deviant behavior of their peers. Continued participation in deviance occurs depending on how deviant actions are reinforced by parents, peers, and others. For example, if an individual is not punished by parents or law enforcement, and receives encouragement or positive social support from their peers, the likelihood of persistent participation in deviance increases.

Criminological research has found significant support for hypotheses derived from social learning theory to account for various deviant and criminal behaviors (see Akers and Jensen 2006). As a consequence, social learning theory has been frequently applied to cybercrimes, including software and movie piracy (Higgins 2005; Higgins, Fell, and Wilson 2006, 2007; Higgins and Makin 2004; Higgins and Wilson 2006), and computer hacking (Holt, Bossler, and Burruss 2010; Skinner and Fream 1997). There is significant value in social learning theory, as individuals who engage in cybercrime "learn not only how to operate a highly technical piece of equipment but also specific procedures, programming, and techniques for using the computer illegally" (Skinner and Fream 1997, 498). While computer and peripheral device technologies have become more intuitive and user friendly, there is still a degree of education required to effectively engage in computer use and abuse (see Holt 2007; Holt et al. 2010). Thus, social learning theory is an intrinsically important framework to understand cybercrime and deviance.

To that end, the social learning literature on cybercrime has found a strong relationship between deviant peer relationships and individual participation in cybercrime (Holt et al. 2010; Skinner and Fream 1997). In addition, studies examining digital piracy have found a significant connection between deviant friends, the acceptance of deviant definitions toward cybercrime, and piracy (Higgins et al. 2006, 2007; Higgins and Makin 2004; Higgins and Wilson 2006). Individuals with definitions that favor the violation of computer laws or norms are more likely to commit computer deviance (Skinner and Fream 1997). The impact of differential reinforcement and imitation is, however, mixed. The severity of punishment used appears to have some influence on hacking activities (Hollinger 1992; Skinner and Fream 1997), while certainty of punishment appears to reduce the likelihood of digital piracy (Hollinger 1992). Individuals who received positive reinforcement for on-line deviance from parents or teachers also appear more likely to engage in cybercrime (Holt et al. 2010; Skinner and Fream 1997).

Though these studies provide some general insights into the utility of social learning theory to account for cybercrime, there is a need for continuing research examining this issue. Specifically, there have been few applications of this theory to assess computer hacking, on-line harassment, or other types of cybercrime (see Holt et al. 2010). Additionally, most studies of social learning and cybercrime do not include measures for imitation and differential reinforcement (see Holt et al. 2010), but instead focus on differential association and definitions (Higgins 2006; Higgins et al. 2006, 2007; Higgins and Makin 2004; Higgins and Wilson 2006). Thus, future studies must utilize and examine full models of social learning theory to expand our understanding of the correlates of cybercrime offending (Holt et al. 2010; Skinner and Fream 1997, 29).

In addition, few studies have explored the theoretical causes and correlates of cybercrime victimization (see Holt 2003). Over the last decade, cybercrime scholars argued that lifestyle-routine activities theory may be useful to account for victimization in light of its success with street crimes and delinquency (see Grabosky and Smith 2001; McQuade 2006; Newman and Clarke 2003; Pease 2001; Yar 2005). Lifestyle-routine activities theory argues that a motivated offender, an absence of a capable guardian, and suitable target must converge in time and space in order for crime to occur. Motivated offenders are individuals and groups who have both the inclination and ability to commit crime for various reasons (Cohen and Felson 1979). Guardianship relates to the capability of persons and/or objects to prevent motivated offenders from harming the target in some fashion. A target is suitable based in part on its attractiveness to an offender, whether based on monetary value, ease of access, or other intrinsic values (see Cohen and Felson 1979; Lauritsen, Laub, and Sampson 1992). This theory has also demonstrated an important link between victims and offenders, in that those who engage in criminal and deviant behavior are at an increased risk of victimization (see Jensen and Brownfield 1986; Lauritsen et al. 1992; Sampson and Lauritsen 1990).

A small body of research has empirically assessed postulates of lifestyle-routine activities theory to cybercrime, and found some success with different forms of victimization. For example, Holt and Bossler found that routine computer use, including spending more time in on-line chatrooms increased the odds of on-line harassment (Holt and Bossler 2009). Similarly, Choi (2008) found individuals who use the Internet more frequently and engage in risky on-line activities were more likely to experience a malicious software infection. Physical guardianship measures appear to have a mixed impact on victimization. Specifically, antivirus programs and other software do not appear to reduce the risk of on-line harassment (Holt and Bossler 2009). With regard to malicious software infections, Choi (2008) found protective software reduced the risk of infection while Bossler and Holt (2010) found no affect. Individual and peer involvement in on-line deviance also appear directly related to an increased risk of victimization (Bossler and Holt 2010; Choi 2008; Hinduja and Patchin 2009; Holt and Bossler 2009). Taken as a whole, these studies suggest that there may be some similarity in patterns of victimization both on and off-line (Holt and Bossler 2009).

The initial studies examining lifestyle-routine activities theory suggest that this framework may have significant utility to account for the risks and correlates of cybercrime victimization. Further research is, however, needed to improve our understanding of this theory, including research utilizing multiple measures of victimization and computer crime to explore and clarify the relationship between computer-based deviance and cybercrime victimization. Additionally, improved measures of computer use, skill, and ownership are needed to delineate what constitutes risky lifestyles and activities in on-line environments.

The Structure of This Book and Its Contributions

Taken as a whole, there is a need for a diverse body of research to understand the correlates and causes of cybercrime, as well as shifts in deviant behavior that can occur over time as a consequence of technology and the Internet (see also Holt 2007; Mann and Sutton 1998; Quinn and Forsythe 2005). The various chapters and contributors of this book discuss these issues in depth by exploring the spectrum of cybercrimes in detail. The organization of this book follows the structure of Wall's (2001) typology by focusing on cyber trespass, deception, obscenity, and violence.

In Chapter 2, West and her colleagues provide a substantive overview of the research literature concerning computer hackers. Since hackers are the primary actors engaged in cyber-trespass, it is critical that we understand their social world in great detail. What is known about the hacker community is, however, clouded by media reports and social stigma surrounding criminal activity online. Thus, this chapter considers the various ways that researchers define and differentiate hackers, their motivations for hacking, and the social environment that they operate within.

Paul Taylor then provides an examination of the philosophical evolution of hacking relative to technology and social mores. Taylor observes that computer hacking can be deconstructed and understood as a response to social alienation as a result of technology. As a consequence, we can better understand how technology as a means of rapid communication has become valued, rather than the information that is communicated.

In their chapter on cyber-theft, Wilson Huang and Andrea Brockman consider the problem of social engineering, a process where individuals are manipulated into disseminating private information, as a means to facilitate on-line fraud. The authors suggest that social engineers can easily structure email messages to convince prospective recipients to provide sensitive personal information that can be used to commit various acts of theft.

Though hackers and data thieves generate significant public concern, they receive much less attention than the activities of pedophiles and child pornographers in on-line environments. There is significant fear over the presence of child predators in cyberspace, which has spurred a variety of social science research to understand this problem. Marcus Rogers and Kathryn Seigfried-Spellar elaborate on this issue in Chapter 5 through a discussion of frameworks to understand pedophilia and child pornography users and creators. They argue that the existing typologies used to investigate and prosecute child pornography in various countries do not adequately account for the role of technology in the acquisition and use of these materials. Rogers and Seigfried-Spellar provide their own framework in this chapter and detail how it can be used to better combat this problem.

Though pornography and obscene materials have always appeared in on-line environments, few researchers have considered how prostitutes and their clients have utilized the World Wide Web to facilitate paid sexual encounters. Scott Cunningham and Todd Kendall discuss the growing problem of the sex trade in virtual environments in Chapter 6. These authors provide a comprehensive overview of the ways that sex workers use computer technology to solicit and screen clients. In fact, Cunningham and Kendall argue that prostitution is fundamentally changing as a consequence of the Internet, causing a shift in the nature of solicitation and the composition of the sex trade generally.

The use of technology in facilitating sexual encounters is also related to the most common forms of cyber-violence. Catherine Marcum details the problem of on-line harassment, bullying, and stalking in Chapter 7, with a distinct focus on the impact of these crimes among juvenile and college populations. Young people are the most likely to utilize emerging technologies to communicate and connect with others, thereby increasing their risk of exposure to unwanted sexual or aggressive content. She also considers the legislative response to these crimes, and discusses how prosecutions will impact free speech and civil rights.

Marjie Britz provides a critical overview on the most problematic and nebulous form of cyberviolence in Chapter 8: cyberterror. She notes that there is no single definition for this term, though various activities have been labeled as cyberterror. Britz provides an overview of the research literature on this issue from the social and military sciences, and gives various examples of terror incidents to give context to this phenomenon.

The final chapter focuses on the capacity of state and local law enforcement agencies' ability to respond to the various forms of cybercrime discussed throughout the book. Thomas Holt, Adam Bossler, and Sarah Fitzgerald utilize a sample of respondents from police agencies across the United States to understand the number of officers trained to investigate cybercrimes, the types of crimes reported, and officer attitudes toward these offenses and the individuals who participate in these activities. The authors argue that local law enforcement agencies have significantly increased their ability to combat cybercrime, though there are several issues that require improvement and investment.

References

Akers, Ronald L. 1998. *Social learning and social structure: A general theory of crime and deviance.* Boston: Northeastern University Press.

Akers, Ronald L. and Gary F. Jensen. 2006. "The empirical status of social learning theory of crime and deviance: The past, present, and future." In *Taking stock: The status of criminological theory*, eds. Francis T. Cullen, John Paul Wright, and Kristie R. Blevins, 37–76. New Brunswick: Transaction Publishers.

Allison, Stuart F.H., Amie M. Schuck, and Kim Michelle Learsch. 2005. Exploring the crime of identity theft: prevalence, clearance rates, and victim/offender characteristics. *Journal of Criminal Justice* 33: 19–29.

AVN Media Network. 2008. Industry Stats. (February 1, 2009), http://www.avn medianetwork.com/index.php?content_about_industrybuzz.

Berson, Ilene R. 2003. Grooming cybervictims: The psychosocial effects of on-line exploitation of youth. *Journal of School Violence* 2: 5–18.

Bocij, Paul. 2004. *Cyberstalking: Harassment in the Internet age and how to protect your family.* Westport: Praeger.

Bossler, Adam M. and Thomas J. Holt. 2009. On-line Activities, Guardianship, and Malware Infection: An Examination of Routine Activities Theory. *The International Journal of Cyber Criminology* 3: 400–420.

Brenner, Bill. 2007. Banks prepare lawsuit over TJX data breach. (October 7, 2008), http://searchfinancialsecurity.techtarget.com/news/article/0,289 142,sid185_gci1294453,00.html.

Brenner, Susan W. 2008. *Cyberthreats: The Emerging Fault Lines of the Nation State.* New York: Oxford University Press.

Britz, Marjie T. 2004. *Computer Forensics and Cybercrime: An Introduction.* Upper Saddle River, NJ: Prentice Hall.

Buchanan, Jim, and Alex J. Grant. 2001. Investigating and Prosecuting Nigerian Fraud. *United States Attorneys' Bulletin*, November, 29–47.

Cappelli, Dawn, Andrew Moore, Timothy J. Shimeall, and Randall Trzeciak. 2006. Common Sense Guide to Prevention and Detection of Insider Threats. Carnegie Mellon Cylab. (November 1, 2007), http://www.us-cert.gov/ reading_room/prevent_detect_insiderthreat0504.pdf.

Cere, Rinella. 2003. "Digital counter-cultures and the nature of electronic social and political movements." In *Dot.cons: Crime, deviance and identity on the Internet*, ed. Yvonne Jewkes, 147–163. Portland, OR: Willan Publishing.

Choi, Kyung-Schick. 2008. Computer crime victimization and integrated theory: An empirical assessment. *International Journal of Cyber Criminology*, 2: 308–333.

Cohen, Lawrence E. and Marcus Felson. 1979. Social change and crime rate trends: A routine activity approach. *American Sociological Review* 44: 588–608.

Computer Security Institute. 2007. "Computer Crime and Security Survey." (June 3, 2007) http://www.cybercrime.gov/FBI2006.pdf.

Conly, Catherine H. 1989. *Organizing for Computer Crime Investigation and Prosecution*. Washington, DC: National Institute of Justice.

Denning, Dorothy E. 2001. "Activism, hacktivism, and cyberterrorism: The Internet as a tool for influencing foreign policy." In *Networks and Netwars: The Future of Terror, Crime, and Militancy*, eds. John Arquilla and David F. Ronfeldt, 239–288. Santa Monica, CA: Rand.

Dhillon, Gurpreet and Steve Moores. 2001. Computer crimes: theorizing about the enemy within. *Computers and Security* 20(8): 715–723.

DiMarco, Heather. 2003. "The electronic cloak: secret sexual deviance in cybersociety." In *Dot.cons: Crime, Deviance, and Identity on the Internet*, ed. Yvonne Jewkes, 53–67. Portland, OR: Willan Publishing.

Durkin, Keith F. 1996. Accounts and sexual deviance in cyberspace: The case of pedophilia. PhD diss., Virginia Polytechnic Institute and State University.

Durkin, Keith F. 1997. Misuse of the Internet by Pedophiles: Implications for Law Enforcement and Probation Practice. *Federal* Probation 61: 14–18.

Durkin, Keith F. 2007. Show Me the Money: Cybershrews and On-Line Money Masochists. *Deviant Behavior* 28: 355–378.

Durkin, Keith F., and Clifton D. Bryant. 1999. Propagandizing pederasty. A thematic analysis of the on-line exculpatory accounts of unrepentant pedophiles. *Deviant Behavior* 20: 103–127.

Edleman, Benjamin. 2009. Red Light States: Who Buys Online Adult Entertainment? *Journal of Economic Perspectives* 23(1): 209–220.

Finkelhor, David, Kimberly J. Mitchell, and Janice Wolak. 2000. *Online victimization: A report on the nation's youth*. Washington DC: National Center for Missing and Exploited Children.

Finn, Jerry. 2004. A Survey of Online Harassment at a University Campus. *Journal of Interpersonal Violence* 19(4): 468–483.

Fontana-Rosa, Julio Cesar. 2001. Legal competency in a case of pedophilia: Advertising on the Internet. *International Journal of Offender Therapy and Comparative Criminology* 45: 118–128.

Franklin, Jason, Vern Paxson, Adrian Perrig, and Stefan Savage. 2007. An Inquiry into the nature and cause of the wealth of internet miscreants. Paper presented at CCS07, October 29–November 2, in Alexandria, VA.

Furnell, Steven. 2002. *Cybercrime: Vandalizing the Information Society*. Boston, MA: Addison Wesley.

Goodin, Dan. 2007. TJX breach was twice as big as admitted, banks say. *The Register.* (October 20, 2008), http://www.theregister.co.uk/2007/10/24/tjx_breach_estimate_grows/.

Goodman, Marc. 2001. Making computer crime count. *FBI Law Enforcement Bulletin* 70 (8): 10–17.

Gopal, Ram, G. L. Sanders, Sudip Bhattacharjee, Manish K Agrawal, and Suzanne C. Wagner. 2004. A Behavioral Model of Digital Music Piracy. *Journal of Organizational Computing* & *Electronic Commerce* 14: 89–105.

Grabosky, Peter N. 2001. Virtual criminality: Old wine in new bottles? *Social and Legal Studies* 10: 243–249.

Grabosky Peter N. and Russell Smith. 2001. "Telecommunication fraud in the digital age: The convergence of technologies." In *Crime and the Internet*, ed. David Wall, 29–43. New York: Routledge.

Grabowski, Peter, Russell G. Smith, and Gillian Dempsey. 2001. *Electronic Theft: Unlawful acquisition in cyberspace.* Cambridge, England: Cambridge University Press.

Higgins, George E. 2005. Can low self-control help with the understanding of the software piracy problem? *Deviant Behavior* 26(1): 1–24.

Higgins, George E., Brian D. Fell, and Abby L. Wilson. 2006. Digital piracy: Assessing the contributions of an integrated self-control theory and social learning theory using structural equation modeling. *Criminal Justice Studies* 19(1): 3–22.

Higgins, George E., Brian D. Fell, and Abby L. Wilson. 2007. Low self-control and social learning in understanding students' intentions to pirate movies in the United States. *Social Science Computer Review* 25(3): 339–357.

Higgins, George E. and David A. Makin. 2004. Self-control, deviant peers, and software piracy. *Psychological Reports* 95: 921–931.

Higgins, George E. and Abby L. Wilson. 2006. Low self-control, moral beliefs, and social learning theory in university students' intentions to pirate software. *Security Journal* 19: 75–92.

Hinduja, Sameer. 2001. Correlates of Internet software piracy. *Journal of Contemporary Criminal Justice* 17: 369–382.

Hinduja, Sameer. 2003. Trends and Patterns among Software Pirates. *Ethics and Information* Technology 5: 49–61.

Hinduja, Sameer, and Justin W. Patchin. 2009. *Bullying beyond the schoolyard: Preventing and responding to cyberbullying.* New York: Corwin Press.

Hollinger, Richard C. 1992. Crime by computer: Correlates of software piracy and unauthorized account access. *Security Journal* 2(1): 2–12.

Holt, Thomas J. 2003. Examining a transnational problem: An analysis of computer crime victimization in eight countries from 1999 to 2001. *In-*

ternational Journal of Comparative and Applied Criminal Justice 27: 199–220.

Holt, Thomas J. 2007. Subcultural evolution? Examining the influence of on- and off-line experiences on deviant subcultures. *Deviant Behavior* 28(2): 171–198.

Holt, Thomas J., and Kristie R. Blevins. 2007. Examining sex work from the client's perspective: Assessing johns using online data. *Deviant Behavior* 28: 333–354.

Holt, Thomas J., Kristie R. Blevins, and Joseph B. Kuhns. 2008. Examining the Displacement Practices of Johns with On-line Data. *Journal of Criminal Justice* 36: 522–528.

Holt, Thomas J., and Adam M. Bossler. 2009. Examining the Applicability of Lifestyle-Routine Activities Theory for Cybercrime Victimization. *Deviant Behavior* 30(1): 1–25.

Holt, Thomas J., Adam M. Bossler, and George W. Burruss. 2010. Social Learning and Cyber Deviance: Examining the Importance of a Full Social Learning Model in the Virtual World. Journal of Crime and Justice.

Holt, Thomas J. and Heith Copes. Forthcoming. Transferring Subcultural Knowledge Online: Practices and Beliefs of Persistent Digital Pirates. *Deviant Behavior.*

Holt, Thomas J. and Danielle C. Graves. 2007. A Qualitative Analysis of Advanced Fee Fraud Schemes. *The International Journal of Cyber-Criminology* 1(1): 137–154.

Holt, Thomas J. and Eric Lampke. 2010. Exploring stolen data markets on-line: Products and market forces. *Criminal Justice Studies* 23: 33–50.

Honeynet Research Alliance. 2003. Profile: Automated Credit Card Fraud. *Know Your Enemy Paper* series. (July 20, 2008), http://www.honeynet.org/papers/profiles/cc-fraud.pdf.

Hughes, Donna M. 2003. Prostitution Online. *Journal of Trauma Practice* 2: 115–131.

IDATE. 2003. Taking Advantage of Peer-to-Peer: What Is at Stake for the Content Industry? (January 7, 2009), http://www.idate.fr/an/_qdn/an-03/IF282/index_a.htm.

Ingram, Jason R. and Sameer Hinduja. 2008. Neutralizing music piracy: An empirical examination. *Deviant Behavior* 29: 334–366.

Internet Crime Complaint Center. 2008. IC3 2008 Internet Crime Report. (March 24, 2009), http://www.ic3.gov/media/annualreport/2008_IC3 Report.pdf.

Jaffe, Greg. 2006. Gates Urges NATO Ministers To Defend Against Cyber Attacks. *The Wall Street Journal On-line.* (June 15, 2006), http://online.wsj.com/article/SB118190166163536578.html?mod=googlenews_wsj.

James, Lance. 2005. *Phishing Exposed*. Rockland: Syngress.

Jenkins, Paul. 2001. *Beyond tolerance: Child pornography on the Internet*. New York: New York University Press.

Jensen, Gary F. and David Brownfield. 1986. Gender, lifestyles, and victimization: Beyond routine activity. *Violence and Victims* 1: 85–99.

Jewkes, Yvvonne, and Keith Sharpe. 2003. "Crime, deviance and the disembodied self: transcending the dangers of corporeality." In *Dot.cons: Crime, deviance and identity on the* Internet, ed. Yvvone Jewkes, 1–14. Portland, OR: Willan Publishing.

Jordan, Tim and Paul Taylor. 1998. A Sociology of Hackers. *The Sociological Review* 46: 757–80.

Jordan, Tim and Paul Taylor. 2004. *Hacktivism and Cyberwars: Rebels With a Cause*. New York: Routledge.

Landler, Mark and John Markoff. 2008. "Digital Fears Emerge After Data Siege in Estonia," *The New York Times*, (May 24, 2007), www.nytimes.com/2007/05/29/technology/29estonia.html.

Lane, Frederick S. 2000. *Obscene Profits: The Entrepreneurs of Pornography in the Cyber Age*. New York: Routledge.

Lauritsen, Janet L., John H. Laub, and Robert J. Sampson. 1992. Conventional and delinquent activities: Implications for the prevention of violent victimization among adolescents. *Violence and Victims* 7: 91–108.

Levy, Steven. 1984. *Hackers: Heroes of the Computer Revolution*. New York: Dell.

Mann, David, and Mike Sutton. 1998. Netcrime: More Change in the Organization of Thieving. *British Journal of Criminology* 38: 201–229.

McKenna, Katelyn Y. A., and John A. Bargh. 2000. Plan 9 from cyberspace: The implications of the Internet for personality and social psychology. *Personality and Social Psychology Review* 4: 57–75.

McQuade, Sam. 2006. *Understanding and managing cyber crime*. Boston: Pearson/Allyn and Bacon.

MENA Business Reports. 2002. Hacktivism: Pro-Islamic hacker groups joining forces globally. (April 30, 2004), http://web.lexis-nexis.com/universe/document?_m=a8bea342a9f56689f3986fa946c79f76&_docnum=3&wchp=dGLbVtbzSkVA&_md5=87f67b999724f1f411e93cee5da58d7f.

Morris, Robert G. and George E. Higgins. 2009. Neutralizing potential and self-reported digital piracy: A multitheoretical exploration among college students. *Criminal Justice Review*, 34.

Motion Picture Association of America. 2007. 2005 Piracy fact sheet. (December 12, 2007), http://www.mpaa.org/researchStatistics.asp.

Nasheri, Hedieh. 2005. *Economic espionage and industrial spying*. Cambridge Publishing.

Newman, Grame and Ronald Clarke. 2003. *Superhighway robbery: Preventing e-commerce crime.* Cullompton: Willan Press.

PandaLabs 2007. Malware infections in protected systems. (November 1, 2007), http://research.pandasecurity.com/blogs/images/wp_pb_malware_infections _in_protected_systems.pdf.

Pease, Ken. 2001. "Crime Futures and foresight: Challenging criminal behavior in the information age." In *Crime and the Internet,* ed. David Wall, 18–28. New York: Routledge.

Putnam, Tonya L., and David D. Elliott. 2001. "International responses to cyber crime." In *The Transnational Dimension of Cyber Crime and Terrorism,* eds. Abraham D. Sofaer and Seymour E. Goodman, 35–68. Stanford: Hoover Institution Press.

Quayle, Ethel, and Max Taylor. 2002. Child pornography and the Internet: Perpetuating a cycle of abuse. *Deviant Behavior* 23: 331–361.

Quinn, James F., and Craig J. Forsyth. 2005. Describing sexual behavior in the era of the internet: A typology for empirical research. *Deviant Behavior* 26: 191–207.

Rob, R. and J. Woldfogel. 2006. Piracy on the high C's: Music downloading, sales displacement, and social welfare in a sample of college students. *Journal of Law and Economics* 49: 29–62.

Roberts, Paul F. 2007. Retailer TJX reports massive data breach: Credit, debit data stolen. Extent of breach still unknown. *InfoWorld.* (October 1, 2007), http://www.infoworld.com/d/security-central/retailer-tjx-reports-massive-data-breach-953.

Rogers, J. 2007. Gartner: Victims of online phishing up nearly 40 percent in 2007. *SC Magazine.* (January 20, 2008), http://www.scmagazineus.com/ Gartner-Victims-of- online-phishing-up-nearly-40-percent-in-2007/article/ 99768.

Rosenmann, Amir, and Marylin P. Safir. 2006. Forced online: Pushed Factors of Internet Sexuality: A Preliminary Study of Paraphilic Empowerment. *Journal of Homosexuality* 51: 71–92.

Sampson, Robert J. and Janet L. Lauritsen. 1990. Deviant lifestyles, proximity to crime, and the offender-victim link in personal violence. *Journal of Research in Crime and Delinquency* 27: 110–139.

Schell, Bernadette H., John L. Dodge, with Steve S. Moutsatsos. 2002. *The Hacking of America: Who's Doing it, Why, and How.* Westport, CT: Quorum Books.

Scott, Maichael S., and Kelly Dedel. 2006. "Street prostitution." *Problem Oriented Policing Guide Series (2).* Washington D.C.: Office of Community Oriented Policing Services, U.S. Department of Justice.

Sharpe, Keith, and Sarah Earle. 2003. "Cyberpunters and cyberwhores: prostitution on the Internet." In *Dot Cons. Crime, Deviance and Identity on the Internet*, ed. Yvonne Jewkes, 36–52. Portland, OR: Willan Publishing.

Shaw, Eric, Keven G. Ruby, and Jerrold M. Post. 1998. The Insider Threat to Information Systems: The Psychology of the Dangerous Insider. *Security Awareness Bulletin* 2.

Siwek, Stephen E. 2007. *The true cost of sound recording piracy to the U.S. economy.* (January 9, 2009), http://www.ipi.org/ipi%5CIPIPublications.nsf/PublicationLookupFullText/5C2EE3D2107A4C228625733E0053A1F4.

Skinner, William F., and Anne M. Fream. 1997. A social learning theory analysis of computer crime among college students. *Journal of Research in Crime and Delinquency* 34(4): 495–518.

Soothhill, Keith, and Teela Sanders. 2005. "The geographical mobility, preferences and pleasures of prolific punters: A demonstration study of the activities of prostitutes' clients." *Sociological Research On-Line* 10(1). http://www.socresonline.org.uk/10/1/soothill.html (October 10, 2005).

Speer, David L. 2000. Redefining borders: The challenges of cybercrime. *Crime, Law, and Social Change* 34: 259–273.

Stambaugh, Hollis, David S. Beaupre, David J. Icove, Richard Baker, Wayne Cassady, Wayne P. Williams. 2001. *Electronic crime needs assessment for state and local law enforcement.* Washington, DC: National Institute of Justice. NCJ 186276.

Stephenson, Peter. 2000. *Investigating Computer-Related Crime.* Boca Raton: CRC Press.

Symantec Corporation. 2003. Symantec Internet security threat report. (October 3, 2005), http://enterprisesecurity.symantec.com/content/knowledgelibrary.cfm?EID=0.

Taylor, Robert W., Eric J. Fritsch, John Liederbach, and Thomas J. Holt. 2010. *Digital Crime and Digital Terrorism, 2nd Edition.* Upper Saddle River, NJ: Pearson Prentice Hall.

Tewksbury, Richard. 2003. Bareback sex and the quest for HIV: Assessing the relationship in Internet personal advertisements of men who have sex with men. *Deviant Behavior* 24: 467–482.

Thomas, Richard and Jerry Martin. 2006. The underground economy: Priceless. *:login* 31: 7–16.

Vamosi, Robert. 2008. Second of 11 alleged TJX hackers pleads guilty. *CNET News.* (October 1, 2008), http://news.cnet.com/8301-1009_3-10048507-83.html?tag=mncol.

Wall, David S. 1998. Catching Cybercriminals: Policing the Internet. International review of Law. *Computers & Technology* 12(2): 201–218.

Wall, David S. 2001. "Cybercrimes and the Internet." In *Crime and the Internet*, ed. David S. Wall, 1–17. New York: Routledge.

Wall, David S. 2004. Digital realism and the governance of spam as cybercrime. *European Journal on Criminal Policy and Research* 10: 309–335.

Wall, David S. 2007. *Cybercrime: The transformation of crime in the information age.* Cambridge: Polity Press.

Wolak, Janice, David Finkelhor, and Kimberly Mitchell. 2004. Internet-initiated sex crimes against minors: Implications for prevention based on findings from a national study. *Journal of Adolescent Health* 35: 424.

Wolak, Janice, Kimberly Mitchell, and David Finkelhor. 2003. *Internet Sex Crimes Against Minors: The Response of Law Enforcement.* Washington, DC: Office of Juvenile Justice and Delinquency Prevention.

Yar, Majid. 2005. The novelty of "cybercrime": An assessment in light of routine activity theory. *European Journal of Criminology* 2(4): 407–427.

Zentner, Alejandro. 2006. Measuring the effect of file sharing on music purchases. *Journal of Law and Economics* 49: 63–90.

2

Hacking into the Hacker: Separating Fact from Fiction

Cassie Wade, Jessica Aldridge, Lindsay Hopper,
Dr. Holli Drummond, Ronald Hopper, and Dr. Keith Andrew

Much has been made of computer hackers in the popular media over the last two decades, promulgating the notion of the hacker as a high-tech thief operating with impunity online (see Furnell 2002). This is a vast departure from the origins of the hacker culture in the late 1950s at the Massachusetts Institute of Technology (MIT) (Meyer 1989; Taylor 1999, 13). The term *hacker* was coined from MIT's Tech Model Railroad Club, where members would "hack" electric trains (Levy 1984; Sterling 1993; Taylor 1999). Some of the members applied these hacking skills to computers and pushed computer programs beyond the initial design limits (Levy 1984; Trigaux 2000). At this time, hacking was seen as impressive and inventive. These hackers lived by an ethic that information should be free, authority always mistrusted, and no harm should come to others (Levy 1984). Two decades later, the counterculture adopted skills from the hacker community to engage in "phone phreaking," using various techniques and devices to make free phone calls (Levy 1984; Meyer 1989; Sterling 1993; Thomas 2002; Turkle 1984). This was one of the first criminals acts related to hacking that began to appear in popular media (Furnell 2002; Holt 2007).

During the 1980s, groups of hackers began to form with the development of personal computers, and the first electronic bulletin board systems (BBS) (Furnell 2002; Meyer 1989). Through BBS, hackers could send messages to one another and upload and download data and software (Mann and Sutton 1998; Sterling 1993; Taylor 1999; Thomas 2002). The first hacker magazines also emerged during the 1980s, further linking participants in the hacker community together (Sterling 1993). In the 1990s, the Internet and World Wide Web grew significantly, allowing hackers to move their tools from BBSs to websites. These technological shifts allowed hackers access to more powerful tools and resources, making the potential for hacks seemed limitless (Jordan and Taylor 1998; Sterling 1993; Taylor 1999; Thomas 2002). Today, a multitude of hacking websites, forums, and videos exist that aid anyone from the novice to the professional hacker (see Holt 2007, 2009a, 2009b; Meyer 1989).

As interest and participation in the hacker community grew and became widely discussed in various media and popular culture, academic examinations of hacking emerged in the 1980s (Levy 1984; Meyer 1989). These initial studies considered the subculture and social organization of hacking, as well as its demographic composition (Levy 1984; Meyer 1989). As the hacker community expanded and changed with the rise of the World Wide Web and simple-to-use computers, researchers continued to attempt to examine hacking (see Jordan and Taylor 1998; Taylor 1999). The hacker community, however, became less tolerant of academic inquiry, particularly as the criminal aspects of hacking became a central focus of much social science research (see Holt 2007; Jordan and Taylor 1998; Loper 2000; Taylor 1999). As a result, explorations of the hacker community are fragmented, utilizing qualitative samples of active hackers and limited survey research with various populations. In an effort to summarize these assessments, this chapter provides a detailed overview of existing social science research on computer hacking. The contribution of such an analysis seeks to provide a more accurate representation of the computer hacker culture, including the historical evolution, socio-demographic characteristics, motives, values, norms, and social organization associated with this unique activity.

Methods

This paper considers the social science research on hacking based on two selection criteria: a discussion of the "methodology" used to select subjects, and content regarding the socio-demographic characteristics, motives, values, norms, and social organization of hackers. First, electronic data bases such as JSTOR, EBSCOhost, ProQuest, and Google Scholar were searched for relevant publications. The search terms used included: hacker, hacking, hacking culture, cybercrime, cybercriminals, crackers, cyberterrorists, cyberterrorism, virus writers, phreakers, computer crime, and internet crime. Next, manual searches were conducted of the reference lists of all publications in order to include research not discovered in the initial searches. This method produced 25 studies, whose findings were synthesized to examine the following issues: 1) defining the activities of a computer hacker, as well as internal and external groupings or typologies, 2) the demographic characteristics of the "average" hacker, 3) the motivations of hackers, and finally 4) the norms and social interaction patters of hackers. A summary of the included publications can be found in Table 2.1.

Defining Hackers

The term *hacker* is not easily defined, as it has different meanings for those within and outside of the hacker community (Furnell 2002; Holt 2007; Meyer 1989). As noted previously, popular media has co-opted the term hacker and use it to refer to any type of computer crime (Furnell 2002). Hackers often object to the use of the term hacker by the media because it is only presented when discussing crime (Holt 2007; Jordan and Taylor 1998; Meyer 1989; Taylor 1999). There is significant debate over how to define hackers, but the most common characteristics include significant curiosity and a strong desire to learn (Holt 2007; Jordan and Taylor 1998; Loper 2000; Schell and Dodge 2002; Taylor 1999; Loper 2000). Holt (2007) suggests that skilled hackers reject the label of 'hacker' because this is an ideal level of knowledge and skill that cannot be achieved in one's lifetime. Thus, for some hacker is viewed as a goal to achieve rather than as a generalized title for computer users with elite skills.

While such labeling is problematic, prior research has determined several activities commonly associated with computer hacking based on perceptions of those within the hacker subculture. Activities often associated with hacking include: breaking into a computer system, copying software (pirating), writing or using computer viruses, destroying or altering data or files, finding security vulnerabilities in software, credit card fraud, and stealing services such as phone service or satellite television (Best 2003; Mann and Sutton 1998; Rogers, Smoak, and Liu 2005). There is, however, debate about which activities can actually be considered hacking. For example, some researchers classify digital pirates as a separate group of offenders from hackers (Furnell 2002; Higgins 2004; Meyer 1989; Turgeman-Goldschmidt 2005). Though hackers utilize pirated materials and interact with pirates, they generally denigrate pirating as an unskilled activity (Furnell 2002; Higgins 2004; Meyer 1989; Turgeman-Goldschmidt 2005). It should also be noted that not all activities associated with hacking are illegal (Rogers et al. 2005). In fact, some hackers contend that those who engage in criminal acts cease to be hackers and become criminal hackers, or crackers (Best 2003; Taylor 1999).

In light of the difficulties inherent in defining hackers, Meyer (1989) suggested that researchers adopt the definition used by those within the hacker community: one who gains unauthorized access to a computer system, file, or network. This definition emphasizes the criminal component of hacking without considering the legitimate applications of hacking as a whole. For exam-

Table 2.1 Summary of the Behavior, Labels, Demographics, Motives, and Theories Discussed in 25 Academic Studies on Hackers

Study	Types of Behavior	Labels and Groups	Socio-demographics	Motives	Theories
Best 2003		Old and New School		Curiosity, improve software, share information	
Furnell 2002	Accessing computer systems	White, Black & Gray Hats, Cyber Warriors, Crackers, Cyberterrorists, Hacktivists		Politics, ideology	
Gordon & Ma 2003				Moral obligation, self-efficacy	Reasoned Action, Planned Behavior, Moral Disengagement
Håpnes & Sørensen 1995	Programming a computer to solve a problem		Male computer science students		Labor Process Theory
Higgins 2004	Software piracy				Low Self-Control, Differential Association
Hollinger 1993	Pirating software, accessing another's computer		Males 2.5–3 times more likely to admit to committing computer crimes, higher levels of piracy among Asians and Hispanics		
Holt 2007	Using malware, port scanning, stealing services			Curiosity, desire to learn, status	Subculture
Holt 2009a					Social organization, subculture
Holt 2009b				Religion, Politics	

Table 2.1 Summary of the Behavior, Labels, Demographics, Motives, and Theories Discussed in 25 Academic Studies on Hackers, *continued*

Study	Types of Behavior	Labels and Groups	Socio-demographics	Motives	Theories
Holt & Kilger 2008	Solve new problems, create new applications	Telecrafters, Makecrafters			Differential Association, Low Self-Control, Neutralization, Subculture
Holt, Soles, & Leslie 2008	Creating malware	Malware writers, Black Hats, Hackers, Crackers	All male sample	Share information	
Jordan & Taylor 1998				Addiction to computers, curiosity, boring life, power, status, ego, ideology, peer acceptance	Neutralization, Subculture
Jordan & Taylor 2004		Hacktivists, Digitally Correct Hacktivists, Mass Action Hacktivists			
Kilger, Arkin, & Stutzman 2004	Denial-of-Service attacks, stealing credit cards			Boring life, money, power, status, ego, peer acceptance	
Loper 2000		Old School Hackers, Bedroom Hackers, Larval Hackers, Newbies, WaRez D00dz, Internet Hackers, Hacktivists, Script Kiddies		Curiosity, desire to learn	Subculture
Mann & Sutton 1998	Breaking into a computer system, software piracy, destroying files	Hackers, Gurus, Parasites, Acolytes, Information Providers, Prophets, and Warners, Growlers, Jostlers, Abusers, Money Makers			Subculture

Table 2.1 Summary of the Behavior, Labels, Demographics, Motives, and Theories Discussed in 25 Academic Studies on Hackers, *continued*

Study	Types of Behavior	Labels and Groups	Socio-demographics	Motives	Theories
Meyer 1989	Software piracy, stealing phone services, unauthorized access to a computer system	Computer Hackers, Phone Phreakers, Software Pirates			Social organization, subculture
Rogers 2001	Computer crimes, software piracy, password guessing				Social Learning, Differential Association, Differential Reinforcement, and Moral Disengagement
Rogers 1999	Write software	Toolkit/Newbies, Cyberpunks, Internals, Coders, Old Guard Hackers, Professional Criminals, Cyberterrorists		Religion, revenge	
Rogers, Smoak, & Liu 2005	Software piracy, accessing another's computer, writing viruses, stealing phone services, obtaining credit card information				Low Self-control, Moral Disengagement
Schell and Dodge 2002	Accessing another's computer, Denial-of-Service attacks, defacing web sites	White and Black Hats, Elites, CyberAngels, Hacktivists, Crackers, Destructive Hacktivists, Cyberterrorists, Cyberstalkers		Politics	Subculture

Table 2.1 Summary of the Behavior, Labels, Demographics, Motives, and
Theories Discussed in 25 Academic Studies on Hackers, *continued*

Study	Types of Behavior	Labels and Groups	Socio-demographics	Motives	Theories
Skinner & Fream 1997	Software piracy, guessing passwords, accessing another's computer, changing files, writing viruses		Males 2–3 times more likely to admit to committing computer crimes, more likely to be White or Asian, no correlation with age		Differential Association, Differential Reinforcement and Punishment, Imitation, Neutralization, Moral Disengagement
Taylor 1999				Knowledge, keeping up with technology, curiosity, boring life, power, status, ego, ideologies, peer acceptance	Subculture
Thomas 2002		White and Black Hats, Phone Phreaks		Hacker ethic, power, curiosity	Subculture
Turgeman-Goldschmidt 2005	Accessing another's computer, software piracy, developing viruses, causing systems to crash, phreaking	Pirates, Hackers, Crackers	Mostly male, young, single, and educated	Revenge, curiosity, money, voyeurism, excitement	Neutralization

ple, Håpnes and Sørensen (1995) found Norwegian university students who engaged in hacking to be obsessed with computers and programming (Håpnes and Sørensen 1995). These self-identified hackers viewed hacking as the ability to program a computer to bring to life an idea or to solve a problem. They wanted complete control over the machine, but did not include manipulation of hardware as a true hacking activity. These hackers claimed to be obsessed with finding knowledge, with no interest in malicious acts as commonly portrayed in the media (Håpnes and Sørensen 1995).

Although media and many academic researchers often use the term *hacker* synonymously with computer criminal, a more comprehensive definition would be a person who has mastery over technology. To that end, Schell and Dodge (2002) define hackers as individuals with a profound interest in computers and technology that have used their knowledge to access computer systems with or without authorization from the system owners (see also Holt 2007, 2009a). Such a definition includes applications of both legal and illegal forms of hacker knowledge, enabling a more robust examination of hacking without necessarily including the stigma of illicit activity. The use of similar definitions in future research would improve our understanding of both the criminal and non-criminal activities of self-identified hackers.

Conceptualizing Hacker Activity

The absence of a unified definition of hacker is related to the complex and diverse labels and frameworks used to conceptualize and identify those who engage in hacking. Individuals within the hacker subculture use distinct definitions to distinguish themselves. Specifically, hackers divide themselves into two schools of thought: old and new. Best (2003) argues that old school hacking culture most often involves contribution to the burgeoning open software movement based on the voluntary contributions of thousands of globally networked programmers to the development of software like Linux. Old school hackers argue that hacking upholds anti-authoritarianism and a dedication to information sharing. Those who follow this school of thought are interested in securing active access to information because of their commitment to open source code (Best 2003). The code itself as information is never the ultimate goal, but rather the ability to actively change, alter, and improve that code and its informational value (Best 2003; Loper 2000). By contrast, new school hackers are disparaged because the invention of the Internet and World Wide Web has tempted many to explore remote systems looking for security holes that need to be fixed. New school hackers subscribe to similar principles espoused by the old school, including the notion that information should be free, authority mistrusted, and curiosity satisfied (Best 2003). Access to all systems must be actively maintained in order to test for security holes and design flaws.

In addition to old and new school frameworks, a common method used to differentiate hackers used by both outsiders and insiders is through the application of the terms white or black hat (see Table 2.2 for detail). White hats are thought to be ethical hackers who work to improve system security, while black hat hackers seek out vulnerabilities and exploit them for malicious purposes (Furnell 2002; Holt 2007; Schell and Dodge 2002; Thomas 2002). Schell and Dodge (2002) also argue that white hats can be categorized into Elites, CyberAngels, and Hacktivists. An Elite hacker is one who is very skilled and can effectively use a computer system, but avoids deliberately destroying data or otherwise damaging systems (Schell and Dodge 2002). CyberAngels are referred to as the "anti-criminal activists" of the hacker community who actively engage in hacking to ensure online safety. White hat Hacktivists pair their need for social action with their computer skills to promote free speech and international human rights worldwide (Schell and Dodge 2002). Similarly, Furnell (2002) argues that Samurais are a form of white hat hackers who are hired to conduct legal cracking jobs, often penetrating corporate computer systems for legitimate reasons.

Schell and Dodge (2002) also argue that black hat hackers can be separated into Crackers, Destructive Hacktivists, Cyberterrorists, and Cyberstalkers. The term "cracker" in the hacking community typically refers to an individual who does one or more of the following: break into others' computer systems without authorization, break copy-protection on software, flood websites to deny access to legitimate users, or deliberately deface web sites for greed or revenge (Schell and Dodge 2002). The term cracker was coined in 1985 by hackers in defense against the journalistic misuse of the term hacker (Furnell 2002). Cracker exploits range from simple and automated to the highly disguised and sophisticated. Destructive Hacktivists are much more driven and demanding of a response of their targets than white hat Hacktivists (Schell and Dodge

Table 2.2 Characteristics of White, Black, and Gray Hat Hackers

White Hats	Black Hats	Gray Hats
• Work within the hacker ethic: Do no harm • Security Experts • Elite Hackers • Do not engage in illegal activities • Improve computer security	• Do not follow the hacker ethic • Will cause damage • Engage in illegal activities • Steal and destroy data • Known to be angry and vengeful	• Those wanting to break away from corporations • Reformed Black Hats • May do security and unethical hacking at the same time

2002). Black hat Hacktivists will also cause destruction and disruption to government and industrial sites to further a political or protest agenda (Schell and Dodge 2002).

Another label used for some hackers is Gray Hat, which originated from members of the L0PHt (a Boston hacker group), who wanted to stand apart from corporate security testers while distancing themselves from the notorious black hats (Fitch 2003). Gray hats are individuals who fall between white and black hats because their motives are unclear and prone to change (Furnell 2002; Holt 2007). There is controversy over the use of this term because some experts feel that any group that creates hacking tools, despite their intent, is not ethical (Fitch 2003). Though the black/gray/white hat labels are used by individuals in and out of the hacker subculture, there are two additional terms used in discussing hacker activity that do not originate within the hacker subculture: cyberterrorist and hacktivist. These terms are commonly used by those in the research, law enforcement, and military communities, but are not clearly defined (Furnell 2002). For example, hackers have breached systems that would be considered very secure, such as military sites, leaving them vulnerable to more insidious threats than other types of hacker attacks (see Furnell 2002; Holt 2009b; Jordan and Taylor 2004). This has led to the emergence of a new class of threat: cyberterrorism (Furnell 2002). A cyberterrorist is someone who commits unlawful attacks and threats against computers, networks, and the information stored therein to intimidate or coerce a government or its people in furtherance of political or social objectives (Gordon and Ford 2005). Cyberterrorists may belong to a group which would provide funding that ordinary hackers would not be privy to. As a consequence, these attacks can produce a more substantial and lasting impact than that of regular terrorism since electronic targets, such as financial systems or power grids, can affect a larger population over a greater period of time than a bomb or physical incident (Furnell 2002).

Since cyberterror involves the use of hacking techniques, it is somewhat similar to the problem of hacktivism. Furnell (2002) states that computer hackers who have a point to make or an axe to grind see cyberspace as a soapbox, and their use of this communications medium for social change can be considered hacktivism (Furnell 2002). Jordan and Taylor (2004) define hacktivism as the emergence of popular political action through the activity of groups of people in cyberspace. It combines elements of grassroots political protests with computer hacking. Hacktivists engage in indirect, non-violent actions, including boycotts, blockades, strikes, and civil disobedience (Jordan and Taylor 2004). Symbolic protests can also be used as a means to register disagreement with something, and form movements to influence others to make social change (Jordan and Taylor 2004).

Hacktivism can be divided into mass action hacktivism and digitally correct hacktivism (Jordan and Taylor 2004). Mass action hacktivism unites politics and inefficient technology in an attempt to defy the lack of physicality in on-line life in favor of a mass collection of virtual bodies that are not in physical proximity in the real world. This is the closest event on-line to traditional mass protests found in the real world (Jordan and Taylor 2004). Digitally correct hacktivism involves the political application of hacking to the infrastructure of cyberspace. According to Jordan and Taylor (2004) hacktivism stays faithful to the ingenuity of "the hack" by using ingenuity to foster more outward-looking political ends.

Given the variety of terms that can be applied to hackers and acts of hacking, some researchers have attempted to develop typologies of the hacker community to better define and differentiate this community. For example, Loper (2000) developed a framework of hackers using terms internal and external to the hacker community based on the time they engaged in hacking, and their overall skill level:

- *Old School Hackers*—Not motivated by profit and crime is incidental. Traditionally they had almost unlimited access to computer hardware.
- *Bedroom Hackers*—Work from home and have limited resources. They will steal services that facilitate exploration yet tend to hold a self conscience ethic.
- *Larval Hackers and Newbies*—Have limited knowledge. They are unsocialized in the hacker subculture and may unknowingly violate the ethic, eager to prove their skills.
- *WaRez D00dz*—Trade pirated software. Activities are specific and conscious violations of law. They have a wide range of skills.
- *Internet Hackers*—Are the contemporary hackers who have internet access. Where bedroom hackers relied on the subculture to maximize scarce resources, internet hackers rely on the subculture for the sense of community.
- *Hacktivists*—Use hacker sills and attitudes to convey a political message. They often subordinate the values of the hacker subculture to their political goals. They range in skill from very low to very high.
- *Script Kiddies*—Have limited knowledge and lack of socialization to the hacker subculture. They lack desire to learn more than the most direct route to an effect.

Additionally, Rogers (1999) proposed a seven-category framework of the hacker community: Toolkit/Newbies (NT), Cyberpunks (CP), Internals (IT), Coders (CD), Old Guard Hackers (OG), Professional Criminals (PC), and Cyberterrorists (CT). The Old Guard hacker groups embrace the ideology of the first hackers and appear to be interested in the intellectual endeavor of hacking (Rogers 1999). By contrast, the Toolkit/Newbies are those who are new to hacking and have very limited skills, while Cyberpunks usually have better computer skills and some programming capabilities (Rogers 1999). Specifically, cyberpunks are capable of writing their own software and intentionally engage in malicious acts unlike Toolkit/Newbies (Rogers 1999). Internals, however, are disgruntled or ex-employees that carry out attacks because they have insider knowledge of networks and systems. Coders are adept at writing malicious code and programming. Professional Criminals and CyberTerrorists are the most dangerous hackers who attack systems for economic, political, or religious reasons.

A final typology created by Holt and Kilger (2008) proposes two new terms for hackers: techcrafters and makecrafters. These terms are value neutral and consider the capacity of the hacker and their use of technology as a basis for evaluation, rather than the arbitrary terms that white and black hat measure (Holt and Kilger 2008). Both the techcraft and the makecraft hacker have a significant interest in computers and technology, though they differ in the ways that they relate to technology. Makecraft hackers may be considered producers, while techcraft hackers are the consumers of technology (Holt and Kilger 2008). The techcraft hacker may be just as skilled as a makecraft hacker, though they apply their knowledge to repair systems or complete a task with known tools and materials. Makecraft hackers are more interested in using their skills to identify and solve new problems, or create and use applications that have not been used before (Holt and Kilger 2008). Holt and Kilger (2008) state that removing the labels of White, Black, and Gray, can allow for more understanding of the methods and tactics of hackers.

Despite the wide range of labels and frameworks applied to hackers, there are underlying patterns of behavior and attitudes that structure these concepts. It is clear that highly skilled hackers, whether referred to as elite, old school, old guard, or simply hackers, have the capacity to develop their own tools, utilize technology in unique ways, and to respect the hacker ethic. Those individuals who are new to hacking, or who subvert technologies for malicious intent may receive less respect within the community because they have much less skill with computer hardware and software. Thus, the categories used to label a hacker, regardless of their origin, help to illustrate who they are and what they do.

The Demographic Composition of Hackers

In addition to the complexities inherent in defining hackers, there is no clear picture of the socio-demographics of a typical hacker. The lack of basic descriptive statistics can be explained by the secretive nature of the hacker subculture. There is, however, strong evidence to suggest hackers are overwhelmingly male (Hollinger 1993; Jordan and Taylor 1998; Skinner and Fream 1997; Turgeman-Goldschmidt 2005). For example, the students in a group of Norwegian hackers studied by Håpnes and Sørensen (1995) were all male and made up of students from physics, computer science, and electronics majors. The female computer science majors used this group as an example of everything they did not like about computer science. Most of the individuals in this group became interested in computers at a very young age and wanted to express their differences from the mainstream culture, and each other (Håpnes and Sørensen 1995; Holt 2007). Norwegian hackers were not very interested in why females were not involved in hacking activities (Håpnes and Sørensen 1995). Females were associated with Macintosh computers which were not of interest to the Norwegian community. This is in part because Macintosh programs are understood to be used for applications, which are seen as feminine activity, rather than the more masculine activity of designing programs (see also Turkle 1984).

Qualitative studies emphasize the gender divide in the hacker community, which is also reflected in limited quantitative research on hacking (see Higgins 2004; Hollinger 1993; Rogers 2001; Rogers et al. 2005; Skinner and Fream 1997). For example, Skinner and Fream (1997) studied US college students from specific departments (including natural and social sciences, business, and engineering), chosen for an assumed higher level of required computer skills. Slightly more than 60% of students surveyed were male, yet males reported committing computer crimes two to three times more than females (Skinner and Fream 1997). White and Asian students were more likely to commit computer crimes than any other racial group. Skinner and Fream (1997) also report that age and year in school did not have a relationship with committing any of the five computer crimes in the study. The likelihood of committing a computer crime was not, however, associated with the student's choice of department. Holt and Kilger (2008) also found their sample of students and active hackers to be primarily male, particularly among those in attendance at hacker conferences.

Studies examining law enforcement perceptions of hacking also reflect the findings of academic research on hackers. In a study commissioned by the National Institute of Justice, researchers interviewed law enforcement officials on their experiences with electronic crime (Stambaugh, Beaupre, Icove, Baker, Cassaday, and Williams 2001). Interviewees suggested hacking was a common form of crime, and hackers were described as mostly being male college students between the ages of 15 and 25 (Stambaugh et al. 2001). Hackers were also viewed as being the most knowledgeable about all aspects of computer crime (Stambaugh et al. 2001).

In light of the significant gender gap reported in research on hackers, Gilboa (1996) provided some guidance on the way that women become involved in hacking. Women participating in hacking were there as girlfriends of hackers or groupies, though some were transients or press doing a story. Additionally, most of the women in the computer underground reported having been stalked and harassed (Gilboa 1996; Holt and Bossler 2009). Chat rooms in general can be hostile places for both men and women, and hacker chat rooms and forums are no different. Segan (2000) reported that women are often sexually harassed in hacker chats, as a lack of respect towards females is prevalent. The Internet offers anonymity, making it difficult for social norms to be enforced (see Holt and Bossler 2009). Because women are greatly outnumbered in the hacker subculture, and hacking is a clearly gendered space, Sollfrank (1999) concluded that female hackers are very difficult to locate. Also, Segan (2000) noted that female hackers face being labeled a "scene whore." From Segan's (2000) perspective, scene whores are hacker groupies who attend conventions and partake in forums, using their sexuality (or engaging in cybersex) to gain status among their male peers (see Holt 2007 for alternative definition). As a result, female hackers who have no interest in being a scene whore struggle to be viewed as a legitimate hacker. In fact, some women pretend to be men on forums, and use more masculine language to avoid being harassed (Segan 2000).

The observed gender composition of the hacker community may be a consequence of the structure of computer science and information technology fields where males highly outnumber females. This is especially true in computer science programs throughout the United States, although there is disagreement as to the cause. Taylor (1999) claims that three factors contribute to why women are less involved in computers and technology: societal factors, masculine environment, and gender in language. Societal factors include the gendered socialization of children, where boys are given technical playthings and girls are given cuddly toys (Taylor 1999). Childhood socialization may play a role as females are not socialized to be technologically savvy. Males are, however, often encouraged to be involved in technology, math, and science. In fact, educating children about computers occurs within the context of a male oriented-jargon (Jordan and Taylor 1998). Computer science is dominated by men, giving it a "locker room" climate in which women would feel uncomfortable. Finally, on-line language is biased towards men, as it is aggressive and short sighted (Taylor 1999). Thus, the masculine language used in computer science reinforces the absence of women by creating barriers for entry to information technology and general socialization into existing gender roles (Taylor 1999).

An alternative explanation for a lack of female hackers is that the introduction of new technology was usually to the disadvantage of females because their work was taken for granted and degraded (Håpnes and Sørensen 1995). Feminists believe this is still the case today, and that males shape technology through control and hierarchy (Håpnes and Sørensen 1995). Given the pressure on males to demonstrate their masculinity in society, they may exert their manliness online through technology if they lack it in real life (Yar 2005). Computer science and technology are competitive fields that require aggressive action to succeed. Females, however, are encouraged to engage in more social sciences and are not often socialized to participate and thrive in hostile environments under intense competition. These two theories have not been explored through empirical research, thus there is a need for future study to clarify the basis for the gender differences observed.

Motives Reported By Hackers

Hackers are motivated by many different reasons. Some of the most common motives identified include addiction, curiosity, excitement, money, power, causes, and peer acceptance (Holt 2007; Jordan and Taylor 1998; Kilger, Arkin and Stutzman 2004; Taylor 1999; Turgeman-Goldschmidt 2007). Each motive will be considered in turn below.

Addiction

Hackers often report an addiction to computers and/or computer networks, a feeling that they are compelled to hack (Jordan and Taylor 1998). One of the most intriguing aspects of hacking is the way in which its apparently obsessive aspects give rise to pejorative portrayals of nerdiness. At the same time, the practical implications of the knowledge gained through obsessive computer use promote a continued public interest in hacking (Taylor 1999). A specific reason why hackers may be viewed as compulsive by outsiders could be a result of the continuous rapid changes in technology (see Holt 2007; Taylor 1999). In order to stay abreast of changes, hackers have to approach technology regularly and with greater intensity than that contemplated by more "nine-to-five-minded" computer people (Taylor 1999).

Curiosity

Hackers often name curiosity as a motive to hack (Jordan and Taylor 1998; Taylor 1999; Turgeman-Goldschmidt 2005). What someone might find on the Internet is a frequent topic of discussion (Taylor 1999). For hackers, their curiosity lies in the desire to learn and know as much as possible, which can only be acquired by exploring and pushing the boundaries of what they can discover (Turgeman-Goldschmidt 2005). Some hackers state that innate curiosity is the fundamental basis for which most technological improvement and adaptations are ultimately derived (Holt 2007; Taylor 1999). Turgeman-Goldschmidt (2005) argues that aside from a general curiosity, hackers engage in voyeuristic or nosy curiosity focusing on the unknown, desirable secrets, or the confidential. Hacking offenses such as unauthorized browsing of systems and networks fall into this type of curiosity (Turgeman-Goldschmidt 2005).

Non-academic research conducted by Grabosky (2001) and Yar (2005) also list curiosity as a motive for hacking. In hackers' self-presentations, they are motivated by factors such as intellectual curiosity (Yar 2005). However, self-attributed motives such as curiosity may be rhetorical devices used by hackers to justify their law-breaking and defend themselves against accusations of criminality and deviance (Yar 2005).

Excitement/Entertainment

Hackers often cite excitement as a motive for hacking. Many claim that their online lives are more exciting than their offline lives (Gordon and Ma 2003; Jordan and Taylor 1998; Kilger et al. 2004; Taylor 1999; Turgeman-Goldschmidt 2005). Hacking for entertainment may produce the least consequences for intended targets because the final objective appears to be more playful than destructive (Kilger et al. 2004). Interviewees from the Turgeman-Goldschmidt (2005) study spoke with genuine excitement and enthusiasm about their hacking experiences. The number of potential schemes deployed in the name of entertainment is limitless, and there is no expectation this motivation will ever die off (Kilger et al. 2004; Stutzman 2004).

Money

Another commonly identified motive among hackers is the desire to make money, or use their skills to fight large burgeoning companies from gaining profit (Gordon and Ma 2003; Holt et al. 2008; Kilger et al. 2004; Turgeman-Goldschmidt 2005). According to Kilger, Arkin, and Stutzman, (2004), in the early history of hacking, there was a strong norm against illegally accumulating large sums of money or other financial resources by utilizing one's computer-hacking skills. There is, however, a decided change in attitudes toward criminal payoffs today, as many people engage in blackmailing companies, launching DoS attacks, and stealing credit cards (Holt et al. 2008; Kilger et al. 2004; Stutzman 2004). There appear to be no current or foreseeable inhibitors that may attenuate this trend, so it is expected that money as a source of motivation for hacking will continue to grow unabated (Kilger et al. 2004). In fact, Holt and associates (2008) found several noteworthy Russian malware writers created tools to be sold for a profit in the larger computer underground. Turgeman-Goldschmidt (2005), however, found that money was not the main motivation in a sample of Israeli hackers. Rather, it served an ideological motivation by opposing bureaucracies and those who price-tag knowledge. The only hackers in her sample who were interested in making a profit were involved in software piracy offences (Turgeman-Goldschmidt 2005).

Power/Status/Ego

Hackers are also commonly motivated by the desire for power and status, either within or outside of the hacker subculture (Holt 2007; Holt et al. 2008; Jordan and Taylor 1998; Kilger et al. 2004; Taylor 1999). The ability to gain power over computer systems is an attraction to hackers, which complements the motive of curiosity (Holt 2007; Jordan and Taylor 1998; Taylor 1999). Curiosity increases knowledge of computer systems, which in turn may lead to an increase in an individual's overall social status within the hacker community (Holt 2007; Jordan and Taylor 1998; Taylor 1999). According to Kilger, Arkin, and Stutzman (2004), status is by far the most powerful social force within the social structure of hacking. Position within the hacker subculture depends on a person's skills in coding, network protocols, and other areas of technical expertise (Holt 2007; Kilger et al. 2004). Those who can demonstrate and apply these skills are the most likely to acquire status and respect from other hackers (Holt 2007; Jordan and Taylor 1998; Taylor 1999).

Expertise and status are also related to the issue of ego maintenance as a motive within the hacker subculture (Kilger et al. 2004). Specifically, hackers gain satisfaction from overcoming technical obstacles and creating innovative solutions to problems (Holt 2007; Jordan and Taylor 1998; Kilger et al. 2004). The tougher the technical challenges faced and overcome, the larger the personal payoff when attempts are successful. The motivating power of ego should not be underestimated, as it may overpower personal restraints against illicit activities (Kilger et al. 2004).

Ideologies

Hackers may be motivated by issues they care strongly about such as politics or religion (Holt 2009b; Jordan and Taylor 1998; Taylor 1999). Ideology is often shaped by different factors, such as geopolitical orientation, cultural influences (whether originating from one's own geopolitical location or from social interaction over the Internet), religion, historical events, and views on current issues. Ideology-driven hacking is becoming more common as Internet connectivity increases and political and social movements utilize online environments as a means of expression (Kilger et al. 2004).

Some hackers claim they are a principled force within society dedicated to opposing the re-establishment of traditional values in the newly emerging information society (Taylor 1999). They argue that such traditional values are based upon physical property rights and are increasingly anachronistic in an emerging information society predicated upon the bodiless transportation of data streams (Taylor 1999). Hackers' more specific claims to be an alternative culture rest with their instinctive dislike for government information-gathering bureaucracies, and their opposition to what they perceive as the unjustified privatization of information (Taylor 1999).

Research by Holt (2009b) on Turkish hackers found their activities were driven in part by a political and religious "mission." In this case, supporting the mission meant attacking targets based on religious and national beliefs, including pornographic websites and resources owned or operated by Israel and the United States (Holt 2009b). Specifically, the targets of these Turkish attacks are mainly websites in countries that slight Muslims, or Turkey specifically (Holt 2009b). As a result, it may be that cause-driven hackers are apt to attack high value or visibility targets, rather than large populations of computer users and general resources (Holt 2009b). Ideology as a motivation in the hacking community should be taken seriously, and occurrence is likely to increase in the future (Kilger et al. 2004).

Peer Recognition

Hackers have been stereotyped to be loners and social outcasts. Research, however, indicates that hackers seek peer acceptance from other hackers (Holt 2007, 2009b; Jordan and Taylor 1998; Kilger et al. 2004; Taylor 1999). The nature of the hacker community does not easily facilitate social recognition and reception, as it is a meritocracy where one's position within the community depends on their level of skill (Kilger et al. 2004). Thus, hackers may feel it necessary to demonstrate their capability to hack, whether through bragging or direct evidence of skill in order to gain acceptance (see Holt 2007, 2009; Jordan and Taylor 1999; Taylor 1999). There are several examples of this sort of activity in the broader research on hackers, as noted by Taylor (1999) who found hackers admitted to peer-encouraged behavior, as well as in Holt (2009b) where Turkish hackers shared information with one another to facilitate group based attacks.

Revenge

Turgeman-Goldschmidt (2005) found that revenge was a motive for some hackers. Revenge is an emotional response wherein individuals desire to get back at those who wronged them in some fashion. The easiest way for hackers to do seek revenge is to engage in malicious attacks, though they may not necessarily direct their attacks against members of the hacker community. Engaging in such activities ensures that the hacker will be successful, as their target does not have the capability to effectively fight back (Turgeman-Goldschmidt 2005).

The Social Organization of Hacking

Hackers are often presented in the media as anti-social loners who have deep relationships with their computers to the detriment of social relationships with friends and family (Furnell 2002; Meyer 1989). Research suggests that these assumptions are, however, myths, as hackers engage in offline relationships and have bonds with others in and outside the hacker subculture (Holt 2009a; Jordan and Taylor 1998; Meyer 1989; Schell and Dodge 2002). Limited research has considered the organizational structure of the hacker subculture utilizing Best and Luckenbill's (1994) social organization framework (Holt 2009a; Meyer 1989). Best and Luckenbill (1982) state that deviant relations with one another can be arrayed along the dimension of organizational sophistication based on associations between deviants, participation in deviance individually or collectively, the division of labor within the group, and how long their deviant activities "extend over time and over space" (Best and Luckenbill 1994). These factors undergird a five point continuum of organizational sophistication:

- *Loners*—The least sophisticated group. They do not associate with other deviants, participate in shared deviance, have a division of labor, or maintain their deviance over extended time and space.

- *Colleagues*—The second-most sophisticated group, because individuals create a deviant subculture based on their shared knowledge. They do not offend together and they are short lived with no division of labor.
- *Peers*—Not only associate with one another, but also participate in deviance together.
- *Teams*—More sophisticated than Peers. They last for longer periods of time and have an elaborate division of labor for engaging in deviance.
- *Formal Organizations*—The most sophisticated deviant organization. They have all the elements of teams, as well as extended duration across time and space.

Using this framework, research suggests that hackers are not loners, but rather operate within loose social networks in the hacker subculture (Holt 2007; Jordan and Taylor 1998; Meyer 1989; Schell and Dodge 2002). The idea that hackers are solitary individuals who are more comfortable relating to machines than to other humans is incorrect (Holt 2009a, 2009b; Jordan and Taylor 1998; Meyer 1989). Hackers often hack in groups, whether in physical proximity in the real world or hacking separately but within an on-line social network (Holt 2009a, 2009b; Jordan and Taylor 1998; Meyer 1989). Additionally, hackers learn from others through exposure to more experienced hackers or by drawing on the collective wisdom of the hacking community through online information (Holt 2007, 2009a, 2009b; Jordan and Taylor 1998; Loper 2000). Hackers also regularly interact at off-line social events, such as the annual DEFCON meeting where thousands of hackers gather for competitions, talks, workshops, sharing skills and information, and non-computer related social activities such as parties and barbecues (Holt 2007; 2009a; Schell and Dodge 2002).

Hackers regularly associate with one another in order to discuss matters of common interest but tend to commit actual hacks alone (Holt 2009a; Jordan and Taylor 1998; Meyer 1989). Hacker groups create and foster relationships between individuals who could provide access to information and resources which suggest peer groups are prevalent in hacker subculture, though they do not necessarily hack together (Holt 2009a, 2009b; Meyer 1989). The structure of the computer underground encourages some to form working relationships, thereby acting as peers by mutually participating in hacker activities (Holt 2009a; Meyer 1989). These peer associations provide support to members, as well as socialization and recruitment functions for newcomers (Holt 2009a; Meyer 1989). The establishment of work groups through mutual participation indicates that the computer underground is largely organized as a network of colleagues, and to a lesser extent, peers (Holt 2009a; Meyer 1989).

Hackers also appear to be selective about their collaborators, usually associating and working with three to five people on average (Holt 2009a; Schell and Dodge 2002). Most hackers, however, acquire information from colleagues on or off-line and work alone on their projects (see also Holt 2009a, 2009b; Schell and Dodge 2002).

In addition, hackers do not typically display the required characteristics of mobs or formal organizations (Holt 2009a; Meyer 1989). The divisions of labor that exist are voluntary and arise on the basis of specialized knowledge rather than a special organizational role (Meyer 1989). The lack of a designated leader prevents hacker groups from being categorized as formal organizations (Meyer 1989). Most relationships and groups in the hacker subculture appear transitory, particularly with regard to web forums (Holt 2009a).

At a broader level it appears that hacking has evolved to constitute a deviant community (Holt 2009a) which is the most sophisticated form of social organization (Best and Luckenbill 1994). Deviant communities share common territories and are institutionally complete, in that they provide resources to facilitate the activities of the community (Best and Luckenbill 1994). Hackers do not necessarily share common territory off-line, though their use of on-line spaces for communication and connections are strong evidence of communal relations (Holt 2009a). Additionally, there are various businesses, websites, and retailers who offer services designed specifically for hackers, including clothing and technological materials (Holt 2009a). Thus, these resources demonstrate that hackers exist within an institutionally complete community.

As a whole, hackers exist in a diverse social environment with relationships that span the continuum of deviant and non-deviant organizational sophistication (Holt 2009a). The on- and off-line social ties between hackers enable individuals to share information, tools, and indoctrinate individuals into the general hacker subculture (Holt 2009a, 2009b). Thus, hackers are not introverts but exist in groups without rigidly defined roles, relying on others for help in understanding and developing different skills.

The Hacker Subculture

The unique nature of hacking, and its social organization suggest that hackers operate within a subculture spanning the globe. A subculture is any group having certain values, norms, traditions, and rituals that set them apart from the dominant culture (Wolfgang and Ferracuti 1967). This includes an emphasis on performing certain behaviors or developing skill sets, as well as rules or codes of conduct that structure how individuals view and interact with different groups (Wolfgang and Ferracuti 1967). These all provide ways to measure an individual's reputation, status, and adherence to the subculture. Researchers have explored various aspects of the hacker subculture, and an in-depth exploration of this subculture was provided in Holt's (2007) assessment of the on- and off-line influences and experiences of the computer hacker. He identified five subcultural values that set the hacker subculture apart from the rest of society: technology, knowledge, commitment, categorization, and secrecy/law. The norms identified appear across multiple studies, and give some insight into the hacker subculture as a whole.

Appreciation of Technology

The hacking community is characterized by a shared appreciation for and attitude towards manipulating technology (Holt 2007; Holt et al. 2008; Jordan and Taylor 1998; Loper 2000; Taylor 1999; Thomas 2002). In fact, hackers define themselves and their activities by their relationship to technology, computers, and communication technology. Hackers adhere to the belief that technology can be manipulated and result in new, unexpected uses (Holt 2007; Holt et al. 2008; Jordan and Taylor 1998; Loper 2000; Taylor 1999; Thomas 2002). The rapid diffusion of technology across the world has enabled hackers to easily use and manipulate computers with support from others around the globe online (Holt 2009b; Taylor 1999). Local peer networks and real world relationships, including those developed at hacker conferences play an important role in developing and improving an individual's relationship to technology (Holt 2007, 2009a, 2009b; Thomas 2002). Thus, the more time hackers devote to understanding new technologies, the more that they can increase their skills.

Knowledge

The importance of technology undergirds the hackers' dedication to learn and understand technology (Holt 2007; Jordan and Taylor 1998). Holt (2007) determined that learning and knowledge also bear great influence on the respect and status a hacker may receive from the hacker community as they are often labeled within the subculture by the level of knowledge they demonstrate. Knowledge directly impacts how a hacker is received within the subculture as unskilled, new hackers are disparaged for asking questions instead of finding the answer for themselves (Holt 2007; Jordan and Taylor 1998; Mann and Sutton 1998). Taylor (1999) contends that cyberspace allows the conditions necessary for cooperation of technologically adept and curious people. The history of hacking is a history of technology as information that has become restricted and is no longer "free." The liberation of information and the hacker ethic are often used as justifications to keep knowledge and information open to all (Thomas 2002, 11). With knowledge comes power, and also the power to monitor those in power and hold those persons accountable (Thomas 2002, 120). Additionally, hackers use contacts made at conferences and local meetings to facilitate information sharing, trading, and the capacity to ask for advice and opinions from other hackers (Holt 2007, 2009a, 2009b).

Commitment

The importance of knowledge of technology is directly related to an individual's commitment to hacking (Holt 2007). Computer hacking skills take a great amount of dedication, effort, and time to learn. In fact, Meyer (1989) recognized that hackers must perpetually learn new skills and master their social and physical environment. Hackers demonstrate their commitment and mastery by referring to the history of hacking and using hacker jargon when talking to others (Loper 2000). New hackers who demonstrate a lack of skill and effort are often berated and given no information whereas a more adept, devoted hacker would be given information because of their commitment to the art of hacking. Newer hackers could fare better in the subculture if they demonstrated that they were prepared to actually learn the 'craft' (Holt 2007; Mann and Sutton 1998). New hackers committed to learn the language, lurk on hacker websites, and respect more esteemed hackers and their idiosyncrasies, were more likely to gain status within the subculture (Mann and Sutton 1998, 218). For example, Schell and Dodge (2002) determined that black hat hackers spent more than twice the time on hacking than did their white hat counterparts. Thus, commitment deeply affects the hacker subculture.

Identity

Holt (2007) contends that the hacker identity based on their commitment to understand technology at profound levels. The variations observed in the terms used by hackers to differentiate themselves are a reflection of the complex nature of hacker identity. Meyer (1989) found that most hackers object to the misuse of the hacker label as presented by the media because the label is only presented when discussing crime. There is a debate within and outside of the subculture over how to define hackers, but the most common characteristics among hackers are curiosity and a desire to learn (Holt 2007; Jordan and Taylor 1998; Loper 2000; Taylor 1999; Thomas 2002). Some skilled hackers, however, reject the label of 'hacker' because they view this term as an ideal that cannot be reached, as one must know all of technology to be deemed a hacker. Additionally, terms like script kiddie, white hat, or black hat are all ways to identify and define hackers based on their skill and knowledge of technology.

Law/Secrecy

The final norm that structures the hacker subculture is the importance of understanding legal risks and maintaining secrecy (Holt 2007). Members of the hacker subculture exert great effort to conceal their illegal behavior from law enforcement, yet there is a desire to brag about hacking accomplishments and share new knowledge online (Jordan and Taylor 1998). While such boasts may increase a hackers' status within the subculture, they also risk detection from law enforcement (Holt 2007). Thus, hackers attempt to reduce legal attention in on- and off-line contexts and frequently discuss law enforcement within the subculture (Holt 2007). Hackers who have been caught are, however, famous for testifying against their fellow hackers in order to receive plea bargains that go against the importance of secrecy (Loper 2000). Individuals within the subculture begrudgingly accept that hackers might "snitch" on others if put under extreme pressure or other circumstances (Loper 2000, 24). Secrecy is also evident when researchers attempt to study hackers as they routinely resist any attempts to gain entry into their secretive subculture (Jordan and Taylor 1998; Loper 2000; Taylor 1999; Thomas 2002). Taken as a whole, secrecy and the law play an important role in structuring the relationships between hackers and law enforcement.

Conclusions

It is clear that research on hackers provide significant insights into the nature of this behavior. Though there are no consistent definitions for hacker, the most basic labels generally used, particularly white hat and black hat, have consistent meanings and applications inside and outside of the hacker community. In addition, hackers exist within a subculture that focuses on technology and values knowledge and applications of skill over and above criminal or malicious activity. Hackers also operate within a relatively collegial social environment on and off-line, where individuals can acquire information, tools, and resources, to facilitate all manner of hacks.

Although our understanding of hackers has advanced in recent years, many questions still remain to be explored in future research. Most importantly, there is very little understanding of the socio-demographics of hackers. While it is clear that most hackers are male, there have been few considerations of the gendered nature of this subculture. Additionally, surveys collecting socio-demographic information are typically given to college students, which may or may not be representative of the larger hacker community. Studies have also focused on illegal computer activities, disregarding other common legal behaviors that could be used to categorize hackers. Thus, research is needed to examine these issues to better understand the social dynamics of legal and illegal applications of hacking.

References

Best, J. and D.F. Luckenbill. 1982. *Organizing Deviance.* Inglewood Cliff, NJ: Prentice-Hall.

Best, J. and D.F. Luckenbill. 1994. *Organizing Deviance, 2nd edition.* Inglewood Cliff, NJ: Prentice-Hall.

Best, K. 2003. The hacker's challenge: Active access to information, visceral democracy and discursive practice. *Social Semiotics* 13(3): 263–282.

Fitch, C. 2003. Crime and punishment: The psychology of hacking in the new millennium. GSEC. http://www.giac.org/certified_professionals/practicals/gsec/3560.php.

Furnell, S. 2002. *Cybercrime: Vandalizing the Information Society.* London: Addison-Wesley.

Gilboa, N. 1996. Elites, lamers, narcs, and whores: Exploring the computer underground. *Wired_Women.* Seattle: Seal Press.

Gordon, S. and R. Ford. 2003. Cyberterrorism? Symantec Security Response. http://www.symantec.com/avcenter/reference/cyberterrorism.pdf.

Gordon, S. and Q. Ma. 2003. Convergence of virus writers and hackers: Fact or fantasy? Symantec. Cupertino, CA.

Grabosky, P. 2001. Computer Crime: a Criminological Overview. *Forum on Crime and Society* 1(1): 35–54.

Håpnes, T. and K. Sørensen. 1995. Competition and collaboration in male shaping of computing: A study of a Norwegian hacker culture. In *The Gender-Technology Relation: Contemporary Theory and Research*, ed. Keith Grint and Rosalind Gill, 174–191. Bristol, PA: Taylor and Francis.

Higgins, G. 2004. Can low self-control help with the understanding of the software piracy problem? *Deviant Behavior* 26: 1–24.

Hollinger, R.C. 1993. Crime by computer: Correlates of software piracy and unauthorized account access. *Security J* 4(1): 2–12.

Holt, T.J. 2007. Subcultural evolution? Examining the influence of on- and off-line experiences on deviant subcultures. *Deviant Behavior* 28: 171–198.

Holt, T.J. 2009a. Lone Hacks or Group Cracks: Examining the Social Organization of Computer Hackers. In *Crimes of the Internet*, ed. Frank Schmalleger and Michael Pittaro, 336–355. Upper Saddle River, NJ: Pearson Prentice Hall.

Holt, T.J. 2009b. The Attack Dynamics of Political and Religiously Motivated Hackers. Paper presented at the 2009 Cyber Infrastructure Conference, June 3–4, in New York.

Holt, T.J., and A.M. Bossler. 2009. Examining the Applicability of Lifestyle-Routine Activities Theory for Cybercrime Victimization. *Deviant Behavior* 30: 1–25.

Holt, T.J. and M. Kilger. 2008. Techcrafters and Makecrafters: A Comparison of Two Populations of Hackers. Paper presented at the Invitation-Only Worldwide Observatory of Malicious Behaviors and Attack Threats Conference, April 21–22, in Amsterdam, Netherlands.

Holt, T.J., J. Soles, and L. Leslie. 2008. Characterizing malware writers and computer attackers in their own words. Paper presented at the 3rd International Conference on Information Warfare and Security, April 24–25, in Omaha, Nebraska.

Jordan, T. and P. Taylor. 1998. A sociology of hackers. *The Sociological Review* 46(4): 757–780.

Jordan, T. and P. Taylor. 2004. *Hacktivism and Cyber Wars*. London: Routledge.

Kilger, M., O. Arkin, and J. Stutzman. 2004. Profiling. In *Know Your Enemy: Learning about Security Threats*, ed. The Honeynet Project. Addison-Wesley Professional. http://old.honeynet.org/book/Chp16.pdf.

Levy, S. 1984. *Hackers: Heroes of the Computer Revolution*. Garden City: Anchor Press/ Doubleday.

Loper, K. 2000. The criminology of computer hackers: A qualitative and quantitative analysis. PhD diss., Michigan State University.

Mann, D. and M. Sutton. 1998. Netcrime: More change in the organization of thieving. *Brit. J. Criminology,* 38(2): 201–229.

Meyer, G.R. 1989. The social organization of the computer underground. Master's thesis, Northern Illinois University.

Rogers, M. 1999. The psychology of hackers: A new taxonomy. Paper presented at the RSA World Security Conference, Feb 1999, in San Jose, California.

Rogers, M. 2001. A social learning theory and moral disengagement analysis of criminal computer behavior: An exploratory study. PhD diss., Manitoba University, Canada.

Rogers, M., N. Smoak, and J. Liu. 2005. Self-reported deviant computer behavior: a big-5, moral choice, and manipulative exploitive behavior analysis. *Deviant Behavior* 27: 245–268.

Schell, B. and J. Dodge. 2002. *The Hacking of America: Who's Doing It, Why, and How*. Westport, CT: Quorum Books.

Segan, S. 2000. Female hackers battle sexism to get ahead. ABC News. http://abcnews.go.com/Technology/story?id=99341&page=1.

Skinner, W. and A. Fream. 1997. A social learning theory analysis of computer crime among college students. *Journal of Research in Crime and Delinquency* 34 (4): 495–518.

Sollfrank, C. 1999. Woman hackers. OBN. http://www.obn.org/hackers/text1.htm.

Stambaugh, H., D.S. Beaupre, D.J. Icove, R. Baker, W. Cassaday, and W. P. Williams. 2001. Electronic crime needs assessment for state and local law enforcement. National Institute of Justice Research Report.

Sterling, B. 1993. *The Hacker Crackdown: Law and Disorder on the Electronic Frontier*. New York: Bantam.

Taylor, P. 1999. *Hackers: Crime in the Digital Sublime*. London: Routledge.

Thomas, D. 2002. *Hacker Culture*. University of Minnesota Press.

Trigaux, R. 2000. A history of hacking. St. Petersburg Times Online. http://www.sptimes.com/Hackers/history.hacking.html.

Turgeman-Goldschmidt, O. 2005. Hacker's accounts: Hacking as a social entertainment. *Social Science Computer Review* 23 (1): 8–23.

Turkle, S. 1984. *The Second Self: Computers and the Human Spirit*. New York: Simon and Schuster.

Wolfgang, Marvin E. and F. Ferracuti. 1967. *The subculture of violence: Towards an integrated theory in criminology*. London: Tavistock Publications.

Yar, M. 2005. Computer hacking: Just another case of juvenile delinquency? *The Howard Journal* 44(4): 387–399.

3

Hacking—The Pervert's Guide to Information

Paul A. Taylor

> Every epoch, in fact, not only dreams the one to follow but, in dreaming, precipitates its awakening. It bears its end within itself and unfolds it—as Hegel already noticed—by cunning. With the destabilizing of the market economy, we begin to recognize the monuments of the bourgeoisie as ruins even before they have crumbled. (Benjamin 1999, 13)

> They find themselves shoved into an everyday life that turns them into henchmen of the technological excesses. (Kracauer 1995, 70)

Benjamin's above quotation is particularly apposite in the midst of a global financial crisis almost exclusively brought about by what Žižek so memorably terms "the mad, self-enhancing circulation of capital, whose solipsistic path of parthogenesis reaches its apogee in today's meta-reflexive speculations on futures" (Žižek 2008, 10). Influenced by the manner in which Benjamin's cultural analysis places dual emphasis upon developing both a prescience for the essential nature of future social epochs and a self-conscious nostalgia for what is being left behind, this chapter proposes that the way we look at the figure of the hacker should be opened up much more broadly. The hacker is presented in this chapter as a revealing trope for the difficult to pin down, but nevertheless profound change in social atmosphere that accompanies the shift from an industrial to an informational society. Society's perception of hacking is one that has evolved from admiration of the ingenious technological curiosity it first exhibited to the subsequent condemnation and marginalization of the hi-tech criminality it subsequently became synonymous with (for a full account of this process of legal and cultural marginalization see Taylor 1999). The purpose of this chapter is to concentrate upon the full implications of hacking as viewed in its earliest, most optimistic cultural representations. This is because today's blanket criminalization of hacking gives us little but an unreflexively negative sense of its cultural significance. By contrast, notwithstanding this chapter's critical deconstruction of early optimistic interpretations of the hacking phenomenon, at least their wrong answers were motivated by the right sort of questions about the true nature of our relationship to our informational environments. Questions not so readily raised once hacking is reduced to a criminal activity.

In psychoanalysis, the term *pervert* refers beyond its usual sexual connotation to one who has an unhealthy overdependence upon rules and structures rather than ultimate ends as succinctly described in Karl Kraus's bons mots: "There is no more unfortunate being under the sun than a fetishist, who yearns for a woman's shoe and has to make do with a whole woman" (Kraus 1977, 225). This chapter argues that insights garnered from philosophical, literary and cultural theory are essential components of the analytical perspective necessary to prevent us from becoming informational perverts in a technological environment that would otherwise pervasively overwhelm our critical faculties—as Marshall McLuhan pointed out: "whoever discovered water, it wasn't a fish." (cited in Merrin 2005, 61) This paper thus takes a step back from the fine grain of contemporary matters surrounding information protection and instead analyses hacking's wider role in the cultural history that preceded it. Using such a historical context, hacking is then re-presented as the recent manifestation of the ambivalence of our on-going engagement and alienation in the face of technology. But more than its technologically-driven exploration of the digital *Matrix* of popular imagination this chapter also demonstrates its place in the Matrix's cultural/economic corollary—the commodity *matrix*. A distinction is made throughout this chapter between the Matrix with a capitalized M and the lower case matrix. This is to emphasise both the distinction but also the commonalities between technocentric nature of the digital Matrix and its underlying economic infrastructure—the commodity matrix (see Taylor and Harris 2005 for a full account). It is argued that exclusive concentration upon the digital Matrix at the expense of the more implicit, but no less real, matrices that pervade our cultural and economic life is a mistake that this paper compensates for by drawing upon the cultural theory of some of the most imaginative sociologists of modern society's technological beginnings.

In its first developments, the size and relative crudity of computing equipment meant that hacking could be seen as a close relation to traditional hands-on craftwork, electronic tinkering etc. (as described in detail by Levy 1984). The inverse relationship between the decreased size but increased opacity of digital technology, however, shifted the focus of hacking away from the hardware itself to the immateriality of the abstract informational spaces created by newly available databases and pervasive connectivity. Legal debates continue to arise in an on-going attempt to codify society's response to the complexities of informational immateriality (the April 2009 prosecution of the Swedish Pirate Bay group is a case in point). To the extent that the early hackers tinkered with prototype computers, the direct and empowering nature of their approach to technology was obvious. Less clear, however, is the status of such engagement when applied to the non-physical spaces of new informational realms. On the one hand, hackers grappled with technological frontiers and went "where no man has gone before," yet on the other hand, exploration and enjoyment of those frontiers appeared to take place at the cost of losing a significant element of autonomy within the environments into which they were immersing themselves so enthusiastically.

Such was the unprecedented nature of early hacking's exploratory activity that it is perhaps unsurprising that fiction has been able to intuit and describe the qualitative novelty of the phenomenon earlier and more easily than conventional social science. The cyberpunk novelist Bruce Sterling hence explained how the work of his colleague, William Gibson, had so successfully gripped the popular imagination and in the process familiarized us with such radical concepts as cyberspace and the Matrix. He argued that: "Gibson's extrapolations show, with exaggerated clarity, the hidden bulk of an iceberg of social change. This iceberg now glides with sinister majesty across the surface of the late twentieth century, but its proportions are vast and dark" (Sterling in Gibson 1986, 11). Fiction's exaggerated clarity is unapologetically utilised in this chapter to demonstrate aspects of technologically-mediated experience unobtainable to more conventional modes of enquiry. Whilst works of fiction are repeatedly referred to, the theme of imagination is used here in the more general sense proposed in C. Wright Mills *The Sociological Imagination* (1958)— a mode of thinking that is based upon a concertedly reflexive attitude to the relationship between particular phenomena and the larger social environments within which they take place. In this seminal critique of social science's myopic deficiencies, Mills counsels those studying society to steer a middle ground between the "abstracted empiricism" of excessively quantitative accounts and the "high theory" of overly speculative and abstract interpretations.

I have attempted to heed Mills' counsel in my own work. It consists of both detailed empirical studies of the early hacker community (Taylor and Jordan 1998, Taylor 1999) and later hacktivist generations (Taylor and Jordan 2004) but also sustained consideration some of the broader issues these socio-technical phenomena raise. With the benefit of additional hindsight, this piece argues that a full understanding of hacking requires further examination of its philosophical implications and the wider resonances of its cultural representations. Along with Mills' call for greater sociological imagination, a further justification for a more faceted interpretation of hacking is found in Heidegger's related philosophical distinction between what is merely *correct* and what is substantively *true*. Thus, accurate and factually informative social science accounts of hacking's various forms and techniques risk suffering from the irony that, their intellectual expertise notwithstanding, they may merely mirror the significant limitations of their object of study and replicate, through a lack of sociological imagination, the reflexively limited nature of hacking's specific form of technical ingenuity. A negative defining feature of hacking (as opposed to its more politically reflexive successor hacktivism—see Jordan and Taylor 2004) is the manner in which it constitutes an activity premised, more than most, upon a blurring of technological means and human ends—an ultimate inability or unwillingness to look beyond the technological framework that is otherwise manipulated so imaginatively—a fault that a social science seeking to understand hacking should avoid.

Empirically dense studies of hacking thus risk replicating Hackers' tendency to over-privilege means over ends. The inherently limited (albeit technically sophisticated) hacking interaction with technological systems is inadvertently matched by technically proficient but similarly unreflexive academic research that fails to engage with hacking's wider cultural significance. An informed theoretical critique needs to consist of a correctively less one-dimensional perspective that takes into account Mills' admonition about the dangers of losing our sociological imagination, and Heidegger's argument that the factually *correct* does not necessarily (in fact, seldom does) equate with what is *true* in a more substantial and phenomenologically richer sense. To provide this broader perspective, the following pages draw upon the philosophy and cultural theory of past thinkers seldom (and rarely, if ever as an interrelated group) discussed in relation to hacking—Walter Benjamin and Siegfried Kracauer. In particular, a close reading and extensive citation of Kracauer's work is used in order to re-problematize hacking and thereby understand better our society's ill-starred relationship with technology.

Cyberspace—A Square without Mercy

> Cyberspace. A consensual hallucination experienced daily by billions of legitimate operators, in every nation, by children being taught mathematical concepts ... A graphic representation of data abstracted from banks of every computer in the human system. Unthinkable complexity. Lines of light ranged in the nonspace of the mind, clusters and constellations of data. Like city lights, receding into the distance ... (Gibson 1984, 67)

The above excerpt taken from the seminal cyberpunk novel *Neuromancer* that first popularized the concept of cyberspace, although much quoted, has been interpreted in a limited fashion. The notion of "consensual hallucination" has frequently been discussed primarily in relation to the computing technology that facilitates it. A deeper reading, however, suggests additional factors that can help to shed extra light upon the significance of cyberspace and the hacking activities that purport to explore it. The phrase "consensual hallucination" repays careful consideration. It simultaneously and paradoxically indicates a voluntary commitment to an unreal environment that nevertheless is a very real part of everyday life for billions of people. The phrase "legitimate" clearly implies that what was once the sole preserve of hacker pioneers is now much more widely accessible. This accessibility is shown to be premised upon a process of abstraction that has its origins as far back in human culture, and is as familiar, even to children, as mathematics. However, whilst the representations are said to be of "unthinkable" complexity the abstract data nevertheless assumes the form of graphic representations.

In philosophical terms, this simultaneous mode of comprehension/incomprehension is reminiscent of the conceptual sleight of hand involved in Kant's category of the sublime. Whilst Kant presents the sublime as something supra-rational—for example, the overwhelming sense of power experienced when witnessing such a phenomenon of nature as a hurricane, our sense of the sublime actually serves to reassert, in an under-acknowledged fashion, the primacy given to reason after all. This is because the purportedly unthinkable is in fact subtly used to reinforce the power of thought. We only temporarily feel overwhelmed before reason reasserts itself as we come to terms with our initial disorientation. Thus, in the midst of Gibson's "unthinkable complexity" we are immediately presented with the compensatory explanatory analogy of "city lights, receding into the distance." The Kantian sublime is divided into two categories. It can either be *mathematical* or *dynamical*. Both of these elements are evident in Gibsonian cyberspace. The mathematical sublime—the overwhelming of our ability to intuit through sheer scale and size—is referred to above in terms of the "unthinkable complexity" of the amount of data being presented to the imagination. The dynamical sublime—the overwhelming feeling derived from the experience of immense power, e.g., the elemental force of the hurricane—is evident in both cyberpunk fiction and, more prosaically, real world hacking culture.

In both hacking fiction and fact, it is the very inhuman qualities and quantities experienced as an inchoate adrenalin rush when accessing the Matrix that are presented as thrilling forms of the dynamical sublime—a misleadingly positive thrill that I have elsewhere critically analysed in terms of excessive *in-*

formational intimacy (see Taylor 2001). Gibson provides the following portrayal of this phenomenologically new mode of accessing information:

> he closed his eyes … It came on again, gradually, a flickering, non-linear flood of fact and sensory data, a kind of narrative conveyed in surreal jumpcuts and juxtapositions. It was vaguely like riding a rollercoaster and phased in and out of existence at random, impossibly rapid intervals, changing altitude attack, and direction with each pulse of nothingness, except that the shifts had nothing to do with any physical orientation, but rather with lightning alternations in paradigm and symbol system. The data had never been intended for human input. (Gibson 1986, 40)

Demonstrating the resonance of Gibson's fiction with the non-fictional real world, Ellen Ullman, a computer programmer describes the experience of writing code in a similar manner:

> We give ourselves over to the sheer fun of the technical, to the nearly sexual pleasure of the clicking though-stream. Some part of me mourns, but I know there is no other way: human needs must cross the line into code. They must pass through this semipermeable membrane where urgency, fear, and hope are filtered out, and only reason travels across … Actual human confusions cannot live here. Everything we want accomplished, everything the system is to provide, must be denatured in its crossing to the machine, or else the system will die. (Ullman 1997, 15)

To reiterate the key philosophical point behind the Kantian sublime, neither its mathematical or dynamical aspects constitute our final experience of it. Rather, our reason is excited by the sublime but still survives the encounter. In the context of hacking and society's wider relationship to our informational environments (in which hackers represented the vanguard), it is thus significant that hackers (and cyberpunks as their fictional counterparts) have typically been presented as embodiments of informational jouissance with much less attention being paid to how that jouissance has then been tamed by the corporate rationale to which it is ultimately subordinated.

In cyberpunk fiction, the hacker figures typically act under the behest of overarching capitalist powers whilst, more prosaically, Douglas Coupland's "factional" novel *Microserfs* (1995) portrays the corporate co-optation of programmers originally driven by Ellen Ullman's sort of programming enthusiasm. Critical theorists explain the roots of such co-optation as residing in the false sense of technological empowerment held by figures such as hackers and their techno-optimist theorist defenders. From such a critical perspective, hacking represents a virtuoso playing *with* but not undermining *of* the system in which it takes place. Thus, writing of the hacker-like radio ham, Adorno is scathing in his assessment of its ultimately quiescent political potential:

> At twenty, he is still at the stage of a boy scout working on complicated knots just to please his parents. This type is held in high esteem in radio matters. He patiently builds sets whose most important parts he must buy ready-made, and scans the air for shortwave secrets, though there are none. As a reader of Indian stories and travel books, he once discovered unknown lands and cleared his path through the forest primeval. As radio ham, he becomes the discoverer of just those industrial products which are interested in being discovered by him. He brings nothing home that would not be delivered to his house. (Adorno 1991 [1938], 54)

Similarly, Baudrillard roundly rejects the notion that widespread familiarity with technological gadgets is likely to lay the basis for the sorts of revolutionary social change that were claimed when computing was first developed:

> … this "revolution" at bottom conserves the category of transmitter, which it is content to generalize as separated, transforming everyone into his own transmitter, it fails to place the mass media system in check. We know the results of such phenomena as mass ownership of walkie-talkies, or everyone making their own cinema: a kind of personalized amateurism, the equivalent of Sunday tinkering on the periphery of the system. (Baudrillard 1981, 182)

The reasons for Adorno and Baudrillard's profoundly negative assessment of any likely positive outcome from the interaction of the hacker mentality and the technological sublime are to be found in the roots of the social and economic system that fundamentally undermines notions of individual autonomy and which pre-dated digital technology. It is to these roots that we now turn.

New Technology—Old Theory

Walter Benjamin's famous essay "The Work of Art in the Age of Mechanical Reproduction" (1936—subsequently referred to as the Essay) represents an early theorization of the key issues later highlighted by the advent of hacking. Writing about the mechanical precursors to digital technology (photography and film) Benjamin describes the decline of a traditional art object or natural event's *aura* (aura being defined as an emanation of presence innately tied to a unique point in space and time). According to Benjamin, the mass dissemination of mechanically reproduced images and sound introduces a qualitatively new phenomenological experience based upon the cultural changes brought about by mass reproducibility compared to humankind's previous dependence upon aura so that: "Uniqueness and permanence are as closely linked in the latter as are transitoriness and reproducibility in the former" (Benjamin 1936, Section 3 [unpaginated]). It is in this context of new technologies of reproduction and the changes they wrought upon society that figures such as the semi-mythical figure of the Parisian flâneur (the proto-hacker of the city) arose. A dandyish figure, who was *in* but not *of* the crowd, the flâneur savored for his own contemplation (*he* was conceived as an exclusively male character) the growing flux and speed of the newly emerging technological urbanization of Paris and the whole new range of sense impressions so created.

Whilst Benjamin's Essay takes a largely optimistic point of view about the profound change to the human condition this radical technologically-facilitated change had created, it also contains the potential for much more ambivalent analysis (see Taylor and Harris 2008)—it provides the early basis of a critical theoretical talk for the practical walk/surf that hackers later came to adopt in this new realm of "transitoriness and reproducibility." Consisting of a diverse range of theoretical and everyday sources—street scenes, feuilletons, advertisements etc, Benjamin's fragmentary magnum opus, *The Arcades Project* (Das Passagen-Werk), provides valuable additional critical insights into the nascent social processes that lay behind the informational environment later traversed by hackers and its potentially deleterious consequences. *The Arcades Project* created an impressionistic account of vestigial capitalist modernity by describing the growth of the urban flows in Paris of the 19th Century that later evolved into the communicational data streams of cyberspace. Benjamin's interest in the flâneur was drawn from the poet Baudelaire who in turn approvingly cited Edgar Allan Poe's depiction of *The Man of the Crowd* (1845) who "hurls himself headlong into the midst of the throng" (Baudelaire 2003, 7) and for whom:

> The crowd is his element, as the air is that of birds and water of fishes. His passion and his profession are to become one flesh with the crowd. For the perfect flâneur, for the passionate spectator, it is an immense joy set up house in the heart of the multitude, amid the ebb & flow of movement, in the midst of the fugitive & the infinite. To be away from home and yet to feel oneself everywhere at home; to see the world, and yet to remain hidden from the world ... the lover of universal life enters into the crowd as if it were *an immense reservoir of electrical energy.* (Baudelaire 2003, 9–10 [emphasis added])

One can see, especially from the final italicized phrase, how Baudelaire prefigures the later, much more explicitly technologized forms of space such as the Matrix as seen in this excerpt from *Neuromancer* (1984) that expresses the comparable informational intimacy experienced by the console cowboy (fictional hacker) Case: "He felt a stab of elation … You're enjoying this, he thought; you're crazy … you could throw yourself into a highspeed drift and skid, totally engaged but set apart from it all, and all around you the dance of biz, information interacting, data made flesh in the mazes of the black market" (Gibson 1984, 26). The flâneur's desire to become one flesh with the crowd is mirrored by the console cowboy's identification of the streets' busy commerce with "data made flesh" and his desire to be simultaneously "totally engaged but set apart from it all."

Using such early European sources as Baudelaire and Benjamin, cyberpunk's fictional portrayal of the real world experience of hacking, which originally appeared as groundbreaking, can actually be seen as part of a continuum of cultural expressions of how we deal with new technologized spaces whether they be the city or the hacker's databases. In the following excerpt, Benjamin expresses this conflation of not only the allegorical and real world phenomenological experience of modern life, but also its political implications as the middleclass values of consumption begin to dominate in their new phantasmagorical guise.

> … the gaze of the allegorist, as it falls on the city, is the gaze of the alienated man. It is the gaze of the flâneur, whose way of life still conceals behind a mitigating nimbus the coming desolation of the big-city dweller. The flâneur still stands on the threshold—of the metropolis as of the middleclass. Neither has him in its power yet. In neither is he at home. He seeks refuge in the crowd. Early contributions to a physiognomics of the crowd are found in Engels and Poe. The crowd is the veil through which the familiar city beckons to the flâneur as phantasmagoria—now a landscape, now a room. Both become elements of the department store, which makes use of flanerie itself to sell goods. The department store is the last promenade for the flâneur. (Benjamin 1999, 10)

Importantly, once can see here the clear identification of the very beginnings of the process in which flanerie conceived as an attempt to achieve distance from modernity's fluxes and flows then merely becomes co-opted into a new commodified modes of selling (thus resonating with the previously cited manner in which the initially emotive experience of the Kantian sublime eventually serves to reinforce the power of rationality). This insight goes straight to the heart of the Benjaminian manner of expressing how both places and people can come to represent symbols of society's failed hopes. Flanerie, initially a mode of playful resistance to modernity's irrepressible march, soon becomes part of that onward surge. Similarly, the early hacker non-utilitarian celebration of technological reverse engineering and dissemination of computing power to the people (the founding days of Apple computers) was soon replaced by corporate success and the strained contradiction of Microsoft (Microserf) programmers with Che Guevarra posters in the bedroom and stock options in their personal investment portfolios (see Taylor 1998).

Prefiguring the womb-like nature of the Matrix (the root of the word coming from the Latin word for mother—*Mater*) Benjamin describes the Parisian shopping arcades as temporary islands of relative calm in the increasingly flux-ridden city. For Parisians of the time, the fantastical new experience of the Arcade's exterior glass and steel lattice work in conjunction with the abundance of shop windows inside provided a foretaste of the subsequent cornucopia of department stores displays and, by extension, the computer screens of online shopping. A large element of Benjamin's *Arcades Project* is its tone of nostalgia. Benjamin portrayed a short-lived moment of tranquility that, by the time of his writing, had already made way for the bulldozing activities of Baron Haussmann who redesigned Paris with wide spacious boulevards—the better for the army to repress revolutionary crowds and for such new channels of transport to act heralds of modernity's various architectural and technological monuments to speed. Benjamin accounts for the origin of both the Matrix of hacking imagination and the over-riding supremacy of commodity values that point to a matrix that increasingly incorporates both our technological and cultural experiences to the extent that the two are increasingly indivisible. He described this enveloping conflation of physical environments and the more general aestheticization of alienation by referring to both such physical events as the World Exhibitions and new social processes whereby people are commodified in unprecedented ways—the combination creating a new cultural framework/matrix that served to lay the basis of the digital Matrix as can be seen here:

> World Exhibitions glorify the exchange value of the commodity. They create a framework in which its use value recedes into the background. They open a phantasmagoria which a person enters in order to be distracted. The entertainment industry makes this easier by elevating the person to the level of the commodity. He surrenders to its manipulations while enjoying his alienation from himself and others.—The enthronement of the commodity, with its luster of distraction … (Benjamin 1999, 7)

A contemporary of Walter Benjamin (and Theodor Adorno's tutor in philosophy), Siegfried Kracauer, conceptualized this changing nature of traditional experience and the rise of a new realm of phantasmagorical distraction. In a series of articles written in the 1920s and early 1930s that came to be known under the title of *The Mass Ornament: Weimar Essays*, he used concepts such as *Ratio* to explain 'the enthronement of the commodity, with its luster of distraction' and the alienating consequences for the individual. He thereby anticipated, with his various cultural concepts describing an incipient matrix, later conceptualizations of the technological environment within which hackers operate—the Matrix.

Siegfried Kracauer

Kracauer's work frequently portrays the increasingly homogenized nature of life within the vestigial commodity matrix also described by Benjamin. He discusses a general society-wide process of increasing immaterial abstraction that nevertheless has profoundly material consequences. He therefore prefigures the later rise of digitally-sponsored im/materiality—the complex interactions and imbrications of the material and its immaterial underpinnings (see Taylor and Harris 2005). Kracauer's analysis is illuminating for the manner in which it represents a continuation of Marx's famous observation that within capitalism "All that's solid melts into air, all that is holy is profaned" into an age when this liquefying of experience was just beginning to gain pace through the effects of mass media. For example, in his essay "Travel and Dance" (originally published in 1925), he describes how the emerging mass media society was beginning to replace experiential ambiguity with the predictable and formulaic. He used language that presciently resonated with such later conceptualizations as cyberspace: "Radio, telephotography, and so forth—each and every one of these outgrowths of rational fantasy aimlessly serves one single aim: the constitution of a depraved omnipresence within calculable dimensions" (Kracauer 1995, 70).

The statement "rational fantasy aimlessly serves one single aim"—contains two apparent oxymorons which, after further thought, reveal an essential thread that underlies Kracauer's idea of the mass ornament and Adorno's more (in)famous notion of the culture industry—the two concepts representing forms of cultural matrices from which the Matrix arose. "Rational fantasy" is an aptly contradictory phrase for the factory-like production of the early Hollywood system of "creative production" that has now passed into the hyper-automated keyboard-processed realms of the studio *imagineers*. Similarly, "aimlessly serves one single aim," provides a succinct expression of the way in which seemingly multifarious media are in fact undergirded by a common, uniform agenda, the phrase acting as the culture industry's negative corollary to Adorno's neo-Kantian definition of art as "purposiveness without purpose." Both statements, however, culminate in the evocative notion of "a depraved omnipresence within calculable dimensions"—which once again both constitutes a critical, negatively-couched precursor of later descriptions of cyberspace, and a re-stating of Kant's notion of the sublime in the context of an incipient commodity matrix. In this instance of the technological sublime, according to Kracauer, new media technologies are both alarming ("depraved ominipresence") but ultimately rational ("within calculable dimensions").

In his essay "Travel and Dance," Kracauer further develops a range of ideas by which to explore this apparent paradox of depraved rationality, referring back to this chapter's epigraph from Benjamin, "we begin to recognize the monuments of the bourgeoisie as ruins even before they have crumbled." Kracauer argues that travelling to "exotic" places in an attempt to escape quotidian reality becomes increasingly constrained by the fact that organized travel, by its very nature, tends to diminish significantly the chance of authentically experiencing the exotic qualities that are nominally being sought. The motivation for experiencing the exotic in the first place stems from a desire to escape the deadening homogeneity of the mechanized world, it being "their sole remaining means of showing that they have outgrown the regions of the Here that enslave them" (Kracauer 1995, 71). Whilst the original motivation for travel is explained by the desire to escape commodity society's homogeneity ("one hotel is like the next, and the nature in the background is familiar to readers of illustrated magazines" (Kracauer 1995, 66)), like a microcosmic experience of the general experience of commodity consumption, it is fated to remain unfulfilled. Travellers, "experience supra-spatial *endlessness* ... Such travel is of the sort that above all and most of the time has no particular destination; its meaning is exhausted in the mere fact of changing locations" (Kracauer 1995, 71 [emphasis added]).

The rise of cyberspace can be viewed as the (il)logical extension of this supra-spatial endlessness. The hacker realizes through cultural perceptiveness Kracauer's original insight. The hacker merely "cuts to the chase" and learns to enjoy rather than be deluded by this experience of travel as an end in itself—supra-spatial endlessness. The physical travel through increasingly homogeneous physical space described by Kracauer mirrors the *self-justifying* movements (whether they be mere eye movements or trips between shops) of both the media viewer and commodity consumer that preceded hacking. A benevolent form of such travel is contained within Benjamin's nostalgic account of the flâneur and his savoring of the city's new flux but Kracauer's appreciation of travel for the post-flâneur is more dire: "The adventure of movement as such is thrilling, and slipping out of accustomed spaces and times into as yet unexplored realms arouses the passions: the ideal here is to roam freely through the dimensions. This spatio-temporal double life could hardly be craved with such intensity, were it not the *distortion* of real life" (Kracauer 1995, 68).

For Kracauer, an individual's authentic experience of reality inevitably consists of an "indissoluble doubleness" akin to Heidegger's notion of *Dasein* (the everyday nature of existence) in which the individual is simultaneously both a being in a particular time and space and also an entity that has a relationship to a Beyond. This realm of the Beyond is produced from a simultaneously immaterial yet very real spatio-temporal tension that surpasses the innate limitations of the here and now (for example, every current moment of reality is imbued with a past that it is influenced by and a future of which it is yet but potential). The consequences for the individual are that:

> The real person, who has not capitulated to being a tool of mechanized industry, resists being dissolved into space and time. He certainly exists in this space here, yet is not utterly dispersed in it or overwhelmed by it. Instead he extends himself across latitudinal and longitudinal parallels into a supra-spatial infinity that should not in any way be confused with the endlessness of astronomic space. (Kracauer 1995, 68)

In contrast to the innate duality of an authentic existence in which the Here and There are inevitably imbricated can be set the sort of flattened-out, etiolated mode of existence that Kracauer sees being produced by a combination of both commodity society and new technology—the M/matrix inhabited by hackers/consumers—the endlessness of an astronomic space inhabited by people reduced to the tools of mechanized industry (the key theme of such novels as Douglas Coupland's *Microserfs* [1995]).

Kracauer offers up a notion of an authentic double life in opposition to the distorted double-life that the traveller (and by extension hacker) craves. Unlike Benjamin's positive interpretation of technology's radical undermining of traditional art, Kracauer perceives an existentially important quality that cannot be authentically replicated by technological reproduction: "Caught in the Here and in need of the Beyond, he leads, in the literal sense of the expression, a *double existence*" (Kracauer 1995, 69 [emphasis in original]). The falsely abstract fluid mobility between the different dimensions of the double existence by the consumer/hacker is a distortion because splitting such a double existence cannot happen authentically: "this duality cannot be split into two positions that could be occupied one after the other, because, when it is understood as man's participation (aroused by an inner tension) in both realms, it defies dissection" (Kracauer 1995, 69). In the inauthentic realm of commodity culture's mass ornament, the relationship between the here and now, and the Beyond's "in-one-another (*Ineinander*) quality, has been reduced to a sequence, to an after-each-other (*Nacheinander*) structure" (Kracauer 1995, 71 [emphasis in original]). This is the distortion of the commodity-form. The substantive meaning of travel is "exhausted in the mere fact of changing locations." The industrial, regimented and formalized nature of the commodity matrix creates a fragmentation of experience for those within the M/matrix—that is, it is a diminution of what could be a fuller experience:

> The forces leading toward mechanization do not aim beyond space and time. They are blessed with an intellect that knows no mercy. Inasmuch as it is convinced that the world can be grasped on the basis of mechanistic presuppositions, this intellect frees itself from all relations to the Beyond and renders pale the reality that man, extended across space and time, occupies. This detached intellect begets technology and aims at a rationalization of life that would accommodate it to technology. But since such a radical flattening out of everything living can only be achieved by sacrificing man's intellectual (geistigen) constitution … in order to make him as smooth and shiny as an automobile, one cannot easily ascribe any real meaning to the bustle of machines and people that it has created. Consequently, technology becomes an end in itself, and a world arises that … desires nothing other than the greatest possible technologizing of all activities. (Kracauer 1995, 69)

The ideological significance of this fragmentation is the false resolution it provides to what should be the irredeemable tension of the authentic double existence. Kracauer's admonition about a mechanized, technologically tautological intellect without mercy, rather than being heeded by our heavily mediated society, instead becomes the implicit manifesto of the flâneur/consumer of the commodity matrix and the hacker of the digital Matrix.

From the perspective of critical cultural theory, the single biggest conceptual error made by techno-optimist advocates of the M/matrix is their mistaken equation of the popularity of this false resolution with authenticity: "The manner in which special spatio-temporal events are currently being savored to the hilt is abundant confirmation that what is at stake in this very enjoyment is a distortion of an increasingly unavailable real existence" (Kracauer 1995, 72). The commodity matrix thus prepares society for the later Matrix since: "these people do not become aware of the limitations of this life Here but instead abandon themselves to the normal contingency within the limitations of the Here" (Kracauer, 72). This claim can be seen in a revealing comparison between critical and more celebratory perceptions of the new technological sublime—Kracauer's negative portrayal of the increasingly mediated experience of early urban centers and a contemporary account of standing in the middle of New York's Time Square. Unlike much of the hacker imaginary, Kracauer dramatically expresses how the excessive mental stimulation caused by a combination of modern technologies and their urban configurations produces a sense of alienation:

> In the centers of night life the illumination is so harsh that one has to hold one's hands over one's ears. Meanwhile the lights have gathered for their own pleasure, instead of shining for man. Their glowing traces want to illuminate the night but succeed only in chasing it away. Their advertisements sink into the mind without allowing one to decipher them. The reddish gleam that lingers settles like a cloak over one's thoughts. (Kracauer 1995, 43)

This description owes something to Simmel's concepts of *neurasthenia, Chokerlebnis* and new *blasé* mental attitudes that urban dwellers need to adopt as a survival strategy with which to deal with the qualitatively new social conditions created by mass living. Avant la lêttre, Kracauer provides here a pre-cyberpunk version of Gibson's previously cited description of the "lightning alternations in paradigm and symbol system. The data had never been intended for human input" (Gibson 1986, 40). Both Gibson and Kracauer in their respective fictional and journalistic manner are attempting to convey the qualitatively new nature of experience in highly technologized environments, engagement with which, hackers subsequently led the way as they pro-actively sought ways to embrace and enjoy the full, jolting experience of technologically-facilitated disorientation. That hackers led the way in dealing with processes that also envelop the more general public is vividly expressed in John Seabrook's updated version of Kracauer's urban scenario:

> The air was fuzzy with the weird yellow tornado light of Times Square by day, a blend of sunlight and wattage, the real and the mediated— the color of Buzz. Buzz is the collective stream of consciousness. William James's "buzzing confusion," objectified, a shapeless substance into which politics and gossip, art and pornography, virtue and money, the fame of heroes and the celebrity of murderers, all bleed. In Times Square you could see the Buzz that you felt going through your mind. I found it soothing just to stand there on my way to and from work

and let the yellow light run into my synapses. In that moment the worlds outside and inside my skull became one. (Seabrook 2000, 5)

The very name *Times Square*[d] alludes to both the speeded up and pervasive nature of experience that hackers both real and imagined (cyberpunks) seek to enjoy. However, despite Seabrook's unalloyed optimism and excitement, after *Neuromancer*, Gibson's work uses female protagonists to revisit Kracauer's initial concerns. Contra Seabrook, Gibson reflects upon the deeply unnatural and alienating nature of the real world trends that appears to accompany the rise of the informational Matrix:

> She's never actually seen soil emerge from any incision they might make in the street, here; it's as though there is nothing beneath the pavement but a clean, uniformly dense substrate of pipes and wiring. She walks on … until she finds herself nearing Kabukicho, the allnight zone they call Sleepless Castle, its streets bright as day, very few surfaces lacking at least one highly active source of illumination … the land of mahjong parlours … sex shops, video porn … but all of it managed with a Vegas-like sobriety of intent that makes her wonder how much fun any of it could really be, even for the committed enthusiast … restless street-level facades seeming to form a single unbroken surface of neon carnival excess. (Gibson 2003, 130–131)

Some of the earliest hints of this new alienating phenomenological realm can again be found in Kracauer's work, this time in his account of the strangely affective town square in which Kracauer and Benjamin found themselves in Marseille. Kracauer nicknamed it in their correspondence the "Place de l'Observance"[1] and he described how: "once its observers have settled into their chairs, it expands toward the four sides of the world, overpowering the pitiful, soft, private parts of the dream: *it is a square without mercy*" (Kracauer 1995, 39 [emphasis added]). We have seen how Seabrook replaces Kracauer's concern with the overpowering, merciless, cerebrally invasive, of such squares with their "reddish gleam that lingers settles like a cloak over one's thoughts" with an uncritically enjoyable "buzz" but for Kracauer, a heavily mediated "collective stream of consciousness" supplants in a disturbing fashion the previous role inhabited by a "liberated consciousness."

---

1. See Levin n. 1 p. 354.

In "The Hotel Lobby" essay, Kracauer compares the disparate entities of modern hotel lobbies and religious congregations in order to highlight the spatio-temporal shallowness and self-referentiality of the eponymous space which he then suggests is emblematic of the wider shallowness of the commodity matrix. Kracauer argues that: "In spheres of lesser reality, consciousness of existence and of the authentic conditions dwindles away in the existential stream, and clouded sense becomes lost in the labyrinth of distorted events whose distortion it no longer perceives" (Kracauer 1995, 173). "The labyrinth of distorted events" that Kracauer associates with the spatio-temporal homogeneity and emptiness of the lobby becomes comparable to the equally homogenous and empty nature of the environment created by the contemporary information society. This can be seen by considering Kracauer's description of the typical denizen of the lobby who embodies his previously discussed concern about the vacuous, spiritually disengaged technological engagement and, then applying it to the hacker's identification with the self-sufficiency of the Matrix:

> The person sitting around idly is overcome by a disinterested satisfaction in the contemplation of a world creating itself, whose purposiveness is felt without being associated with any representation of a purpose … Just as the lobby is the space that does not refer beyond itself, the aesthetic condition corresponding to it constitutes itself as its own limit. It is forbidden to go beyond this limit, so long as the tension that would propel the breakthrough is repressed and the marionettes of *Ratio* … isolate themselves from their bustling activity." (Kracauer 1995, 177)

The notion of *tension* is an important one. It is present in the congregation but absent from the hotel lobby. It has existential connotations in so far as it refers to an object or process's relationship to a spatio-temporal continuum beyond its immediate present. The concept of the existential tension/torsion of Being is based upon the idea that any object as it is viewed in a particular moment of time is significantly constituted by what it also necessarily lacks at that same moment in time—the past that helped make it what it is today and its future that has yet to unfold. Such an existential tension is applicable to the depth of the congregation poised as it is between the communal history of a religion and the future confrontation with eternity for which it is preparing itself. Tension thus refers to a relationship with a realm of symbolic meaning whether it is understood in terms of a transcendent deity, pure art, or Hegel's spirit of history (*Geist*) etc. Since entities within the commodity matrix or travel within the digital Matrix are designed for immediate and repetitive consumption such a tension is neither desirable nor possible.

An essential aspect of the M/matrix is its removal of the tension to create an existentially empty, tensionless space—cyberspace and commodity culture:

> What is presented in the hotel lobby is the formal similarity of the figures, an equivalence that signifies not fulfillment but evacuation. Removed from the hustle and bustle, one does gain some distance from the distinctions of "actual" life, but without being subjected to a new determination that would circumscribe from above the sphere of validity for these determinations. And it is in this way that a person can vanish into an undetermined void, helplessly reduced to a "member of society as such" who stands superfluously off to the side and, when playing, intoxicates himself. This invalidation of togetherness, itself already unreal, thus does not lead up toward reality but is more a sliding down into the doubly unreal mixture of the undifferentiated atoms from which the world of appearances is constructed. (Kracauer 1995, 179)

Like cyberspace, the hotel lobby acts as a spatial trope for the wider commodity matrix's lack of an essential grounding—an evacuation of real life. The denizen of the hotel lobby points to similar representative figures. The flâneur both immersed and removed himself from the hustle and bustle and later the hacker embraced yet more fully, how, with the advent of the Matrix, one can "vanish into an undetermined void" in a state of intoxication.

Marx describes capitalism's abstraction from the use-values of objects and the way in which it replaces them with the abstract, decontextualized notion of exchange value. Similarly, the spaces under consideration here—the hotel lobby, cyberspace, the society-wide commodity matrix—represent illustrations of the same essential processes at various levels of technologically-facilitated speed. In the hotel lobby/commodity matrix there are only two modes of operation available. One can stand *superfluously off to the side* or immerse oneself to the extent of intoxication. The togetherness implied by social bonds of substance are replaced in this new situation with an *invalidation of togetherness*. In a mode of cultural preparation for the later technological extremes of cyberspace, formerly socialized people are now reduced to undifferentiated atoms in terms that again predates even Baudrillard's late work in which he defines this invalidation of togetherness as a process of *telemorphosis*. Kracauer's prescient account of the spatially limited hotel lobby, becomes for Baudrillard a society-wide phenomenon although its essential value of circumscription is indicated by the penchant for such invalidly together Reality TV formats to be situated in "any enclosed space where an experimental niche or zone of privilege is recreated—the equivalent of an initiatory space where the laws of open society are abolished" (Baudrillard 2005, 191). Early cyberspatial organizations such as the aptly named *Electronic Frontier Foundation* embodied this initiatory, law-free, space but there is underacknowledged link between such clear engagements with the Matrix and the wider commodity matrix of our more general culture.

Referring to the French Reality TV programme *Loft Story*, Baudrillard provides us with the (il)logical extension of Kracauer's "formal similarity of the figures, an equivalence that signifies not fulfillment but evacuation." Baudrillard describes how this evacuation affects our whole society: "Loft Story is both the mirror and the disaster of an entire society caught up in the rush for insignificance and swooning to its own banality" (Baudrillard 2005,190). The existential tension that Kracauer finds in the congregation is evacuated in the hotel lobby just at it is in the Loft where: "this existential micro-situation serves as a universal metaphor of the modern being enclosed in a personal loft that is no longer his or her physical and mental universe but a tactile and digital universe … of digital humans caught in the labyrinth of networks, of people becoming their own (white) mice" (Baudrillard 2005, 193). Kracauer's hotel lobby and his own "labyrinth of distorted events" thus foresaw both Baudrillard's caustic analysis of Reality TV and the underlying, complex process of abstraction that undergirds both cultural and technological matrices—the matrix and Matrix:

Kracauer refers to the *universal concepts* that relate to the manner in which the commodity matrix escapes the existential tension of the authentic human experience and instead replaces it with the "inessential foundation" that can be read as the systemic nature of the global matrix that can reproduce tensionless commodities, TV formats, cyberspatial environments etc. not only on a mass scale within nation states but on an increasingly global scale heraldically indifferent to geographical or cultural barriers.

> … in the hotel lobby what emerges is the inessential foundation as the basis of rational socialization. It approaches the nothing and takes shape by analogy with the abstract and formal *universal concepts* through which thinking that has escaped from the tension believes it can grasp the world. These abstractions are inverted images of the universal concepts conceived within the relation; they rob the ungraspable given of its possible content, instead of raising it to the level of reality by relating it to the higher determinations." (Kracauer 1995, 179–180)

We can see here the roots of the hyperreal, society of pseudo-events and spectacles and the ultimate social price paid in terms of "the ungraspable given" deprived of its potential content and replaced instead with an all-grasping, all-consuming system. Kracauer's *mass ornament* represents a systemic ersatz replacement for reality in terms of an "unreal" that anticipates much later conceptions of *hyperreality*. In Baudrillard's definition of this term, the hyperreal is marked by the absence of a model upon which the fake is based. This absence is what Kracauer proceeds to describe when he suggests that: "The desolation of Ratio is complete only when it removes its mask and hurls itself into the void of random abstractions that no longer mimic higher determinations, and when it renounces seductive consonances and desires itself even as a concept." (Kracauer 1995, 180) Here we see that the previous imitation of reality is replaced by a realm of "random abstractions" that are now independent of any "higher determinations."

In Kracauer, as with Baudrillard, previous forms of traditional life are now eviscerated by a self-referential matrix that generates its own meanings so that: "the intellect that has become totally self-absorbed create[s] the appearance of a plenitude of figures from zero" (Kracauer 1995, 180).

The differentiations between essentially similar commodities that the commodity matrix creates are thus based upon ultimately false distinctions. In a perversion of Benjamin's hopes for the emancipatory power of a media matrix that both sprang from and helped to create the masses, substantive quality is replaced through the "energy" of mass reproduction to produce the homogenous society now discussed in terms of McWorld and prefiguring the exact term of the one-dimensional used by Marcuse and Reality TV's rationalization of the irrational, Kracauer asserts that:

> The intellect reduces the relations that permeate the manifold to the common denominator of the concept of energy, which is separated merely by a thin layer from the zero. Or it robs historical events of their paradoxical nature and, having leveled them out, grasps them as progress in one-dimensional time. Or, seemingly betraying itself, it elevates irrational "life" to the dignified status of an entity in order to recover itself, in its delimitation, from the now liberated residue of the totality of human being, and in order to traverse the realms across their entire expanse. (Kracauer 1995, 180–1)

The liberated consciousness Kracauer opposes to life under *Ratio* becomes overwhelmed by the manipulation of *the liberated residue of the totality of human being*. We now see the ability of the matrix *to traverse the realms across their entire expanse* in its rapacious appetite for creating new, ever-more contrived and explicit formats of reality TV that ironically become more surreal the more they chase after the real. Although illogical from the perspective of an authentic reality, the logic of *Ratio,* is identifiable through the discernible efficiency with which it constructs commodified meaning from an essentially empty ground that lacks the spatio-temporal depth of religion, high art etc.: "the deployment of empty abstractions that announces the actual position of a thinking that has slipped out of the tension. The visitors in the hotel lobby, who allow the individual to disappear behind the peripheral equality of social masks, correspond to the exhausted terms that coerce difference out of the uniformity of the zero" (Kracauer 1995, 181). This *uniformity of the zero* is a succinct summary of the ultimate emptiness of the binary logic of the M/matrix's content and the suspicion that hackers may merely have been the vanguard explorers of a society-enveloping lobby in which we are all now visitors.

In the Destructive Element Immerse—The Nostalgia of Social Science Fiction

A man that is born falls into a dream like a man who falls into the sea. If he tries to climb out into the air as inexperienced people endeavor to do, he drowns—*nicht wahr?* ... No! I tell you! The way is to the destructive element submit yourself, and with the exertions of your hands and feet in the water make the deep, deep sea keep you up. So if you ask me—how to be? ... I will tell you! ... *In the destructive element immerse.* (Conrad 1971 [1900], 163–164 [second emphasis added])

... a book about order and disorder more of a, sort of a social history of mechanization and the arts, *the destructive element ...* (Gaddis 2003, 244 [emphasis added])

The first of the above quotations is taken from Conrad's *Lord Jim,* as the trader Stein describes his philosophy of survival. The second is taken from Gaddis's *JR,* at the point where the character Jack Gibbs replies to a question as to what type of book he is in the process of writing. Both highlight in literary form the very real world problem of engaging positively with an essentially negative force.

The dandyish nature of the flâneur, the hard-boiled characteristics of the console cowboy (a descriptive term obviously redolent of the frontier mentality of the American dream/consenusal hallucination), and the socially rebellious connotations of hacking, can all be seen as a form of displacement from the more concerning aspects of this destructive element of the M/matrix that such cultural figures are seeking to master. Parallels can also be drawn with the film noir genre. Frequently involving a world-weary investigator and a femme fatale (matched in cyberpunk by such characters as Molly Millions) film noir also arose during a time of great social upheaval as society attempted to come to terms with the implications of growing urbanization and the increasingly rapid technological flows that this brings. Likewise, flâneurs, hackers, cyberpunks, all represent in their different ways prototypical explorers of rapidly evolving social landscapes. Under-represented in those studies that do trace the links between socio-technical change and its cultural representation is adequate recognition of the negative consequences for human autonomy. This is vividly illustrated in Robert Von Musil's significantly (for the purposes of this chapter) named novel *Der Mann ohne Eigenschaften* (*The Man without Qualities*). Published in two volumes in 1930 and 1932, Musil provides an epic account of the end of the Austro-Habsburg Empire due to modernism's irresistible incursions.

In the following excerpt, Musil describes the context of the apparent (we do not learn of his actual fate) death of a pedestrian (who represents the now anachronistic values of the flâneur) knocked down by a lorry in a Vienna that is rapidly assuming an anonymizingly inhumane, threatening scale/sense of sublimity:

> Motor-cars came shooting out of deep, narrow streets into the shallows of bright squares. Dark patches of pedestrian bustle formed into cloudy streams. Where stronger lines of speed transected their loose-woven hurrying, they clotted up—only to trickle on all the faster then and after a few ripples regain their regular pulse-beat ... the general movement pulsed through the streets ... Like all big cities, it consisted of irregularity, change, sliding forward, not keeping in step, collision of things and affairs, and fathomless points of silence in between, of paved ways and wilderness, of one great rhythmic throb and the perpetual discord and dislocation of all opposing rhythms, and as a whole resembled a seething, bubbling fluid in a vessel consisting of the solid material of buildings, laws, regulations, and historical traditions. (Musil 1979 [1930], 3 & 4)

Musil's fictional format enables him to counterposes the human and biological (like blood the crowd "clotted up" and has a "regular pulse-beat") with the technological and its inhuman movement of increasing abstraction in order to attempt to express the sort of immaterial (but no less real) new social forces and systems that hackers later came to tackle. Like the geometric lattices of light used by Gibson to portray the Matrix created by global information systems ("... and still he'd see the matrix in his sleep, bright lattices of logic unfolding across the colourless void ..." [Gibson 1984, 11]), in Musil early antecedents of later informational flows can be read into the "stronger lines of speed" that transect and contrast with the more organic movements of the crowd to create the "seething, bubbling fluid" to which traditional forms are reduced in a mode of expression that resonates with Marx's previously cited description of capitalism's effects as "all that's solid melts into air" (Marx & Engels 1977 [1848], 38). Musil's description thus represents more than just the literary curiosity afforded by being able to read of the fictional death of the semi-fictional flâneur, rather, it is represents a vivid portrayal of the fatal real-world implications that cybersociety's flows have for traditional life-worlds and their values.

Musil's scene neatly encapsulates the literary point in history at which the flâneur's fascination and desire to become one with Baudelaire's immense reservoir of urban energy is overwhelmed by the sheer intractable power of forces that do not lend themselves readily to conscious contemplation. Musil is thereby describing a new form of technology-induced sublimity that combines both Kantian categories of the dynamical and the mathematical. The dynamical element is patent (the pedestrian feels its full power!) whilst the mathematical element is present in Musil's subsequent description of character who witnesses events from the balcony of his town house:

> ... for the last ten minutes, watch in hand, he had been counting the cars, carriages, and trams, and the pedestrians' faces, blurred by distance, all of which filled the network of his gaze with a whirl of hurrying forms. He was estimating the speed, the angle, the dynamic force of masses being propelled past, which drew the eye after them swift as lightning, holding it, letting it go, forcing the attention—for an infinitesimal instant of time—to resist them, to snap off, and then to jump to the next and rush after that ... "It doesn't matter what one does," the Man Without Qualities said to himself, shrugging his shoulders. "In a tangle of forces like this it doesn't make a scrap of difference." (Musil 1979 [1930], 7–8)

In Gibson's oeuvre, his initial explicit confrontations with the buzz of information in *Neuromancer* has made way for subtle and deliberately vague allusions and a Benjamin-like nostalgia that also resonates with the resignation exhibited by the Man Without Qualities. Indicative of Gibson's changed literary emphasis from the Matrix to the matrix, the character Bigend appears in both *Pattern Recognition* and *Spook Country* and is an informational impresario who refers to "pre-ubiquitous media" to distinguish between a "state in which 'mass' media existed, if you will, within the world" rather than "comprising it" (Gibson 2007, 103). This is a comment that resonates with Baudelaire's previously cited intuition of this passage from pre-ubiquitous to ubiquitous media that the flâneur is one of the first to experience directly in his enthusiasm: "To be away from home and yet to feel oneself everywhere at home; to see the world, and yet to remain hidden from the world ... the lover of universal life enters into the crowd as if it were an immense reservoir of electrical energy" (Baudelaire 2003, 9–10).

Commentary upon Gibson's agenda-setting oeuvre tends to be disproportionately weighted towards the early novels, which despite containing plenty of dystopian warnings are predominantly cited as celebratory endorsements of the information society's exciting buzz. It is significant, however, that Gibson's later work is marked by consistently less futuristic settings and full of critical representations of the human effects of the informational order. *All Tomorrow's Parties*, for example, contains the following unequivocal statement of the anomic effect (or perhaps an illustration of Jameson's "waning of affect") a heavily informationalized society has upon the character Laney:

> Laney is in drift.
> That is how he does it. It is a matter, he knows, of letting go. He admits the random.
> The danger of admitting the random is that the random may admit the Hole.
> The Hole is that which Laney's being is constructed around. The Hole is absence at the fundamental core. The Hole is that into which he has always stuffed things: drugs, career, women, information.
> Mainly—lately—information.
> Information. This flow. This ... corrosion.
> Drift.
> (Gibson 1999, 40)

Postmodern literature abounds with variations upon this theme. The aptly-named Guy Swift[2] from Kunzru's *Transmission* (see Taylor 2006) is a latter day perversion of the flâneur's increasing disassociation from society and similar portrayals can be found in a spate of characters from the novels of such authors as Ballard and Houellebecq.

Eagleton explains this aesthetic representation of the subject in postmodernity in terms of a self-devouring process to match at a human level what this chap-

---

2. In this context it is interesting to note that "The Painter of Everyday Life" who inspired the title of one of Baudelaire's most famous essays on the nature of modernity was called Constantin Guys.

ter has traced in detail as capitalism's general hunger for abstraction at the expense of matter:

> With postmodernism, the will turns back upon itself and colonizes the strenuously willing subject itself. It gives birth to a human being every bit as protean and diffuse as the society around it. The creature who emerges from postmodern thought is centreless, hedonistic, self-inventing, ceaselessly adaptive ... Postmodernists oppose universality, and well they might; nothing is more parochial than the kind of human they admire ... The human subject finally breaks free of the restriction which is itself. If all that is solid must be dissolved into air, there can be no exceptions made for human beings. (Eagleton 2003, 190)

As shown throughout this chapter, the flâneur/cyberpunk/hacker's inability to make a significant difference is perhaps the most underacknowledged aspect of social science commentary upon hacking. Whist cyberpunk fiction had a highly influential impact upon the early hacking imagination, its overwhelmingly positive reception came at the cost of the lost irony of the genre's frequent depiction, amidst the buzz of informational intimacy, of the harmful consequences to both society and the individual. The importance of a fuller appreciation of the above literary aesthetic for our understanding of the information society is the way in which it helps us maintains a level of Gibsonian irony that we fail to recognize at our peril.

Conclusion—From Jugendstil to a Melancholic Dialectical Standstill

> Ambiguity is the manifest imaging of the dialectic, the law of dialectics at a standstill. This standstill is utopia and the dialectical image, therefore, dream image. Such an image is afforded by the commodity *per se*: as fetish. Such an image is presented by the arcades, which are house no less than street. Such an image is the prostitute—seller and sold in one. (Benjamin 1999, 10 [emphasis in original])

> "... the flâneur ... abandons himself to the phantasmagorias of the marketplace ... humanity will be prey to a mythic anguish so long as phantasmagoria occupies a place in it." (Benjamin 1999, 14–15)

This chapter has deliberately avoided the relatively unproblematic but overwhelming negative contemporary connotations of hacking. Instead, it has concentrated upon some of the first cultural representations of hacking because they still retain an element of Benjamin's above notion of ambiguity. Amongst many of its other aspects, Benjamin's work illuminates the relationships between artistic movements such as Jugendstil/Art Nouveau and the newly emerging technologies to which such movements respond. The preceeding pages have sought to follow a similar path. Speculative cultural theory and literary sources have been mined for the valuable insights they offer to which methods deemed nominally more empirical tend, nevertheless, to be impervious. Following Benjamin and Kracauer, we have seen how the hacker (especially in fiction) represents a dream image of the information society to the extent that like Benjamin's prostitute, as a microserf employee of Microsoft he became "seller and sold in one." Although at a standstill, the dialectical image continues to invite a degree of speculation and reflexivity largely absent from mainstream social science accounts of the hacking phenomenon.

The apparent unwillingness to recognize the implicit warnings contained within fictional accounts of the information society can be interpreted as an ideological consequence of the typically upbeat rhetoric that dominates cybersociety discourse. Thus, it is perhaps unsurprising that the continued relevance of theorists such as Benjamin and Kracauer is overlooked whilst concepts like online democracy and digital citizenship systematically confusing the symptom of society's various participatory failures with the "cure" of the faux-participations of a point-and-click polity. Despite some of the originally utopian aspirations invested in hacking, hackers have been presented here as uncritical embodiments of a transmission model of communication in which the efficiency of the mode of communication supplants adequate consideration of the value of the very thing being transmitted so that communication in any authentic sense fails to occur (producing environments akin to Kracauer's hotel lobby. Unreflexive social science studies of hacking risk making academics the accomplices rather than the analysts of a perverted informational order.

Benjamin's notion of melancholy provides a resource with which to avoid this perversion and to find at least a partially effective mode of dealing with our unavoidable mythic anguish. The problem for which the hacker provided advance cultural warning was not a dearth of information, but its excess—what Bataille (1991) refers to as each society's problematic surplus—it's *accursed share*. Similarly, Žižek observes, "As for the melancholic subject, like the miser he possesses the object, but he loses the reason that made him desire it. Most tragic of all, the melancholic has free access to all he wants, but finds no satisfaction in it" (Žižek 2008, 77). The solipsistic and narcissistically entranced individualism of cyberspatial interactions is a frequent theme of the hacking imaginary but underacknowledged in empirically-minded studies. In this chapter's detailed consideration of the flâneur as a prototype hacker who is *in the* crowd but not *of* the crowd, one can see how: "the necessity of this solitary perambulation corresponds to the flâneur's predisposition for states of melancholy, a melancholy from which he seeks escape in a deluge of images—searching in these images for points of orientation, markers of life" (Glebber 1999, 59–60). Since William Gibson gave us the original dream image of cyberspace with Case as its über-hacking male explorer, it is fitting to end with the female perspective of Cayce Gibson's later exemplum of the melancholic flâneur.

In Gibson's *Pattern Recognition*, Cayce finds herself experiencing a sublime moment of calm amidst the tumult of New York seconds before the 9-11 disaster occurs within her earshot. Whilst it may be far too "New Ageist" to suggest that cultural commentators of the information society need to take more time out from celebrating cyberspatial fluxes and flows to go and smell the flowers, there are, however, strong grounds to argue that the on-going reduction of life's rich ambiguity to the pre-enframed qualities of the M/matrix should be counterbalanced by theory/literature's sensitivity to what "empirical" methodologies *systematically* fail to perceive:

> She had watched a single petal fall, from a dead rose, in the tiny display window of an eccentric Spring Street dealer in antiques ... The dead roses, arranged in an off-white Fiestaware vase, appeared to have been there for several months. They would have been white, when fresh, but now looked like parchment ... the objects in the window seemed to change in accordance with some peculiar poetry of their own, and she was in the habit, usually, of pausing to look when she passed this way. The fall of the petal, and somewhere a crash, taken perhaps as some impact of large trucks, one of those unexplained events in the sonic backdrop of lower Manhattan. Leaving her sole witness to this minute fall. Perhaps there is a siren then or sirens, but there are always sirens, in New York. (Gibson 2003, 135–136)

References

Bataille, Georges. 1991. *The Accursed Share: An Essay on General Economy.* London: Zone Books.

Baudrillard, Jean. 1981. *For a Critique of the Political Economy of the Sign.* Telos Press, St. Louis.

Baudrillard, Jean. 2005. *The Conspiracy of Art.* New York. Semiotext(e).

Baudelaire, Charles. 2003 [1859]. *The Painter of Modern Life and Other Essays.* London: Phaidon Press.

Benjamin, Walter. 1936. The Work of Art in the Age of Mechanical Reproduction Available at: http://www.jahsonic.com/WAAMR.html. Accessed 08/05/2008.

Benjamin, Walter. 1999. *The Arcades Project*, London: Harvard University Press.

Conrad, Joseph. 1971 [1900]. *Lord Jim*. London: Penguin.

Coupland, Douglas. 1995. *Microserfs*. London: Flamingo.

Eagleton, Terry. 2003. *After Theory*. London: Allen Lane.

Gaddis, William. 2003 [1976]. *JR*. London: Atlantic Books.

Gibson, William. 1984. *Neuromancer*, London: Grafton.

Gibson, William. 1986. *Count Zero*, London: Grafton.

Gibson, William. 1999. *All Tomorrow's Parties*. London: Viking.

Gibson, William. 2003. *Pattern Recognition*. London: Viking.

Gibson, William. 2007. *Spook Country*. London: Viking.

Gleber, Anke. 1999. *The Art of Taking a Walk: Flanerie, Literature, and Film in Weimar Culture*. Princeton: Princeton University Press.

Kracauer, Siegfried. 1995. *The Mass Ornament: Weimar Essays*. London: Harvard University Press.

Kraus, Karl. 1977. *No Compromise: Selected Writings of Karl Kraus*. New York: Ungar Publishing.

Levy, Stephen. 1984. *Hackers: Heroes of the Computer Revolution*, New York: Bantam Doubleday Dell.

Merrin, William. 2005. *Baudrillard and the Media*. Cambridge: Polity.

Mills, Charles Wright. 2000 [1959]. *The Sociological Imagination*. Oxford: Oxford University Press.

Marx, Karl, and Friedrich Engels, F. (1977 [1848]) *Manifesto of the Communist Party*, Moscow: Progress Publishers.

Musil, Robert. 1979 [1930]. *The Man without Qualities*, vol. 1, London: Picador.

Seabrook, Jon. 2000. *Nobrow: The Culture of Marketing and the Marketing of Culture*. London: Methuen.

Taylor, Paul A. 1998. "Hackers: cyberpunks or microserfs?," *Information, Communication and Society*, 1(4): 401–19.

Taylor, Paul A., and Tim Jordan. 1998. "A Sociology of Hackers," Sociological Review, 46 (4): 757–80.

Taylor, Paul A. 1999. *Hackers: crime in the digital sublime*, London: Routledge.

Taylor, Paul A. 2001. "Informational Intimacy & Futuristic Flu: Love & Confusion in the Matrix," *Information, Communication and Society* 4(1): 74–94.

Taylor, Paul A., and Tim Jordan. 2004. *Hacktivism & Cyberwars: Rebels with a Cause?* London: Routledge.

Taylor, Paul A., and Jan Harris. 2005. *Digital Matters: Theory and Culture of the Matrix*, London: Routledge.

Taylor, Paul A. 2006. "Pattern Recognition in Fast Capitalism: Calling Literary Time on theorists of flux," *Fast Capitalism*, 2(1).

Ullman, Ellen. 1997. *Close to the Machine: Technophilia and its Discontents.* San Francisco: City Lights Books.

Žižek, Slavoj. 2008. *Violence: Six Sideways Reflections.* London: Profile Books.

4

Social Engineering Exploitations in Online Communications: Examining Persuasions Used in Fraudulent E-mails

Wilson Huang and Andrea Brockman

Over the past two decades, the Internet has greatly simplified both personal and business communications. A click of a mouse can deliver letters and images to thousands of recipients around the world in a matter of minutes and at virtually no cost to the sender. Along with such benefits, the Internet has brought new challenges and sometimes harmful consequences to online users. As demonstrated in many statistics, fraud and other crimes committed on or through the Internet are indeed common and rising.

According to the Consumer Sentinel (U.S. Federal Trade Commission 2008), 221,226 complaints associated with Internet-related fraud were filed by consumers in 2007, up from 205,269 in the previous year. The Internet Crime Complaint Center also reported quadruple the number of electronic-fraud complaints in 2007 than 2001 (Anderson 2007). The most recent Internet Crime Report (National White Collar Crime Center 2008, 1) showed that citizen complaints of Internet fraud increased by 33.1%, from 206,884 submissions in 2007 to 275,284 of 2008. Not only have the numbers of online frauds increased, but the cost to victims has also escalated. A survey of 503 computer security practitioners discovered that the monetary amount reportedly lost to Internet crime in 2002 was almost $456 million, compared with $378 million in 2001 and $265 million in 2000 (Swartz 2002). A study by Ultrascan Advanced Global Investigation (UAGI, 2010) found that the global cost for advance-fee frauds was $9.3 billion in 2009, with an overall loss of $27 billion since 2005. The median value of monetary losses for all online fraud was $931 per complaint, but for specific types, such as check fraud, computer fraud, and confidence fraud, median monetary losses exceeded $1,000 (National White Collar Crime Center 2008, 5). Similarly, another report (Howell 2006) revealed that the average amount lost per Internet scam victim had increased from $256 to $1,244 between 2005 and 2006.

Online communications by e-mail play an important role in the above crimes. The Internet Crime Report found that e-mail was the most frequent contact method used by perpetrators. About 74% of complainants utilized e-mails as their contact method, followed by Web pages at 28.9% (National White Collar Crime Center 2008, 10). Other methods, including telephone, instant messenger, fax and chatroom, were used in a much smaller percentages, ranging from 2% to 15%. Spamming, or sending out unsolicited bulk e-mail, has been the primary means employed by scammers. A content analysis of spam mails showed that 90% of received spams lacked legitimacy (Wall 2004, 314); 28% involved investment schemes, pyramid selling schemes, working-at-home scams, advance-fee frauds, and phishing attacks. About one third of the spams were misrepresentative or deceptive. These figures are not surprising considering how easily and inexpensively fraudsters can reach millions of e-mail inboxes via bulk e-mails (see Chu, Holt, and Ahn 2010).

Research in recent years has attempted to uncover characteristics of online frauds involving e-mails. Investigators have utilized either content analyses (Blommaert and Omoniyi 2006; Holt and Graves 2007; King and Thomas 2009; Ross 2009; Wall 2004) to evaluate writing techniques found in e-mail messages, or descriptive analyses (Edelson 2003; Zook 2007) to identify sources and distributions of fraudulent e-mails. This stream of research has provided descriptive information about the content of deceptive e-mails and operational schemes of frauds. However, systematic patterns of identifiable factors have not been established to explain correlates of different kinds of online fraudulent communications. The current study attempts to make a contribution by offering a psychological perspective known as social engineering to the explanation of the correlates of fraudulent e-mails.

The notion of social engineering is frequently referred to as a deception or persuasion used to obtain personal privileged information or gain access to institutional confidential data. Using persuasive, deceiving techniques based on social engineering, online fraudsters have been able to swindle money from vulnerable victims. This chapter will discuss the major persuasive techniques of social engineering, and their applications in various e-mail frauds. The chapter will end with suggestions and implications for the prevention of social engineering exploitations in the online environment.

The Concept of Social Engineering

Social engineering is a persuasive mechanism constructed on the assumption of people's emotional weaknesses. Social engineering can be considered collectively as a process in which individuals are persuaded or deceived into disseminating private information to a manipulator (Long 2008; Mann 2008; Mitnick and Simon 2002). When exploiting human weaknesses rather than system weaknesses, fraudsters or tricksters may sometimes be referred to as social engineers. Playing on victims' emotions, social engineers employ a diversity of tactics to impact the emotional state of the victim, thus influencing their willingness to divulge confidential information (Workman 2008). Social engineers have become experts at utilizing the Internet to influence the decisions made by users. Their attacks can occur at an individual (private) or a corporate (company) level. Through deception and persuasion, social engineers manipulate situations to gain personal and organizational data for the commission of frauds (Thompson 2006).

The major goals of social engineering attacks are not limited to gaining access to or control of an information system; they may also gain money or other valuable items such as financial records. The social engineer utilizes his/her ability to develop a trusting relationship with the target (Mitnick and Simon 2002; Thompson 2006). Social engineering attacks take place at the physical and psychological level. The workplace, telephone, trash cans, and Internet are common settings for the social engineer to seek unauthorized information, access, and work toward a psychological attack (Workman 2008).

The social engineer relies on cognitive biases, i.e., errors in mental processes, to initiate and execute the attack (Raman 2008). By triggering these cognitive biases, social engineers produce an automatic emotional response in their victims. A cognitive bias may be characterized as choice-supportive bias, confirmation bias, exposure effect, and/or anchoring (Raman 2008, 10–11). *Choice-supportive bias* is based on an individual's tendency to remember past experiences as being more positive than negative (Mather, Shafir, and Johnson 2000, 136). For example, an individual who uses an online system to make purchases or pay bills, may unintentionally disclose credit card information to a fraudulent site or an individual in response to an e-mail from a company claiming they have not received payment. *Conformation bias* states that individuals will base findings, information, and evidence on their personal views (Nickerson 1998, 176). For instance, when employees become accustomed to seeing service personnel in specific uniforms and identification badges, they may fail to question an imposter. Thus, the social engineer is not challenged and is able to gain access without identifying himself. *Exposure effect* suggests that individuals are attracted to familiar items and people (Zajonc 1968, 24). For example, users who find an interest in online social networks may be more willing to visit a malicious website which claims to have "online dating services." *Anchoring* is defined as the individual's tendency to identify a noticeable trait, such as a bank name (Tversky and Kahneman 1974, 1128). For example, a fraudulent website displaying a popular logo of an actual bank will deceive visitors.

In addition to these cognitive biases, schemas, and internal representations of our social information, also influence the decision-making processes. The world is a vast community of people, places, and things. To quickly describe what is seen, individuals place information into numerous categories based on physical characteristics and individual experience. For example, a child who sees a dog calls it a dog; a child who sees a wolf, calls it a dog. For adults, schemas are often based on occupations, roles, and stereotypes. For instance, law enforcement officers may be viewed as conservative and arrogant. These schemas may link with errors in judgment, especially when dealing with stereotypical beliefs. Common errors due to social schemas can come from sources like fundamental attribution bias, salience effect, and pressing conformity. Fundamental attribution bias assumes that individuals perceive the behavior of others as permanent characteristics which define the individual (Gilbert and Malone 1995, 3). Therefore, the social engineer will work to make a positive first impression to gain the trust of the victim. The salience effect suggests that the presence of a widely recognized badge/logo, famous slogan, or other clearly visible item or characteristic will cause the person or a company to stand out quickly. The social engineer can work to blend in physically or virtually to convince their targets (Taylor and Fiske 1975, 441). Pressures of conformity, compliance, and obedience lead to a change in behavior (Raman 2008, 11). The social engineer has learned to use authority and manipulation to accomplish entry into a network or computer account through pressure. For example, a social engineer may pretend to be an executive or computer security consultant, making the victim may feel obligated to provide information regardless of their credentials.

The social engineer studies the existing cognitive biases, schemas, and the individual to better determine the "best" approach for an attack. One's perception plays a large role in the decision-making process. If someone or something is perceived to be bad, it is avoided; which that is perceived to be familiar, good, or normal is accepted. The social engineer takes advantage of human nature by presenting him/herself in a positive manner. Through the application of social sciences and knowledge of cognitive biases and schemas, effective social engineers have discovered meaningful ways to influence behaviors of others.

Persuasions in Social Engineering Exploitations

Social engineers exploit psychological weaknesses of human nature through persuasions (Workman 2008). While social engineering can involve direct (physical) or indirect (e-mail, telephone) contact to initiate their persuasion, most social engineers rely on indirect means to carry out the attack (Mitnick and Simon 2002). The indirect route allows a greater usage of persuasion without a need for explanation, simply relying on a strong emotion such as excitement or fear (Peltier 2006, 14). A skillful social engineer would utilize information familiar to the victims to avoid their suspicion (Peltier 2006, 15).

Persuasion encompasses a wide array of factors deployed to generate trust and acceptance by the victims. Persuasion in the form of authority enables social engineers to establish legitimacy or produce fears that encourage individuals to obey commands. Authority is used to work off the confidence of the victim. The victims disclose information to social engineers as they are perceived to have credibility along with institutional affiliation. A social engineer will focus on individuals who are trusting as they are more likely to fall prey to a scheme. The consistency factor is also important as psychological commitment creates the natural tendency that individuals would respond consistently to trust. Persuasion may also be formed to develop likeability, where perceived credibility and expertise are combined to gain trust (Cialindi 2001).

Through various techniques the social engineer can build friendly rapport with targets to gain more trust (Mann 2008). Individuals who may not fall for a friendly demeanor may be responsive to authority or fear. Consequently, an individual who believes an authority figure (e.g., supervisor, bank, or credit card company) is involved, who fears punishment, or that their credit will be harmed if they do not respond quickly, is more likely to become a victim of a social engineering exploitation (Workman 2008, 671). Forging a sense of urgency to the target by the social engineers is, therefore, a crucial element in the persuasion attack.

In addition to authority discussed earlier, other persuasive techniques can include appeals to pity and tradition (Capaldi 1971, 47–56). The social engineer may use appeals to pity where they claim to need assistance or describe a problem working to build sympathy in the victim. The pity factor may also appeal to one's sense of charity. An appeal to tradition focuses on ideal values such as honor, recognition, or legacy. The social engineer concentrates on the moral difference between right and wrong, thus developing a scheme in which the victim bases his/her decision on ideal values. The use of tradition can defend and reinforce legitimacy and credibility of multiple appeals. The authority, tradition, and institutional significance portrayed by the social engineer is often seen as an indicator of trust, therefore influencing the victim's willingness to meet the demands requested by the exploiters.

Social engineering exploitation works to gain the attention of the victim by operating off his/her perceptions or emotions. Most social engineering attacks employ multiple persuasions to target the victim and achieve a significant emotional response (Capaldi 1971; King and Thomas 2009; Long 2008; Mitnick and Simon 2002; Workman 2008). A seasoned social engineer utilizes several persuasions and operates them simultaneously to cause the greatest emotional impact. Through intensive research the social engineer gains insight into common weaknesses of victims. The extensive knowledge obtained ensures social engineers' ability to manipulate the victims into releasing confidential information or cooperate with swindlers voluntarily.

Social Engineering Exploitations and Fraudulent E-mails

Social engineering exploitations can be conducted on or off-line, usually impersonating someone in authority to gain private information. Help desk employees are common victims due to their tendency to be friendly (Mitnick and Simon 2002). Further, they are trained to focus on the customer and will more readily release information. Dumpster diving or trashing can be used by social engineers, as an act of gathering information by going through company dumpsters (Long 2008). Potential security leaks in trash come from company phone books, organizational charts, memos, company manuals, printouts of sensitive data (e.g., social security numbers, birth dates), and outdated hardware (Granger 2001). The most straightforward method of social engineering is probably shoulder surfing where attackers simply look over the shoulder of a user when he/she enters privileged information into a computer account (Okenyi and Owens 2007, 304). A common mistake is that online users often repeat the use of a common ID and an easy password on their accounts (e.g., e-mail accounts and social networks). Thus, once a social engineer has spotted a user name and password, he/she often gains access to multiple accounts of the user.

Recent schemes of social engineering rely on electronic technology rather than person-to-person contacts. For example, a pop-up window showing a virus warning on the user's screen can trigger him/her fear to click immediately on the link out of fear, without considering the consequences of such action. Social engineers can also set up a spoofed website, called a Lobsterpot (Rusch 2004), to wait for victims to fall into their trap. This deceptive replica of an authoritative website can easily make victims to log in with their account names and passwords, which are then forwarded automatically to scammers (Peltier 2006, 17). Mail attachment is another common tool used by social engineers to trick innocent users. A spam e-mail may claim that the attachment must be opened to receive messages, pictures, videos, or digital cards. Once the victim clicks the attachment, his/her system is infected by a Trojan horse to be utilized by the scammer (Peltier 2006, 17).

One of the most undesirable consequences of a Trojan is the invasion of malicious codes known as malware or spyware into the computing system. These viruses can take possession of an invaded computer and send signals of keystrokes entered by the users to remote hackers (BitDefender, 2007). The programs, referred to as keyloggers, allow hackers to display and store privileged data such as account IDs, passwords, and credit card numbers without the knowledge of online users. Using the infected computer along with the stolen account name/password, a hacker can embark on social engineering attacks to unlimited numbers of users for their personal confidential information. This continuously expanding process can harvest numerous accounts and passwords and further many other criminal acts like spamming and bank frauds (Chu et al. 2010; Symantec Corporation 2007).

The most common social engineering ploy is phishing e-mails (Granger 2006; Okenyi and Owens 2007, 304). Phishers must use social engineering deception to trick and trap the victim without showing criminal intent (Long 2008). Fraudulent e-mails may look like they are from a creditable, trustworthy online service (e.g., PayPal, eBay, AOL) claiming security updates, missing information, a late payment, or news alert. If the phishing e-mail is sent by a financial institution (e.g., Bank of America, Citibank, HSBC), the e-mails would depict a bank's logo/slogan and other well known features of the financial institution involved. Operating on victims' pressing conformity and fear, the social engineer provides a clickable link for victims to easily enter their account name and password. Coupled with the convenient link are messages urging victims to supply confidential information as quickly as possible. This urging mail subsequently impacts the victims' decision-making abilities, increasing the chances they will unwittingly follow the link and relay sensitive information to the fraudulent site (Drake, Oliver, and Koontz n.d.). The entire social engineering process for phishing is short and fast, making this online e-mail fraud a method of choice for social engineers.

Another commonly encountered social engineering attack online is advance-fee scams executed primarily by e-mail persuasions. Social engineers have engaged in a number of strategies to persuade online users to advance money to scammers before a promised larger fund or incentive can be received. The advance-fee frauds can be initiated through different incentives including large sums of cash through lottery winnings, investments or inheritances, work-at-home jobs, business representatives, and a few others like overpayments and gift cards (Federal Bureau of Investigation 2009; Holt and Graves 2007; Wall 2004). Many of these e-mails are related to funds available in an African country, or secured by Nigeria nationals and their associates. These scams have been known as Nigeria 419 frauds, corresponding to the fraud section in the Nigerian criminal codes. Generally, the design of e-mail persuasions in advance-fee frauds relies on authority, attraction, pity, and other rhetorical appeals combined with an urgent reminder to put forth the operations (Ross 2009). A phony account, certificate, serial number, business proposal, or other credentials is presented with e-mail messages to convince the recipients. By following the written instructions provided by the social engineers, the e-mail recipients anticipate excess funds from the senders. The recipients, however, receive no returns and lose the connection with the fraudulent senders.

Analyzing Social Engineering Persuasions in Fraudulent E-mails

The current study attempted to analyze five types of persuasive techniques commonly found in fraudulent e-mails: authority, pity, tradition, attraction, and urgency. Definitions of these persuasions, below, are based on studies by Capaldi (1971) and Ross (2009). *Authority* involves the use of persuasive statements to create legitimacy, trust, and credibility. It is used to establish a frame of reference for the rest of the case (Capaldi 1971, 22). Institutional markers such as official affiliations and professional titles can also be considered authority. *Pity* refers to sympathy and charity expressed in the messages. It relies on simple presentation of the case in its appeal to the audience (Capaldi 1971, 19). *Tradition* appeals to an ideal value people endorse (Capaldi 1971, 28); it can include honor and legacy commonly recognized by the public. *Attraction* refers to an incentive which can draw excitement or a sense of subversive joy (Ross 2009, 32); examples are huge cash prizes, easy job offers or opportunities for profits. *Urgency* involves a stress on the exigency of the situation (Ross 2009, 35). Urgent statements are used to stress the requirement to respond promptly to receive the offer or award. For example, they can be written in a negative tone, such as threatening to disable an account if a request is not fulfilled.

To evaluate how written persuasions were presented by fraudsters, this study examined three categories of e-mails: phishing, advance-fee, and lottery winning frauds. E-mails that included a clickable link requesting an account ID, password or other personal information, were classified under the phishing category. E-mails involving advance-fee scams used attractive offers to persuade recipients to respond. In their solicitations, fraudsters typically wrote a lengthy narrative to explain the recipient selection and urgent situation to establish the credibility of the fabricating story (King and Thomas 2009, 216–220). Recipients were then asked for action by giving contact information such as a mailing address and phone number to the scammer. Lottery reward notification is a special case of advance-fee fraud. The focal appeal of the notification to the recipients is a clearly specified large quantity of money. Winning numbers, ticket serial codes, claiming procedures, names of sponsoring organizations and contact persons are always included to increase the authority and trust of the deceitful notification. The appearance of this notification is distinct from other types of advance-fee e-mails due to these fake authority features.

Data and Methods

The current analysis involves a convenient sample of 35 fraudulent e-mails collected from individual accounts and a data archive. Because most current e-mail servers have installed filters, only a small number of the three categories of e-mails were found in the authors' email accounts. Over the past two years, 2008 and 2009, only 20 emails were gathered from the inboxes or spam boxes of the authors' university or Google e-mail accounts. To expand the sample size, 15 more were selected purposely from a database maintained by an anti-phishing site, MillerSmiles, in Great Britain. Other data archives such as Anti-Phishing Working Group, Scambuster, and 419Legal were reviewed for possible case selection, but they provided only partial or revised messages. Archived data at these sites are not as comprehensive and complete as are MillerSmiles'. E-mails at the MillerSmiles archive site were reviewed retrospectively in the order of time. Any redundant e-mails were skipped. This review process led to 15 e-mails, an appropriate number compared to the number of e-mails collected from the first data source. This small supplement also helps illustrate the diversity in content of persuasive tactics presented in the results section.

The selection and review process for the previously mentioned 35 e-mails were consistent with that of prior studies (Blommaert and Omoniyi 2006; Ross 2009). To be included, the emails had to be written in English despite grammatical errors or typos found in the text; appear to be full letters, showing an e-mail address, subject line, salutation, body text, and closing; and reflect the sender's control of funds, power of monetary distribution, and knowledge of scheme procedures. Spamming e-mails that did not fit into solicitations for personal, privileged information or monetary funds were excluded. These exclusions, for example, included e-mails promoting low home mortgage rates, brand name products at extremely low prices, online dating, online drugs, sex enhancement pills and adult entertainment.

Content analyses were conducted to examine the persuasive language used in the body of the messages. Statements that met the definitions of the five persuasive techniques were classified by the three e-mail types. Because letters of advance-fee scams vary in their appeals and offerings, we reported the results of this analysis in two subcategories: one emphasizing authority persuasion, and the other focusing on pity. Distributions of the 35 cases are 15 phishing; 10 advance-fee, authority-based; 5 advance-fee, pity-based; and 5 lottery winning. The classification scheme also contained descriptive items of each e-mail. These included the institutional affiliation of the sender, subject line, greeting, closing, and receiving date of the mail. These items are used to demonstrate how fraudsters have utilized familiar features of e-mail in their social engineering exploitations. The relationships between persuasion techniques/features and types of fraudulent mails are depicted in the tables discussed below.

Analyses and Findings

Table 4.1 introduces the primary features of phishing e-mails excluding the body of the text. All statements in the table are in original writing of the senders. Cases are sorted alphabetically by the name of the target institution. As shown, these institutions are not necessarily banks or investment companies; they can be online stores whose services require credit cards for purchases or membership enrollments. E-mail service providers (e.g., Case A15) can become institutional victims when their users fall prey to scammers and supply their e-mail addresses and passwords at the spoof site. The subject line highlights the main concern of the message. Sometimes alarming words like alert (A7, A13), warning (A1), attention (A10), disabled (A13), or limited (A10) are used in conjunction with multiple exclamation points to strike fear in affected recipients. In other cases, social engineers use friendly salutations (e.g., Dear Member/Customer) and closures (e.g., Best Regards, Sincerely) to make a positive, familiar appearance. Regardless of the approach, the e-mails all show institutional affiliations. The senders have worked to enhance fundamental attributions (Gilbert and Malone 1995) to encourage recipients to comply with the e-mail's request for action.

In Table 4.2, original messages sent by social engineers were included and classified. Following the content of the subject line, authority persuasions are a common method to achieve rapid recipient conformity with their request. For example, in the A9 case, users are informed why they have received the messages, commanded to take proper action and threatened with an undesirable consequence if they do not comply immediately. This logical sequence is consistent with the notions of conformity, compliance, and obedience (Raman 2008). Security upgrades are a very common authority technique utilized by social engineers (e.g., A1, A6). This suggests that security issues are a central concern to many users, thus such warnings are more likely than other reasons to prompt responses. An authority persuasion may sometimes build on a fake, specific episode as shown in the A12 case. This suggests that a particular claimed expense with a real monetary value can trigger an emotional response leading to the designated action expected of the social engineers. The urgency statement shown throughout the fifteen mails imposes a time limit and/or encourages swift action. It seems to be a reinforcer used to strengthen the desired responses. Messages threatening a penalty such as account suspension are common in phishing e-mails.

Authority persuasions have been used more elaborately in advance-fee fraud e-mails. As shown in Table 4.3, social engineers attempt to explain the nature and source of the funds in detail to convince the recipients that the offer is creditable. To create an impression of legitimacy, social engineers claim that the funds came from governmental debt (B2, B3), inheritance funds left by people who died in a plane crash (B1), or natural disaster such as a tsunami (B5). Social engineers maintain that they are executives of corporations, fund managers, retired governmental officials, or attorneys—all positions that help further their credibility. Different from the conformity/compliance/obedience model found in phishing e-mails, the advance-fee model used direct incentives such as large amounts of money (B1–B7), work from home jobs (B8), job offers (B9), and business opportunities (B10) to attract the attention of the recipients. The large sum of cash used by advance-fee social engineers implies that cash bait is more effective than non-monetary offers.

Another major persuasion used in advance-fee scam e-mails is pity (or sympathy). The five cases reported in Table 4.4 are sorted by the date of the e-mail. In cases C1 and C2, social engineers resorted fabricating stories of the death of their husbands or concerns for personal safety/health for help. To dramatize their pity appeal, these social engineers used ideal values to recognize their late husbands. These recognitions include "my husband was one of the best farmers in the country" (C1), "my late husband worked with the Chevron/Texaco

Table 4.1 Initiation and Appearance in Phishing E-mails

Case #	Institutional Affiliation	Subject Line	Greeting	Closing	Sender Affiliation
A1	Amazon	Upgrade for Your Amazon.com Account	Dear Amazon.com Customer	Thank you	Amazon Online Shopping Security Team
A2	AOL	AOL Recent Change in Your Account	Dear AOL Member	n/a	n/a
A3	Bank of America	Bank of America Notification	Dear Bank of America member	Thank you for your cooperation	BOA Security Service
A4	Ebay Support	Official notification from eBay	Dear EBAY.COM Member	Thank you	CIPP Senior Counsel, Global Privacy Practices eBay Inc.
A5	HSBC Bank	Update your Online Banking	n/a	n/a	HSBC Internet banking
A6	HSBC Bank plc	Urgent Security Message Notice	Valued HSBC Customer	Sincerely	Customer Service
A7	HSBC Bank UK	Important Message Alert (Secure)	Dear Valued Customer	Best Regards	HSBC UK Plc Security Department
A8	InterSwitch	InterSwitch VERVE Security Upgrade	Dear InterSwitch Card Holder	Thank you	InterSwitch Limited
A9	National Savings and Investment	NS&I Limited Account Status Notification	Dear BS&I Customer	Sincerely	Customer Account Review Dept, NS&I
A10	Paypal	Attention! Your Paypal account has been limited!	Dear Paypal Member:	Sincerely	Paypal Account Review Department
A11	Paypal	Paypal Email & Details Upgrade Notification	Dear Customer	Thank you	Paypal Online Banking Security Team
A12	Paypal	Your purchase to XXX XXX	Dear Paypal Member:	Thank you for using Paypal	The Paypal Team
A13	Paypal	Alert! Your Paypal account has been disabled!	Dear Paypal Member:	Sincerely	The Paypal Team
A14	Western Union	Western Union: Your account has been limited	Dear Valued Customer	Thank you for using Western Union	n/a
A15	Windows Live Hotmail	Warning Warning!!! Account Verification!	Dear Account Owner	Sincerely	The Windows Live Hotmail Team

Note: The first and last names of an individual are replaced by XXX.

Table 4.2 Persuasions by Authority and Urgency in Phishing E-mails

Case #	Subject Line	Authority	Authority Continued	Urgency
A1	Upgrade for Your Amazon.com Account	upgraded to a more secure and encrypted SSL servers	You are requested to update your account information by following the reference below	failure to verify account details will lead to account suspension
A2	AOL Recent Change in Your Account	Time has come to update your information	That requires you to verify the billing information	Failure to verify your records will result in account suspension
A3	Bank of America Notification	You have 1 new security message from Security Center	update your information	n/a
A4	Official notification from eBay	This is your official notification from eBay	Your online has expired	If not, your online will be limited and deleted
A5	Update your Online Banking	Your account has been flagged, due to recent changes we have made	your security is important to us, we are proactively notifying you of this activity	All flagged account requires immediate activation for Online Banking to remain active
A6	Urgent Security Message Notice	for the safety and integrity of the HSBC account we have issued this warning message	failure to update your records will result in account suspension	Please update your internet Banking user ID before Dec 15, 2009
A7	Important Message Alert (Secure)	Important warning about internet Banking Fraud. Click here to read.	HSBC will never send you an e-mail asking you to update, reconfirm or change your security details	You have 1 new message waiting in your inbox folder
A8	InterSwitch VERVE Security Upgrade	An extra verification has been introduced to make your transaction more secure and protect you	you are requested to verify/register your ATM DEBIT CARDS, X-CHANGE CARDSs and CASH CARDS	must be registered on or before 1st January 2010. Failure to register your card will lead to card suspension
A9	NS&I Limited Account Status Notification	account was flagged for inactivity	accounts inactive over a long period of time will be disabled	immediately login to your account, protecting the security of your account is our primary concern
A10	Attention! Your Paypal account has been limited!	We recently contacted you after noticing an issue on your account	Our system detected unusual charges to a credit card linked to your Paypal account	This is the last reminder to log in to Paypal as soon as possible
A11	Paypal Email & Details Upgrade Notification	upgrade to a more secure and encrypted SSL servers	Using our new secure and safe SSL servers to validate your online banking account	It is compulsory to follow as failure to verify account details will lead to account suspension
A12	Your purchase to XXX XXX	This email confirms that you have paid XXX XXX $337.50 USD using Paypal	This credit and transaction will appear on your bill as "PAYPAL XXX XXX"	If you haven't authorized this charge, click below to cancel the payment and get a full refund

Table 4.2 Persuasions by Authority and Urgency in Phishing E-mails, *continued*

Case #	Subject Line	Authority	Authority Continued	Urgency
A13	Alert! Your Paypal account has been disabled!	It has came to our attention that your Paypal billing information are out of date	This billing update is also a new Paypal security statement	A failure to update your records may result on a suspension of your account
A14	Western Union: Your account has been limited	Your account access has been limited due to a login attempt failure	We will need to confirm your Credit Card CVV from your profile. You will need your new User Name and Password next time you sign in	If not, your account with us will be suspended
A15	Warning Warning!!! Account Verification!	sending it to every hot-mail email user account owner for safety	We are having congestions ... We are shutting down some hotmail accounts	account will be suspended within 48 hours for security reasons

in Russia for 20 years," "I and my husband were married for 15 years," and "he made a vow to use his wealth for the down trodden and the less privileged in the society" (C2).

In the C3 case, the social engineer claimed to be a helpless orphan sheltered in a pastor's house. She had lived in constant fear because her stepmother intended to take over the funds she inherited from her father, who had been killed by military rebels. Then she used the ideal values "appreciations to you throughout my lifetime" and "always remember your goodness to me all the entire days of my life" to broaden her pity persuasions. Her appeal was closed by a strong statement for immediate attention.

Case C4 called himself a school teacher of a missionary college. This social engineer claimed that he adopted a son whose deceased father was a "good catholic" and a knight. The social engineer urgently sought someone who could be a foster father of the son as well as an account holder on behalf the adopted son in a foreign country. This social engineering letter utilized all of the five persuasions in the messages. Different from prior cases, the last appeal (C5) resorted to charity. She was raised in an orphanage, inherited funds from her doctor husband, and thus was willing to establish a charitable foundation. Similar to prior cases, this social engineer employed multiple persuasions in the appeal. Examinations of the five cases suggest that pity-based, advance-fee solicitations are more complex and diversified than phishing e-mails and the authority-based advance-fee letters.

Table 4.5 presents persuasion techniques used in lottery reward notifications. Authoritative items routinely included in this type of solicitation are the

Table 4.3 Persuasions by Authority, Urgency, and Attractiveness in Advance-Fee E-mails

Case #	Subject Line	Authority	Authority Continued	Authority Continued	Attraction	Urgency
B1	URGENT ATTENTION NEEDED	In my department we discovered an abandoned sum of USD$18.3M from our foreign customer who died along with his wife and children in the plane crash	The request of foreigner in this transaction is necessary because our late customer was a foreigner and a Burkinabe cannot stand as next of kin to a foreigner	On the account of your reliability and trust worthiness, I have decided to contact you in order to transfer the said amount of into your nominated bank account	18.3 million	I am assuring you that with my position this money will hit your account before 21 banking working days
B2	From: Former CBN Governor Very Important	I have successfully resigned as the Governor of Central bank of Nigeria CBN	fund has been moved into your Account.... the accumulated interest of 2.5 Million has been deposited to your ATM Master Card	Once you comply with the bank arrangement then the card will be send to you	2.5 million	Contact him immediately
B3	From Governor Central Bank Nigeria	Following the protest of the international community, the world bank and IMF ... all the outstanding foreign debt especially contract payment should be release to the beneficiaries with unconditional	The world bank has given us the instruction to transfer your fund as well, your inheritance funds of $1,000,000 USD	funds has been gusseted to be released, via key telex transfer (KIT)—direct wire transfer to you by the senate committee for foreign over due fund transfer	$1,000,000	Your immediate respond is needed before it will be too late
B4	Attention, Attention, Attention	This is the United Parcel Service mailing you	your ATM INTER SWITCH CARD with funding is now in our office	We need your residential address and delivery fee to send your card	$1,600,000	within 2 days
B5	I am XXX XXX	I am an attorney	my client and his family died in the 2004 tsunami disaster	n/a	$18,000,000	n/a
B6	Important Message from Dubai Oil Investment Corporation	I have contacted New Zealand financial advisor XXX XXX for this contact	confirm that funds are legitimate	funds would be only under the control of the second party which is you the partner	$25,000,000	n/a

Table 4.3 Persuasions by Authority, Urgency, and Attractiveness in Advance-Fee E-mails, *continued*

Case #	Subject Line	Authority	Authority Continued	Authority Continued	Attraction	Urgency
B7	Very Very Urgent From ICB Bank. Please Reply Immediately	your fund is confiscated in ECOWAS porce	the bill has been waved meaning you can be able to get the fund wired into your account	I will be sending you a waver form certificate and the fund released order	unspecified amount	very very urgent
B8	Representatives and agents wanted for appointment!!!	Global Platinum Credit and Loan Financial S.L	We need representatives and agents in your area	description of task and formal contact info are listed in the mail	work at home	n/a
B9	International Expatriate Official Job Online Interview	Your name has been chosen to the International Expatriate Official Job Online Interview	formal contact info is provided	we will issue you the Success Letter and the Contract Document	job offer	get back to me as soon as possible
B10	Business proposal	I am Director of operation Ghana National Petroleum Corporation	I have a business proposal which will be lucrative to both parties	n/a	lucrative business	n/a

Table 4.4 Pity and Other Persuasions Used in Advance-Fee E-mails

Case#	C1	C2	C3	C4	C5
Subject Line	Family request for urgent help and business assistance	Dear Beloved Urgent Reply Needed	Waiting for your reply	Hello	Please Reply Urgently
Pity	the president supporters invaded my husband's farm burnt down everything, killed him and confiscated all his investments	find a place in your Heart to assist me in fulfilling My Late Husband's Last Wish will	My life is not safe down here ... hid myself here in a pastors house	I have an adopted son who wants to continue his education in your country	presently, I'm hospitalized
Pity Continued	my Son and I have decided to move out of Zimbabwe for the safety of our lives	Presently, I am in hospital ... For Esophageal cancer (treatment)	I think about my dead parent because I miss them so much	his uncles are searching seriously for this young boy to kill him (for the fund left by his deceased father)	I am undergoing treatment for my up coming breast cancer surgery operation
Pity Continued	we as asylum seeker here in South Africa cannot open an account of any sort	my Doctor told me that I have a short time to live	My sufferness is too much for me to withstand, comparable to my age and an orphan lady	n/a	I was raised from a motherless baby home.... my desire to establish a charity foundation
Pity Continued	n/a	Please I beg you to help me stand as the beneficiary and collect the Funds	I am feeling pains all over my bodies	n/a	n/a
Tradition	My husband was one of the best farmers in the country	my late husband worked with the Chevron/Texaco in Russia for 20 years	my late father XXX XXX, who the Epmgigo rebels killed recently in political crisis in our country	I am a secondary school teacher of St. Pauls Missionary College	n/a
Tradition Continued	n/a	I and my husband were married for 15 years without a child	I will always be of enough appreciations to you throughout my lifetime	the late father was a good catholic	n/a
Tradition Continued	n/a	he made a vow to use his wealth for the down trodden and the less privileged in the society	and I will always remember your goodness to me all the entire days of my life	he was a knight of the order of saint molumba	n/a

Table 4.4 Pity and Other Persuasions Used in Advance-Fee E-mails, *continued*

Case#	C1	C2	C3	C4	C5
Authority	I got your contact address from the South African chambers of commerce	the funding is concealed in a Diplomatic Box and Lodged with a Security Company abroad	I have a substantial capital I honorably inherited from my late father	When the father died, we discovered through his lawyer a deposit	I inherited from my late husband Dr. XXX XXX
Authority Continued	detailed contact information was listed	I want you to take Custody of the fund and use it for Charity Works	I want you to be rest assured that everything is in order and legitimate	also discovered a written Testament/ Will establishing his only child as the sole heritor to the said fund	I will give you all the relevant information that will authorize the release and transfer of the money to you
Attraction	$48,000,000	$12,500,000	$11,500,000	$6,700,000	$48,000,000
Urgency	n/a	time is of essence due to my present health condition	do urge you to give the matter your immediate attention it deserves	send your direct telephone number so that I will give you a call today	I hope to hear from you urgently

Table 4.5 Persuasions by Authority, Attraction, and Urgency in Lottery Winning Notifications

Case #	Subject Line	Claim Agency	Authority	Authority Continued	Attraction	Attraction Continued	Attraction Continued	Urgency
D1	Congratulations!	Toyota International Lotto Headquarters	You are among the winners of the Toyota Car International Promotion Program	Participants were selected through a computer ballot system	$1,000,000	2nd prize	a Toyota highlander	call our claim agent or send email immediately
D2	Congratulations	Nokia Mobile Corporations	Your E-mail Address has won you a cash prize on our online lottery	draws was conducted from an exclusive list ... by an advanced automated random computer selection	$500,000	2nd prize	5 Nokia phones	please contact us for due processing
D3	Reminder	Sponsor Global Networks	This is the second time we are notifying you about this said fund	Your email address was picked as one of the twenty winning email addresses	$2,550,000	3rd prize	n/a	without any delay otherwise it rolls over to the next draw
D4	Official Winning Notification	NLF Online International Lottery program	Your e-mail address drew lucky numbers/ you have therefore been approved for a lump sum pay	participants were selected through a computer ballot system	$800,000	1st prize	automatically qualified to take part in our next year USD 5 million international lottery programs	as soon as possible/within 7 working days
D5	Congratulations!	NLF Online International Lottery program	Your e-mail address drew lucky numbers/ you have therefore been approved for a lump sum pay	participants were selected through a computer ballot system	$800,000	1st prize	a Toyota Camry Car 2009 model	as soon as possible/within 7 working days

program name and sponsoring agency of the lottery drawing event, frequency of the event (e.g., yearly), winning lottery numbers, prize level, ticket number, and reference code. Recipients are asked to provide name, address, gender, age, and other personal information to the claim agent. But the focus of the letters is on the large cash prize and additional awards. As revealed in Table 4.5, additional incentives can be cars or cellular phones. Social engineers used these extras in the hopes that they will prompt recipients to supply the requested information, thus falling into the scammer's trap. Recipients were also reminded to respond promptly in order to avoid the expiration of their award.

Discussion and Implication

This study reveals that the social engineer employs an array of tactics to gain a degree of trust or excitement from the victims. Social engineers often introduce their scheme by an institutional marker with a proper header, courteous greeting, and adequate presentation of facts. Then through attractive means of gaining individual advancement (e.g., security upgrades, inherence funds, cash prizes) social engineers prey on the emotional desires of their victims. The findings are consistent with prior studies (Gilbert and Malone 1995; Holt and Graves 2007; King and Thomas 2009; Raman 2008; Workman 2008) indicating that social engineers have a tendency to engage in familiar and friendly behaviors (e.g., account updates, salutations, closings) for infiltration into human minds.

On the other hand, unfriendly language may have the same persuasive power as friendly tones. The study's analysis showed that the rhetoric of authoritative and, most of time, urgent persuasions were used quite often in fraudulent e-mails. The finding is similar to that of previous research which reported that a large percentage of the fake e-mails have utilized this timeless technique. For example, one study indicated an 83% prevalence in their sample of e-mails involving urgent persuasions (Holt and Graves 2007, 147), while another discovered that almost every single e-mail examined had used that technique (Ross 2009, 30). This universal application signifies the importance of such persuasion on victims. The appeal to pity is another important technique used by social engineers to exploit victims' sympathy for illegal gains (Blommaert and Omoniyi 2006; Holt and Graves 2007; Ross 2009; Workman 2008). The study revealed that scammers had employed multiple persuasions, expressed in either positive or negative tones, to exhaust psychologically the user's defenses, making them more likely to fall for the scam (Ross 2009, 31).

A unique finding of the study was the differential usage of persuasion in advance-fee frauds. Prior research has treated advance-fee scheme as a single category without taking into account the variability of appeals applied in different advance-fee solicitations. This study reveals that persuasions have been tailored to the unique features of an advance-fee ploy to maximize the attractiveness of the offer. In the lottery reward solicitation, for example, the authority and attraction appeals work to generate a strong sense of trust and worthiness in e-mail readers. For the pity-based solicitation, appeals to tradition and sympathy are formed to show decency of the involved family and the care and assistance needed to complete the monetary transaction. In authority-based advance fee solicitations, gaining and reinforcing the sense of credibility of the fake funding are highlighted in the body of the messages. Generally, multifaceted persuasions have been oriented toward the maximization of success in each unique type of e-mail scam.

It is clear that social engineers have strategized, and carried out emotional attacks through skillful manipulation of the cognition of innocent users. As the scammers prepare for attack with their advantage of persuasive, deceptive skills, the potential victims must also be cognizant of social engineering exploitation and ready to counter an attack at any given time under any circumstances. Previous research has consistently looked at the social engineer with a limited amount of acknowledgment for the victims. Thus, future research should identify potential victims by looking at the characteristics of individuals who have fallen for social engineering victimization.

Besides research, public education has been a constant strategy used by governments and businesses to prevent online fraudulent acts. These organizational efforts include raising public awareness of social engineering through speeches, pamphlets, web pages, and the delivery of security messages in e-mails sent to users. Cautions have been raised concerning the psychological effects the educational campaign may produce on users, especially bank customers (Bardzell, Blevis, and Lim 2007; Emigh 2007; Mann 2008). From the standpoint of the customer, banks have been perceived as security providers who are assumed to offer protection advice and warnings to users. When a user receives an e-mail about security or updates from the bank, he/she has been pre-programmed to follow the instructions or visit suggested links (Mann 2008, 134). It has been customary for ordinary users to react correspondingly to the request of the bank. They would exercise their familiarity or emotion naturally to make decisions, often ignoring the security threat, faulty traps, or future financial loss they are facing. Thus, expecting that users can distinguish between phishing and legitimate e-mails and not follow instructions from a phisher is an unattainable assumption (Emigh 2007, 260). Social engineers have taken advantage of this gap and manipulated it against the victim.

Focusing the human elements on awareness and learning of social engineering exploitations remains the most prevalent and influential approach to combat the problem of fraudulent communications other than criminal justice responses and technological improvements. Educating users about the operations and mindsets of social engineering in elementary schools may reduce the likelihood of victimization from various on-line scams. Training students in proper use of online communications helps develop their "healthy skepticism" for persuasive messages used in fraudulent mails (Bardzell et al. 2007, 247). This early orientation can set up stronger internal defences against external, deceptive manipulations. Beyond public education, government and private sectors should implement security measures based on not only hardware and software devices but also a comprehensive protection system designed for various users (Bardzell et al. 2007, 241–259). More innovations and implementations for user-centered designs are needed to meet the security and emotional needs of users.

Conclusion

The study has showed that social engineering attacks using psychological persuasions can occur in online and offline environments. The social engineer learns, practices, and executes strategic attacks through manipulation of the victims' emotions. As the engineer prepares for an attack the potential victim, including corporations and individuals, must also prepare for an attack. Although security measures typically focus on the technological aspect of computer interaction, this study stresses the need to also focus on the user. Individuals allow their emotions to influence their decisions often ignoring the psychological threat they are facing. Social engineers have become witness to this phenomenon and have used it to their advantage.

This research further revealed that the social engineering methods used are active and multifaceted. The findings further provided information on the specific tactics the social engineer uses, the human weaknesses he/she looks for, and the manipulative nature of an attack. As we learn more about the social engineer, corporations and individuals can better prepare themselves for an attack. Additionally, research has uncovered the victims' cognitive and emotional weaknesses. Taking this information collectively, potential victims can learn to identify likely attacks, system vulnerability, and individual weaknesses. Change within social engineering will occur once the social engineer has limited access to victims. Through research, the knowledge gained will negatively impact the social engineer, as potential victims physically and psychologically prepare themselves for attacks.

References

Anderson, Troy. 2007. "Online fraud crimes soaring: D.A. sounds alarm on electronic theft." *The Daily New of Los Angeles*. (October 13, 2007), http://www.galileo.usg.edu.

Bardzell, Jeffrey, Eli Blevis and Youn-Kyung Lim. 2007. "Human-centered design considerations." In *Phishing and countermeasures*, ed. Markus Jakobsson and Steven Myers, 241–259. Hoboken, New Jersey: John Wiley & Sons, Inc.

BitDefender. 2007. "BitDefender Lab's top 10 malware list for 2007 spotlights botnet as top security threat." *Market Wire.* (December 18, 2007), http://www.galileo.usg.edu.

Blommaert, Jan and Tope Omoniyi. 2006. "E-mail fraud: Language, technology, and the indexicals of globalization." *Social Semiotics* 16 (4): 573–605.

Capaldi, Nicholas. 1971. *The art of deception*. New York: Donald W. Brown Inc.

Chu, Bill, Thomas J. Holt, and Gail Joon Ahn. 2010. "Examining the Creation, Distribution, and Function of Malware On-Line." Technical Report for National Institute of Justice. NIJ Grant No. 2007-IJ-CX-0018. (April 20, 2010), http://www.ncjrs.gov/pdffiles1/nij/grants/230112.pdf.

Cialindi, Robert B. 2001. *Influence: science and practice*. Boston: Allyn & Bacon.

Drake, Christine E., Jonathan J. Oliver, and Eugene J. Koontz. n.d. *Anatomy of a phishing email: A technical white paper*. (December 1, 2009), http://www.mailfrontier.com/docs/MF_Phish_Anatomy.pdf.

Edelson, Eve. 2003. "The 419 scam: Information warfare on the spam front and a proposal for local filtering." *Computer and Security* 22(5): 392–401.

Emigh, Aaron. 2007. "Mis-education." In *Phishing and countermeasures*, ed. M. Jakobsson and S. Myers, 260–275. Hoboken, New Jersey: John Wiley & Sons, Inc.

Federal Bureau of Investigation. 2009. *New E-scams & warnings*. (December 18, 2009), http://www.fbi.gov/cyberinvest/escams.htm.

Gilbert, Daniel T. and Patrick S. Malone. 1995. "The correspondence bias." *Psychological Bulletin* 117: 21–38.

Granger, Sarah. 2006. *Social engineering reloaded*. (February 22, 2010), http://www.securityfocus.com/infocus/1860

Granger, Sarah. 2001. *Social engineering fundamentals, Part I: hacker tactics*. (December 1, 2009), http://www.securityfocus.com/infocus/1527.

Holt, Thomas, and Danielle Graves. 2007. "A qualitative analysis of advance fee fraud e-mail schemes." *International Journal of Cyber Criminology* 1 (1): 137–154.

Howell, Donna. 2006. "Line on phishing scams." *Investor's Business Daily.* (November 9, 2006), http://www.galileo.usg.edu.

King, Anthony, and Jonathan Thomas. 2009. "You can't cheat an honest man: Making ($$$s and) sense of the Nigerian e-mail scams." In *Crime of the Internet,* ed. Frank Schmalleger and Michael Pittaro, 206–224. Saddle River, New Jersey: Prentice Hall.

Long, Johnny. 2008. *No tech hacking: A guide to social engineering, dumpster diving, and shoulder surfing.* Rockland, MA: Syngress Publishing.

Mann, Ian. 2008. *Hacking the human: Social engineering techniques and security countermeasures.* Burlington, VT: Gower Publishing Company.

Mather, Mara, Eldar Shafir, and Marcia K. Johnson. 2000. "Misremembrance of options past: Source monitoring and choice." *Psychological Science* 11: 132–138.

MillerSmiles, http://www.millersmiles.co.uk.

Mitnick, Kevin D. and William L. Simon. 2002. *The art of deception: Controlling the human element of security.* New York, New York: Wiley Publishing.

National White Collar Crime Center. 2008. Internet crime report. Washington, DC: Bureau of Justice Assistance. (July 11, 2009), http://www.ic3.gov/media/annualreport/2008_IC3Report.pdf.

Nickerson, Raymond S. 1998. "Confirmation bias: A ubiquitous phenomenon in many guises." *Review of General Psychology* 2 (2): 175–220.

Okenyi, Peter O. and Thomas J. Owens. 2007. "On the anatomy of human hacking." *Information Systems Security* 16: 302–314.

Peltier, Thomas R. 2006. "Social engineering: Concepts and solutions," *Information Security and Risk Management,* November 2006. http://www.peltierassociates.com.

Raman, Karthik. 2008. "Ask and you will receive." *McAfee Security Journal,* 1–12.

Ross, Derek G. 2009. "ARS dictaminis perverted: The personal solicitation e-mail as a genre." *Journal of Technical Writing and Communication* 39 (1): 25–41.

Rusch, Jonathan J. 2004. Phishing and Federal Law Enforcement. Washington, DC: U.S. Department of Justice. (February 22, 2010), http://www.abanet.org/adminlaw/annual2004/Phishing/PhishingABAAug2004Rusch.ppt.

Symantec Corporation. 2007. Symantec internet security threat report: Trends for January–June 07. (February 20, 2010), http://www.symantec.com/business/theme.jsp?themeid=threatreport.

United States Federal Trade Commission. 2008. Consumer fraud and identity theft complaint data: January–December, 2007. Federal Trade Commission.

(December 1, 2009), http://www.ftc.gov/sentinel/reports/sentinel-annual-reports/sentinel-cy2007.pdf.

Swartz, Nikki. 2002. "Cybercrime soars." *Information Management Journal,* 36(3): 6.

Taylor, Shelley E. and Susan T. Fiske. 1975. "Point of view and perception so causality." *Journal of Personality and Social Psychology* 32: 439–445.

Thompson, Samuel T. C. 2006. "Helping the hacker? Library information, security, and social engineering." *Information Technology and Libraries,* 222–225.

Tversky, Amos, and Daniel Kahneman. 1974. "Judgment under uncertainty: Heuristics and biases." *Science* 185: 1124–1130.

Ultrascan Advanced Global Investigations. January 2010. "419 Advance Fee Fraud Statistics 2009." (March 1, 2010), http://www.ultrascan-agi.com/public_html/html/public_research_reports.htmleport.

United States Federal Trade Commission. 2008. Consumer fraud and identity theft complaint data: January–December, 2007. Federal Trade Commission. (December 1, 2009), http://www.ftc.gov/sentinel/reports/sentinel-annual-reports/sentinel-cy2007.pdf.

Wall, David. 2004. "Digital realism and the governance of spam as cybercrime." *European Journal on Criminal Policy and Research* 10: 309–335.

Workman, Michael. 2008. "Wisecrackers: A theory-grounded investigation of phishing and pretext social engineering threats to information security." *Journal of American Society for Information Science and Technology* 59 (4): 662–674.

Zajonc, Robert B. 1968. "Attitudinal effects of mere exposure." *Journal of Personality and Social Psychology* 9 (2): 1–27.

Zook, Matthew. 2007. "Your Urgent assistance is required: The intersection of 419 spam and new network of imagination." *Ethics, Place and Environment* 10 (1): 65–88.

5

Internet Child Pornography: Legal Issues and Investigative Tactics

Marcus K. Rogers and Kathryn C. Seigfried-Spellar

The protection of children has historically been an important part of any society; the same holds true today (Finkelhor, Mitchell, and Wolak 2000). With the incredible growth in science and technology over the last two decades, there has been an increased emphasis on the protection of children (Finkelhor, Mitchell, and Wolak 2000; Seigfried-Spellar, Lovely, and Rogers 2010). The Internet and its accompanying technologies (e.g., World Wide Web, Twitter, Face-Book) have introduced some complexity and possibly new avenues for the potential abuse of childen and other historically victimized segments of our population. The notion that the Internet has become both a tool for advancing our society and culture as well as a tool for criminal or nefarious purposes is well documented (Ferraro and Casey 2005; Rogers and Seigfried-Spellar 2009; Taylor 1999, September; Wolak, Finkelhor, and Mitchell 2009). Criminals and other deviant segments of society have traditionally been early adopters of technology as a means to extend and improve their criminal tradecraft (Ferraro and Casey 2005). Information and Internet technologies are no exception to this. One only has to look at the various media reports on identity theft, credit card fraud, or some other electronic banking attack (see Holt and Graves 2007; Holt and Lampke 2010; Newman and Clarke 2003).

As it relates to the notion of protecting children, the Internet and its technologies have been in the media forefront. Federal, state, and local law enforcement agencies have created specialized units, and task forces (e.g., Internet Crimes Against Children-ICAC Task Force) to investigate crimes against children where the attacker has used technology to target their victims (Breeden and Mulholland 2006). The Federal government has passed new legislation (e.g., Adam Walsh Act) and provided funding to centers focused on combating child exploitation (National Center for Missing and Exploited Children) (Finkelhor et al. 2000; Wolak, Finkelhor, Mitchell, and Ybarra 2008).

Despite these seemingly proactive approaches to child protection, very little if any research has been conducted on the nature of these types of crimes and on the characteristics of these offenders (Lanning and Burgess 1984; Quayle and Taylor 2005). While there has been some empirical based research exploring pedophilia in online environments (Durkin and Bryant 1999; Holt, Blevins, and Burkert 2010; Jenkins 2001), most of the evidence cited to justify the focus on the Internet and its technologies is anecdotal or single case in nature. This has resulted in a gap in our understanding of the offenders, uncertainty regarding how to protect the victims, and ignorance as to how best to investigate, prosecute, and deter these types of offenses (Ferraro and Casey 2005; Taylor and Quayle 2003).

There has been some limited debate as to whether there is truly an increase in pedophilia and sexual deviancy that can be attributed to the corresponding increase in society's dependency on technology and the Internet. Current research indicates that regardless of the correlation versus causation debate, consumers of online child pornography are using Internet technologies to further their deviant sexual behavior (Taylor and Quayle 2003; Wolak et al. 2009).

In an attempt to shed some much-needed light on this societal issue, this chapter examines the role that the Internet and Internet-related technologies play in child pornography, pedophilia and sexually deviant Internet based paraphilia. We examine the emerging typology of online consumers of child pornography and how this is being manifested in the technology and online behaviors exhibited by these individuals. The chapter provides a brief overview of the context and possible scope of online child paraphilia, summarizes the current research related to investigative profiles of online predators and consumers of child pornography, advances in understanding and categorizing offenders and their offenses, suggestions for modifying current sentencing guidelines and provides guidance on using digital evidence in support of these types of investigation. Two cases studies are also included to illustrate the concepts discussed.

Scope and Context

The threat of online predators and the correlation between the Internet and pedophilic behavior has caused much alarm in the law enforcement and general public domains. One would assume that the media and political attention focused on this problem would have led to statistics and meaningful metrics regarding the frequency and prevalence of these activities; or that we would

have a body of empirical research regarding offender characteristics, victi-
mology, and the effectiveness of investigative techniques. Sadly this is not the
case (Seigfried-Spellar, Lovely, and Rogers 2010; Wolak et al., 2008; Wolak et
al. 2009). There does not seem to be a large body of research or evidence based
public or law enforcement policy regarding this type of criminal behavior
(Wolak et al. 2009). To be fair, federal agencies such as the FBI have published
various law enforcement related reports (Lanning 2001; Lanning and Burgess
1984), dealing with predatory offenders and consumers of child pornography,
but these reports are restricted to those cases that have been officially reported
to authorities; like other sex crimes, pedophilic related or predatory offenders
crimes tend to be under reported (Wolak et al. 2008; Wolak et al. 2009).

This lack of statistics has resulted in some dubious and obviously inflated
claims by organizations whom, have taken on the task of trying to protect children and/or educate parents as to the risks of the Internet to children and adolescents. As an example of some these claims, several websites provide the
following statistics (Enough 2009; Media 2009):

- Average age of first Internet exposure to pornography—11 years old;
- Largest consumers of Internet pornography—35–49 age group;
- 15–17 year olds having multiple hard-core exposures—80%;
- 8–16 year olds having viewed porn online—90% (most while doing
  homework);
- 7–17 year olds who would freely give out home address—29%;
- 7–17 year olds who would freely give out email address—14%; and
- Children's character names linked to thousands of porn links—26
  (Including Pokemon and Action Man).

It is unknown where these statistics came from, or how the sample was selected (assuming some type of actual empirical/survey based research was conducted) as no information was available on the methodology or sampling
procedures. At first glance, these statistics seem very frightening with 80% of
adolescents having hardcore experiences, and 11 year olds viewing pornography. Even if these figures are valid and reliable, they do not tell us anything
about the risk of these children and adolescents becoming victims of online
predators or about the consumption of child pornography. Other websites
offer even more disturbing supposed statistics (Healthymind 2009):

- 100,000 websites offer illegal child pornography;
- Child pornography generates $3 billion annually;
- 90% of 8–16 year olds have viewed porn online (most while doing homework);

- Average age of first internet exposure to pornography is 11 years old; and
- Largest consumer of Internet pornography 12–17 age group.

These statistics are equally frightening, but again, where did they come from? How can we possibly know or estimate the annual revenue from child porn, do these individuals and businesses file tax returns with their respective countries? How did they confirm the age range for the consumers of child porn? Unfortunately, as is the case with emotionally and politically charged topics, personal, corporate, and political agendas can get in the way of meaningful metrics and statistics that are essential for garnering a true understanding of the risks to children and adolescents and the actual role that the Internet and its technologies play (e.g., Quayle and Taylor 2005; Skenazy 2009). As Lanning so eloquently stated:

> Some professionals [dealing with child sexual abuse], however, in their zeal to make American society more aware of this victimization, tend to exaggerate the problem. Presentations and literature with poorly documented or misleading claims about one in three children being sexually molested, the $5 billion child pornography industry, child slavery rings, and 50,000 stranger-abducted children are not uncommon. The problem is bad enough; it is not necessary to exaggerate it. Professionals should cite reputable and scientific studies and note the sources of information. If they do not, when the exaggerations and distortions are discovered, their credibility and the credibility of the issue are lost. (Lanning 1992, 15)

From a global perceptive, the problem of child pornography only escalates due to the differences in national and international legislatures. The possession, distribution, and production of Internet child pornography is criminally sanctioned in several countries, such as the United States and United Kingdom; however, it is not illegal but is in fact readily available in others. For example, Japanese law only criminalizes the production or distribution of child pornography, thereby allowing personal possession without intent to distribute. In addition, similar laws accepting the personal use of child pornography are prevalent in Russia, Thailand, and Korea (Akdeniz 2008).

At the same time, several international entities have criminalized the possession, distribution, and production of Internet child pornography all together, such as the European Union, Council of Europe, and United Nations (Akdeniz 2008). The Canadian Criminal Code has included "viewing" or "accessing" as a criminal offense even if the individual did not permanently possess (e.g., download) the child pornography image. Overall, child pornography has become a global problem due to the advancement in technology and the differences in regulatory policies and sanctions.

The lack of reproducible empirical research in this area often leads to difficulties in determining the real severity of the offense, the danger posed by the offender, and what sentences are appropriate or in the United States, constitutional (Akdeniz 2008). Therefore, it is important to turn our discussion to possible solutions to this gap in knowledge.

The COPINE Project

In 1997, funding from the European Commission ignited the Combating Paedophile Information Networks in Europe (COPINE) project to research and explore the relationship between technology, more specifically the Internet, and the victimization of children (Taylor, Holland, and Quayle 2001). As part of the COPINE project, researchers began to quantitatively analyze and review child pornography images collected by offenders in order to explore the level of child victimization and severity of possession for the offenders. In 2001, Taylor et al. (2001) developed a continuum or categorization system, which placed seemingly innocent, non-sexualized images at one end of the spectrum while the sexually explicit and aggressive images appeared at the polar end. COPINE's continuum includes 10 levels based on the increase in severity of the child's sexual victimization: indicative, nudist, erotica, posing, erotic posing, explicit erotic posing, explicit sexual activity, assault, gross assault, and sadistic/bestiality (Taylor et al. 2001).

Level 1, or the indicative category, refers to any non-pornographic or innocent image, such as the advertisements for Disneyland. The nudist category (Level 2) includes images of naked or semi-naked children in appropriate nudist settings from a legitimate source (Taylor et al. 2001), such as an Art gallery or family photo album. Level 3, or the Erotica category, refers to images secretly taken of children in safe environments with varying degrees of nakedness, such as pictures covertly taken of children playing at the park or on the beach. However, the images contained in Levels 1, 2, and 3 are usually not considered "chargeable" offenses due to the lack of obscenity or difficulty in identifying the context or intent of the image (e.g., child pornography vs. real family photographs; Taylor et al. 2001).

Levels 4, 5 and 6 specifically refer to images where the children are deliberately posed. In Level 4 (posing), the images involve children that are intentionally posed in either complete, partial, or no clothing. According to Taylor et al. (2001), the amount, context, and organization of the Level 4 images may suggest whether or not the collector has a sexual interest in children. In addition, Level 5 (erotic posing) refers specifically to the deliberate sexual nature of the child's pose, which may include varying degrees of nakedness (e.g., child's legs are spread open). The explicit sexual posing category (Level 6) includes images, which stress the child's genital areas, once again, regardless of the degree of nudity. As the categories increase in the level of child victimization, the legality of the images becomes more cohesive with current legal definitions of child pornography. Again, Levels 4 and 5 may or may not be considered illegal; however, there still exists a psychological abuse due to the broken boundaries between the adult and child. With Level 6, images are more likely to be considered chargeable depending on the age of the minor. Currently, the majority of international and national legislature defines a minor as under the age of 18 years (Akdeniz 2008).

Finally, for most international and national legislatures, it is illegal to possess, distribute, or produce images of minors in Levels 7, 8, 9, and 10 of the COPINE continuum. These categories include images in which the level of victimization is considered to be more severe because of the direct interaction between the victim and the producer, which involves both physical and psychological abuse. Level 7, or explicit sexual activity, involves images of "touching, mutual and self-masturbation, oral sex, and intercourse by a child" (Taylor et al. 2001, 101), which do not involve the participation of any adult. In the assault category (Level 8), the child is sexually assaulted by an adult through digital touching. Level 9 (gross assault) includes grossly indecent images in which an adult is sexually assaulting the child by penetrative sex, masturbation, or oral sex. Finally, Level 10 (sadistic/bestiality) refers to images in which (1) the child is being "tied, bound, beaten, whipped, or otherwise subject something that involves pain" or (2) images of a child involved in some form of sexual activity with an animal (Taylor et al. 2001).

Overall, the continuum suggested by Taylor et al. (2001) is the best descriptive analysis to date regarding the types of child pornography images available via the Internet. As the spectrum suggests, not all child pornography images are the same especially in regards to their level of victimization. In addition, the classification system includes images, which may or may not be criminally sanctioned. By not solely focusing on the pictures that are illegal, science can begin to emphasize the psychological perspectives of the offender (Taylor et al. 2001). In the end, the preferred type of image and the collection itself may provide researchers with a better understanding of the offenders' personality traits and psychological characteristics.

In addition, Taylor et al. (2001) suggest each level should be assessed regarding size, novelty, and the age of the victim. The size and quality of the offender's collection may indicate their level of involvement in child pornography. For instance, the collection may reveal the offender's sexual interest with children or level of addiction or obsession with the Internet. In addition, the presence of novel images may indicate the offender's ability to network on the Internet. In essence, the more novel the images, the more involved the offender may be in the Internet child pornography rings. Finally, younger children are more likely to be the victims of child pornography because they are easier to control and manipulate, and research indicates the age of children involved in pornography is decreasing (Taylor 1999). Overall, the level of severity within each category of the COPINE continuum may differ depending on these three additional factors.

The Courts and COPINE

The COPINE classification system has influenced research on this topic as well as legislative decisions regarding the sentencing of child pornography offenders. For instance, Frei, Erenay, Dittmann, and Graf (2005) gathered data on 33 male child pornography offenders in Switzerland who were identified and arrested by law enforcement for using the Internet child pornography company, "Landslide Production Inc," which required the clients to provide identifiable information. The authors conducted a qualitative analysis of the pornographic material collected by the offenders using the COPINE classification system. Almost half of the offenders (45%) collected Level 9 images, or gross assault, and 27% of the offenders collected Level 10 images or "sadistic/bestiality" pictures. 9% of the offenders collected erotica (Level 3) images, 3% collected erotic posing (Level 5) images, and 3% collected explicit sexual assault (Level 7) images. Finally, 12% of the offenders either did not collect any child pornography, or the level of the child pornography images was unknown due to lack of data. Thus, the majority (72%) of the offenders collected images, which depicted greater levels of child victimization as indicated by the COPINE classification scale (Frei et al. 2005).

In 2002, the COPINE scale was adopted and modified into England and Wales' sentencing guidelines for child pornography related offenses. *In R v. Oliver and others*, the Court of Appeal determined the seriousness of a child pornography offense should be based on the "nature of the material involved and the extent of the offender's involvement with it" (*R v. Oliver* and others 2003). Based on the COPINE classification system, the "nature of the material" was defined in the Oliver image description scale as five categories: (1) erotic posing with no sexual activity, (2) sexual activities involving a child or children, (3) adult and child non-penetrative sexual activity, (4) adult and child penetrative sexual activity, and (5) sadism or bestiality (Akdeniz 2008). Levels 1, 2, and 3 of the COPINE scale, which involve less sexual victimization, were not included in the Oliver image description scale.

In addition, England and Wales adopted sentencing guidelines, which assess the content (i.e., level) and amount (i.e., quantity) of the images seized in child pornography related offenses based on the Oliver image description scale (Akdeniz 2008). In addition, the sentencing guidelines take into account the various child pornography offenses (i.e., possession, distribution, or production) as well as whether the child in the image is a real or computer-generated victim. In general, images involving real children, in contrast to computer-generated images, are considered by the courts as a more serious offense (Akdeniz 2008). Taking these four factors into consideration, the Oliver guidelines may suggest a punishment anywhere from a fine to a ten-year maximum sentence. However, as indicated by their name, the Oliver guidelines are merely "rules of thumb" for the courts to consider.

Judges have discretionary power to contemplate other aggravating factors, such as the defendant posting the images in a public domain of the Internet. In 2004, the *R v. Thompson* guidelines further clarified the Oliver guidelines by requiring indictments to include either an exact or representative count of the number of images at each level of the Oliver image description scale (*R v. Thompson* 2004). This guideline resulted from questions regarding the definition of "small or large quantities" in the Oliver guidelines (Akdeniz 2008).

In 2005, the Provincial Court of British Columbia Canada, adopted a similar system as the U.K.'s Oliver image description scale for categorizing the images seized in child pornography cases (see Table 5.1). According to the adopting court, the guidelines for categorizing images were meant to act as a deterrent for offenders by focusing on the harm experienced by the child in the images (Akdeniz 2008). Despite using a similar nomenclature in which the levels increase in their degree of child sexual victimization, the court documents do not make any reference to the COPINE scale or U.K.'s Oliver images description scale (Akdeniz 2008).

Currently, the United States does not utilize the COPINE scale, or any similar system, in the federal courts. However, the United States Sentencing Commission (U.S.S.C.) developed sentencing guidelines for offenses related to the sexual exploitation of a minor. Specifically, harsher sentences are implemented if the offense involves "material that portrays sadistic or masochistic conduct or other depictions of violence" (U.S.S.C. 2009). In addition, the guidelines recommend harsher sentences for offenses involving collections with a large quantity of images with 10–149 images at the lower end of the spectrum and

Table 5.1 The Suggested Canadian System for Classifying Images
Seized in Child Pornography Related Cases

Level	Description
1	Non erotic, non sexualized material including nudity
2	Material where the dominant characteristic demonstrates a sexual purpose
3	Explicit sexual activity and assaults between adult-child, child-child
4	Gross assaults, penetrative assaults involving adults
5	Sadistic images

more than 600 images at the polar end (U.S.S.C. 2009). Overall, the current federal sentencing guidelines in the United States focus on violent images of child sexual victimization and the total number of images in the offender's collection.

A Hypothetical Case Study

In order to better understand the classification system developed by Taylor et al. (2001), we created a hypothetical collection of images to clarify the various levels of the continuum. The doll images used for this case study were obtained from an actual law enforcement case in which the defendant was accused of child molestation, and during the investigation, hundreds of hard-copy images were discovered of dolls in various degrees of nakedness. The original case file was provided to the author by the investigating detective with direct orders to use the materials for educational and teaching purposes. The possession of child pornography by academics for the purpose of research is illegal in the United States by federal law. Thus, the hypothetical collection includes both non-child pornography images obtained via the Internet as well as the doll images obtained from a law enforcement case.

To set up the scenario, the reader is to assume the collection of images was obtained during a search of a suspect's computer, who was accused of possessing and distributing child pornography. As show in the Figure 5.1 (from left to right), the collection contains the following images:

- the Coppertone girl, a famous ad for an American sunscreen;
- a young girl with her arms raised above her head, which reveals her underpants;
- Olympia Nelson, then at the age of six, photographed nude by her mother, which appeared on the cover of an Australian art magazine (Marks, 2008);
- a young girl with her dress pulled down, which reveals her undergarments

- a girl's genitals; and
- two young girls on the beach in bikinis.

The images in Figure 5.1 will be discussed in the hypothetical order they might appear based on the COPINE's continuum of increased sexual victimization.

Figure 5.1 A Hypothetical Collection of Images

Using COPINE's scale, the Coppertone ad is an excellent example of the Level 1 or indicative category. Despite the girl's partial nudity, the image of the Coppertone girl ad is clearly innocent and non-pornographic in nature. Therefore, this image would not be considered illegal by most jurisdictions in view of the fact that it was obtained from a legitimate commercial source. For instance, this type of image would not fall into a category according to the U.K.'s Oliver Image Description Scale. In addition, it would most likely be labeled as a Level 1 image in the Canadian courts, which encompasses images not subject to criminal sanctions (Akdeniz 2008). However, as suggested by Taylor et al. (2001), these types of images should not be ignored by investigators, for the "context or organization of pictures by the collector [may] indicate inappropriateness" (p. 101).

The image of Olympia Nelson, whose nude photograph appeared on the cover of an art magazine, is more controversial than the Coppertone girl. Recently, this photograph sparked controversy as to the distinction between "art" and child pornography (Marks 2008). Although society continues to debate this fine line between legal and illegal, this image is an excellent illustration of the Level 2 or nudist category according to COPINE. In this hypothetical collection, such an image would be labeled a Level 2 because it is from a legitimate, verified source, an art magazine. In most instances, this image would not apply to the U.K.'s Oliver scale, and it would be labeled a Level 1 by Canadian courts.

Next, the image of the two girls on the beach becomes more difficult to classify according to the COPINE continuum. Assuming the image is from a legitimate source, such as the collector's family album, the image would be considered a Level 1 since the girls are semi-naked (wearing bikinis) at an appropriate setting (the beach). However, if this picture was not from the collector's family album, but was instead secretly taken of the two girls while they were playing at the beach, the image would be categorized as a Level 3 (erotica).

Thus, the investigators would have to determine the source of the image (i.e., family album or covertly taken) in order to accurately classify the image using COPINE's scale. In addition, investigators should once again consider the amount or context of other images, which are of a similar nature, in order to understand the collector's intent of possessing the innocent images.

Investigators would probably label the image of the girl raising her hands above her head as a Level 4 (posing). She appears to be posed in a non-provocative manner although her underwear is slightly revealed. In addition, this category is not concerned with the degree of nakedness of the child in the image. Although, this image would not be considered illegal in most jurisdictions, Taylor et al. (2001) suggest investigators should be aware of the "amount, context, and organization" of the images, which may suggest the collector has a sexual interest in children (p. 101).

As shown in Figure 5.1, the image of the partially nude girl with her dress pulled down would best be labeled as a Level 5 (erotic posing) using COPINE's scale. The girl is deliberately posed in a sexualized manner since her dress has been pulled down around her ankles, which reveals her undergarments. Again, this image may or may not be considered a chargeable offense in most jurisdictions. In the U.K., this image may be identified as a Level 1 (erotic posing with no sexual activity) according to the Oliver guidelines. However, this image may be labeled as a Level 2 (material demonstrates sexual purpose) according to the Canadian sentencing guidelines.

Lastly, the image focusing on the girl's genitals would be an example of a Level 6 (explicit erotic posing), since the genital area is clearly emphasized in this image, and no sexual activity is apparent (e.g., touching, masturbation). Images identified at this level are more likely to be considered illegal depending on the age of the minor. Based on the Oliver scale, this image would most likely be labeled as a Level 1, whereas it would fall under the Level 2 category according to the Canadian guidelines.

Criticisms of Court Image Classifications

Overall, the sentencing guidelines in the United States, England and Wales, and Canada, base sentencing decisions on the *quantity* of images as well as the *content* of the images in the collection. More specifically, the guidelines recommend harsher sentences for collections, which include more violent images (e.g., sadism). The COPINE continuum was originally developed as a way of discriminating images within a collection by identifying the level of sexual victimization. In addition, it offered a "means of judging severity within the broad

offense of possession" while providing a "basis on which systemic picture qualities may be related to offender behavior" (Taylor et al. 2001). For example,
utilizing a classification system allows researchers to better understand the
trends in child pornography collections; Taylor (1999) suggests the children
in child pornography images are becoming younger. In other words, newer
images of child pornography feature younger children, which may be related
to the imbalance of power between adults and young children (Taylor and
Quayle 2003).

The authors' original intention of "judging severity" has clearly been adopted
by the courts to mean that collectors with more violent images, or images at
the higher levels of COPINE, should receive harsher sentences within their
child pornography related offenses. In addition, the courts rationalization for
the increased punishment is the belief that the types of images in the collection must be reflective of the offender's behavior or personality. For instance,
collections including more violent images may be related to more violent offenders or at least offenders who are at the greatest risk of recidivism. In addition, the sentencing guidelines appear to place some of the blame on the
possessors of child pornography because they are fueling a commercial industry. Another argument is based on supply and demand—if there was no
demand for the sadistic images, there would be no need to produce them.
Thus, the possessors of child pornography should receive harsher sentences
for being a part of this child pornography supply-demand chain.

However, research suggests there is no evidence to support the enhancement
of sentences because more violent collections reflect more violent offenders
(Beech, Elliott, Birgden, and Findlater 2008; Friendman and Supler 2008; Quayle
2008). According to Friedman and Supler (2008), there is a lack of research or
empirical validation for the sentencing guidelines implemented in the United
States. Instead, the sentencing guidelines reflect political agendas and societal
panic in response to the increased availability of Internet child pornography (Akdeniz 2008; Friendman and Supler 2008). In addition, there is no evidence that
collections including more violent images should act as an aggravating factor
when determining offender risk for recidivism (Beech et al. 2008). Overall, more
research needs to be conducted in order to better understand the relationship
between the offenders and their collections; otherwise, sentencing guidelines will
continue to be based on moral and emotional responses rather than empirical data.

If the purpose of the sentencing guidelines is to punish offenders because
they are fueling a commercial industry, then it may be appropriate to consider
the level of child victimization in the image. After all, as the images become
more violent, the child is not only being exposed to emotional or psychological abuse but physiological abuse as well. In addition, the harsher sentences

require that the possessor and distributor of the images take some responsibility for the increased demand in images with higher degrees of sexual victimization. Thus, the various guidelines implemented by the United States, United Kingdom, and Canada may be appropriate if they are solely focusing on the level of harm experienced by the child (Beech et al. 2008; Taylor and Quayle 2003).

Classification System for the United States

The United States judicial system is in dire need of an image classification scale based on the COPINE scale. By classifying the images seized in child pornography related offenses, research and empirical data may be generated regarding trends in the content as well as comparisons between cases and countries. In addition, a detailed classification system may assist the various stages of the legislative process from the initial investigation to the sentencing procedures. Based on the previous scales adopted by the U.K. and Canada, we developed a similar classification system, which includes a description and example as well as the individuals involved at each level (see Tables 5.3 and 5.4). This model includes the technical activities of the offender to contact others or obtain materials. We hope this modified scale will ignite academic research and interest for qualitatively analyzing the content of images collected by offenders in the United States. First, new trends in the child pornography market may be identified. In addition, informed policy decisions regarding the level of severity in the offender's actions and behaviors along with the psychological perspectives of the offenders' sexual interest in children may be better understood.

Technical Investigations

Prior to an offender coming before the court system, investigators must identify evidence and determine that in fact an offense has been committed. Investigating online criminal behavior in general is somewhat problematic (Furnell 2002; Rogers 2005; Rogers, Seigfried, and Tidke 2006; Stambaugh et al. 2001). Crimes involving technology and technical advances such as the Internet and the World Wide Web require that investigators, be they law enforcement, military or private sector, have a strong understanding of the underlying structure of networks and networking protocols, operating systems, file systems, storage devices (e.g., hard drives, thumb drives, DVDs) and software/application development (Rogers and Seigfried, 2004). Each of these areas is a specialization in and of itself, and to assume that investigators can be experts in all of these is unrealistic.

Apart from the challenge of having properly trained investigators, the fact that technology evolves and changes at an incredible rate, causes investigators, and forensic tool developers to make constant changes to their methods, techniques and applications. Each time an update is made to an operating system (e.g., Microsoft Windows 7, Apple Snow leopard), the location of potential evidence, encryption capabilities and new privacy enhancements (e.g., over writing of web browser history files, shredding of deleted files) can result in the tool or investigator missing crucial evidence or misinterpreting the context of any evidence found (Rogers and Leshney 2009; Rogers and Seigfried 2004; Slade 2004).

Size limitations of this chapter preclude us from conducting an in depth discussion about all possible investigative strategies such as online sting operations, across all platforms.[1] Instead we focus on investigations involving Microsoft Windows and its NTFS file system. The NTFS files system is the most widely used file system in the world and is the default file system found on Windows XP, VISTA and Windows 7. In order to assist investigators several offender investigative profiles have been developed. These include the Lanning FBI model, the Krone model and the Rogers and Seigfried-Spellar Hybrid model (Rogers and Seigfried-Spellar 2009). Each model will be discussed in detail.

Lanning Model

The model developed by Lanning (2001), is based on the FBI's dichotomous offenders framework. This model uses the primary categories of situational and preferential sexual offender as the two extremes. The motivation of the offender is placed on a continuum of needs consisting of Biological/Physiological Sexual needs, Power/Anger Nonsexual needs, Psychosexual/Deviant Sexual needs (Lanning 2001). Lanning clearly indicates that his model should be thought of in terms of investigative typologies used to assist investigators and not for use in clinical diagnosis or developing psychological profiles.

Lanning's model states that preferential offenders include those with specific preferences or paraphilia that can include a preference for children and pornographic pictures of children, more commonly known as pedophilia (Lanning 2001). He further sub-divides the category of situational offender into: Regressed, Morally Indiscriminate, and Inadequate. Regressed offenders are characterized by low self-esteem, poor coping skills, and seek children as sexual

---

1. Please see Ferraro and Casey 2005, Hagy 2007, and Hart 2004 for more information.

Table 5.2 Lanning Computer Offender Typology

Type	Sub-Category
Situational	Normal adolescent/adult Morally indiscriminate Profiteers
Preferential	Pedophile Diverse Latent

partners to offset their inability to have a mature/age appropriate relationship (Lanning 2001).

Morally indiscriminate offenders are habitual "users and abusers of people" (Lanning 2001, 26). The sexual victimizations fit their pattern of general abuse directed at spouses, offspring, co-workers, etc. The sexual abuse is often opportunistic but the preference is for children. Common examples of this type of offender include incestuous fathers or mothers. Inadequate offenders can be suffering from mental disorders such as psychosis, mental retardation, senility, or other personality disorders (Lanning 2001). The sexual relations with children can be the product of curiosity, insecurity or built up impulses.

Lanning evolved his model to include computer-based offenders (Lanning 2001) (see Table 5.2). For those Situational offenders using computers and computer technology, two additional types were added from his earlier model: "Normal"—adolescent/adult who were curious about sex and pornography and used computers to search for pornography online; and "Profiteers" who make easy money from commercial opportunities for selling child pornography online (Lanning 2001).

Under the category of Preferential computer offenders, the model again lists two additional types: "Diverse"—offender with a wide variety of paraphiliac or deviant sexual interests, but no strong preference for children (referred to as the sexually indiscriminate in his previous model); and "Latent"—individuals with potentially illegal but previously latent sexual preferences (manifested through online activities such as chats, which weakens their inhibitions; Lanning 2001).

Krone Model

Similar to Lanning's computer offender typology, Krone's model is used specifically with offenders who are familiar with technology, and use technology to view, collect, distribute, and produce child pornography in an online environment (i.e., Internet). The model is based on work that was conducted in Australia, but nothing in the model precludes it from being used internationally. Krone focuses on the type of involvement of the offender, amount of networking, the level of technical expertise, whether the offender took technical precautious to avoid being traced or caught, and the nature of the abuse. The model consists of nine types of offenders, Browser, Private Fantasy, Trawler, Non-Secure Collector, Secure Collector, Groomer, Physical Abuser, and Distributor (Krone 2004).

According to Krone, a browser would fall under the umbrella of Lanning's situational offender. This is one of the only categories in this model that would be considered non-preferential offenders. Browsers stumble upon illicit pictures of children during their web browsing or via spam/rootkits but then fail to get rid of the pictures or intentionally seek more out (Krone 2004). Browsers generally, do not take steps to secure or hide their activities while online and do not have well-established networks in order to trade pictures. This type of offender does not usually participate in actual contact offenses with children.

Private fantasy offenders are preferential offenders under the Lanning model. They harbor thoughts and fantasies regarding sex with children (i.e., pedophilia) and collect pictures, movies and stories depicting naked children and children engaged in sexual activities (Krone 2004). Again this group does not actively hide their online behaviors or secure their computer systems against the possibility of being investigated. Private fantasy offenders do not have networks established for trading purposes. These offenders try and keep off the radar of law enforcement and do not usually move onto contact offenses with children.

Trawlers actively seek out child pornography and are considered preferential offenders. The major difference, according to Krone, between trawlers and private fantasy offenders is that trawlers take a more active approach to seeking out child porn. The private fantasy offender sits at a level of intentionality between Browsers and Trawlers. The Trawler also tends not to have a deep network of other offenders established, but may have connections in the "community." Trawlers are a low risk for contact offenses. The level of security and privacy knowledge and techniques are also very minimal (Krone 2004).

Non-secure collectors make use of peer-to-peer networks, chat rooms and other more open sites. These offenders have set up relationships with other offenders for the purpose of trading and collecting. This category does not typically employ any sophisticated security or privacy controls to hide their online activities and is not considered a high risk for contact offenses (Krone 2004).

Secure collectors are more cautious than the non-secure group. They are well connected in the "community" and prefer trusted sources and more secure networks in order to collect and trade their pictures (Krone 2004). They are usually concerned with security and privacy, have moderate to high levels of technical knowledge and abilities and may attempt to cover their tracks. However, this group is still unlikely to commit contact offenses.

The Groomer category is the first level in this model that has a high risk of contact offending. Groomers use technology and the Internet to make initial contacts in order to have sex with children. According to Krone they may have a level involvement across the entire range in the model. Groomers may have complex networks that include children or other offenders looking to actually engage in sexual activity with children. At this level the Krone model is vague as to whether security refers to technology or physical security in the context of the child involved (Krone 2004).

Physical abusers use pornography to facilitate the abuse, have connected networks to establish contact with children and again the security component is more focused on the physical contact of the child (Krone 2004). Technology is often involved for use in documenting the abuse in more of a private diary format than for distribution.

Producers are effectively at the top level of the model. They use technology to seek out victims and produce media that can be shared with other pedophiles. The level of networking depends upon whether the media produced is used more for private use or to feed the demands of the "community." They are involved in the actual abuse of the children and security is more related to technology used in the production of the media and the physical security in context of the child involved (Krone 2004). Although not directly listed in the model, it is logical to assume that the technical knowledge of this group would be significant.

Distributors in Krone's model are a bit of an odd category and could also fall under the category of situational offenders under Lanning's model. Distributors in Krone's model may or may not be pedophiles, but could be thought of as opportunistic business people (similar to Lanning's Profiteers). Money seems to be the primary motive and as such, they have regular clients and producers that they deal with. They do not ordinarily engage in any contact offenses, and as a business, they take steps to protect their computer systems and web sites (Krone 2004).

Other researchers have further generalized the typologies of Lanning and Krone into four higher order categories (Beech et al. 2008, 225):

1) individuals who access abusive images sporadically, impulsively and/or out of curiosity;
2) those who access/trade abusive images of children to fuel their sexual interest in children;

3) individuals who use the Internet as part of a pattern offline contact offending; and
4) individuals who access abusive images for seemingly non-sexual reasons (e.g., commercial profit).

Rogers and Seigfried-Spellar Hybrid Model

Though the Krone model is a useful typology, there may be greater value in a more comprehensive model. The Rogers and Seigfried-Spellar hybrid model was first introduced in July 2009 at a workshop conducted at John Jay College of Criminal Justice in New York City (see Tables 5.3, 5.4; Rogers and Seigfried-Spellar 2009). The model was also presented at the US-Indo Conference and Workshop on Cyber Security, Cyber Crime, and Cyber Forensics in Kochi, India in August 2009. The model extends the work of both Lanning and Krone and focuses on how and where different offenders will store evidence related to their online offenses on their computer systems. The model uses Krone's concept of security employed by the various offender types, but the hybrid model restricts the focus to technology and not physical security. The model is considered a hybrid in that it extends the work of Krone, who expanded the work of Lanning.

The hybrid model is primarily designed as an investigative tool for investigators and not as a diagnostic classification or treatment typology. While the focus is on technology, the model does not deal with networking technologies (e.g., routers, switches, firewalls or other servers that log user activity). It is acknowledged that these areas can provide crucial information, however, the starting point for most investigations is the suspect's computer system.

Table 5.3 Classification System Suggested by Rogers and Seigfried-Spellar

Level*	Adult Involved	Description	Example
1	No	No sexual activity; may involve sexual posting	Naked child laying on bed
2	No	Child-Child sexual activity or solo masturbation	Child touching his/her genitals
3	Yes	Non-penetrative sexual activity between adult-child	Adult touching a child's genitals
4	Yes	Penetrative sexual assault between adult-child	Sexual intercourse between adult-child
5	Maybe	Sadistic activity or child-animal sexual activity	Child tied and beaten OR beastiality

The model considers the offenders computer system, and specifically the file system to be analogous to geographical or physical space (Rogers and Seigfried-Spellar 2009). Offenders (and all computer users) interact with metaphors of the real world/physical space. When we log in we are taken to a desktop, we have files, folders, recycle bins. Our data and files are abstracted and presented to us in hierarchies, with various levels of nesting. The basics behind the graphical user interface (GUI) have purposely mimicked the real world that most users (at least older generations) were already comfortable with.

The computer operating systems (e.g., Windows XP, Windows 7, Leopard, Unix) and their file systems (e.g., NTFS, HFS+, EXT3) have other constraints and defaults around where data structures and files are stored. Due to the interaction of the GUI and the file system, there is actually a fairly well mapped out geography of a typical computer's hard drive. This mapping allows the hybrid model to predict the most likely location of evidence given the technical abilities of the offender in question and the operating and file system being used.

The assumption that system defaults for files systems locations of certain data is based on research findings that most online child pornography offenders do not employ any type of encryption, data wiping, or other kinds of security and/or privacy software to cover their activities (Carr 2004; Wolak, Finkelhor, and Mitchell 2005). Studies have also found that the majority of those arrested for child pornography did not have sophisticated computer systems and were not considered to have a high degree of technical knowledge or capabilities (Wolak, Finkelhor, and Mitchell 2005).

As stated earlier, due to its large market share, our discussion of the hybrid model will be limited to Microsoft Windows operating system (e.g., Windows XP) and the NTFS file system. Table 5.4 illustrates the model. The first two columns are identical to Krone's, and the third column provides investigators with artifacts that have the highest probability of being of an evidentiary nature. Investigators now have some type of a basic workflow model to help guide their investigations. This workflow is not considered a checklist and is designed to only act as suggested minimum types of data that should be located, examined and analyzed. As was mentioned previously, the artifacts and their locations within the file system are the result of defaults set by the system. However, it should be noted that data, such as pictures and documents, could be relocated by the end user to non-default locations. This is why it is important to understand the technical knowledge of the suspect. If the suspect has a high level of technical knowledge and sophistication, then investigators need to look in non-default locations (other than "C:\Documents and Settings\User Account\<USERS>").

Table 5.4 Rogers Seigfried-Spellar Hybrid Model

Category	Features	System Artifacts	
Browser	Response to spam, accidental hit on suspect site—material knowingly saved.	• Internet History logs • Temporary files • Web Cache • Cookies	• Thumbnails • Deleted files • Recycle Bin • Default User account folders (e.g., pictures, movies)
Private Fantasy	Conscious creation of online text or digital images for private use.	• Internet History logs • Temporary files • Web Cache • Cookies • Deleted files • Recycle Bin • Mobile Phone	• Thumbnails • P-2-P folders • email • Registry/Typed URLS • Default User account folders (e.g., pictures, movies) • External storage devices
Trawler	Actively seeking child pornography using openly available browsers.	• Internet History logs • Temporary files • Web Cache • Cookies • Deleted files • Recycle Bin • IRC folders • Mobile Phone	• Thumbnails • P-2-P folders • email • Registry/Typed URLS • Default User account folders (e.g., pictures, movies) • Non-default folders • External storage devices
Non-secure collector	Actively seeking material often through peer-to-peer networks.	• Internet History logs • Temporary files • Web Cache • Cookies • Deleted files • Recycle Bin • IRC folders • Mobile Phone	• Thumbnails • P-2-P folders • email • Registry/Typed URLS • Default User account folders (e.g., pictures, movies) • Non-default folders • External storage devices
Secure collector	Actively seeking material but only through secure. Collector syndrome and exchange as an entry barrier.	• Internet History logs • Temporary files • Web Cache • Cookies • Deleted files • Recycle Bin • IRC folders • Mobile Phone • Encrypted folders	• Thumbnails • P-2-P folders • email • Registry/Typed URLS • Default User account folders (e.g., pictures, movies) • Non-default folders • External storage devices
Groomer	Cultivating an online relationship with one or more children. The offender may or may not seek material in any of the above ways. Pornography may be used to facilitate abuse.	• Internet History logs • Temporary files • Web Cache • Cookies • Deleted files • Recycle Bin • Mobile Phone	• Thumbnails • P-2-P folders • email • Registry/Typed URLS • Default User account folders (e.g., pictures, movies) • Non-default folders • External storage devices

Note: Table A is a reduced version of the model and only provides an overview of the offender type (based on Krone's model) and what system artifacts the investigator should look for. The full model provides the investigator with the location of where these files are kept—assuming the system in question is using the standard defaults (Rogers and Seigfried-Spellar 2009).

Table 5.4 Rogers Seigfried-Spellar Hybrid Model, *continued*

Category	Features	System Artifacts	
Physical abuser	Abusing a child who may have been introduced to the offender online. The offender may or may not seek material in any of the above ways. Pornography may be used to facilitate abuse.	• Internet History logs • Temporary files • Web Cache • Cookies • Deleted files • Recycle Bin • Digital cameras • Mobile Phone	• Thumbnails • P-2-P folders • email • Registry/Typed URLS • Default User account folders (e.g., pictures, movies) • Non-default folders • External storage devices
Producer	Records own abuse or that of others (or induces children to submit images of themselves).	• Internet History logs • Temporary files • Web Cache • Cookies • Deleted files • Recycle Bin • IRC folders • Mobile Phone • Digital cameras	• Thumbnails • P-2-P folders • email • Registry/Typed URLS • Default User account folders (e.g., pictures, movies) • Non-default folders • External storage devices
Distributor	May distribute at any one of the above levels.	• Internet History logs • Temporary files • Web Cache • Cookies • Deleted files • Recycle Bin • IRC folders • Mobile Phone • Digital cameras	• Thumbnails • P-2-P folders • email • Registry/Typed URLS • Default User account folders (e.g., pictures, movies) • Non-default folders • External storage devices

Case Study

The utility of the hybrid model is best understood in the context of a small case study. The case study looks at an investigation in which the suspect falls into the offender type of "Browser." According to Lanning's typology, a Browser could be classified as a situational "Normal adolescent/adult." According to Krone, Browsers do not usually employ any kind of physical or technical security and are not technically sophisticated (Krone 2004).

Figure 5.2 shows the directory listing of the Browser's system. The investigation would initially focus on the "Documents and Settings" directory to locate the user accounts on this system. The "Recycler" directory, which contains files that have been placed in the "recycle bin" would also be of interest, as these files are grouped by a unique security ID and can be easily recovered (see Figure 5.3).

According to Figure 5.4, in this case the system has three user accounts that are not default system accounts (e.g., all users, guest, administrator).

Figure 5.2 Directory Listing

Figure 5.3 Recycle Bin

Name	Date Modified	Size	Kind
S-1-5-21-842925246-1844823847-725345543-1003	Nov 30, 2008, 2:02 AM	--	Folder
$I30	Sep 6, 2008, 5:43 PM	4 KB	Unix ...ble File
Dc1	Nov 30, 2008, 12:56 AM	--	Folder
$I30	Aug 6, 2008, 9:40 PM	4 KB	Unix ...ble File
08&dad.jpeg	May 18, 1999, 10:02 AM	52 KB	JPEG image
08&dad5.jpg	May 18, 1999, 10:02 AM	52 KB	JPEG image
abby-01.jpg	Jun 12, 1999, 10:02 AM	52 KB	JPEG image
abby-03.jpg	Jun 12, 1999, 10:02 AM	52 KB	JPEG image
abby-04.jpg	Jun 12, 1999, 10:02 AM	52 KB	JPEG image
adina-03.jpg	Dec 15, 1998, 10:02 AM	52 KB	JPEG image
adina51.jpg	Dec 15, 1998, 10:02 AM	52 KB	JPEG image
Dc2	Nov 30, 2008, 12:56 AM	--	Folder
amber060.jpg	May 6, 1999, 10:02 AM	52 KB	JPEG image
amber067.jpg	May 6, 1999, 10:02 AM	52 KB	JPEG image
Dc3	Nov 30, 2008, 12:56 AM	--	Folder
Dc4.jpg	May 12, 1999, 10:02 AM	52 KB	JPEG image
Dc5.jpeg	May 18, 1999, 10:02 AM	52 KB	JPEG image
Dc6.jpg	May 18, 1999, 10:02 AM	52 KB	JPEG image
Dc7.jpg	Jun 12, 1999, 10:02 AM	52 KB	JPEG image
Dc8.jpg	Jun 12, 1999, 10:02 AM	52 KB	JPEG image
Dc9.jpg	Jun 12, 1999, 10:02 AM	52 KB	JPEG image
Dc10.jpg	Dec 15, 1998, 10:02 AM	52 KB	JPEG image
Dc11.jpg	Dec 15, 1998, 10:02 AM	52 KB	JPEG image
Dc12.jpg	May 6, 1999, 10:02 AM	52 KB	JPEG image
Dc13.jpg	May 6, 1999, 10:02 AM	52 KB	JPEG image
Dc14.jpg	May 19, 1999, 10:02 AM	52 KB	JPEG image
Dc15.jpg	May 12, 1999, 10:02 AM	52 KB	JPEG image
Dc16	Nov 30, 2008, 12:56 AM	--	Folder
babysit3.jpg	May 6, 1999, 10:02 AM	52 KB	JPEG image
Thumbs.db	Nov 19, 2008, 1:56 PM	8 KB	Datab...ument
Dc17	Aug 25, 2008, 10:27 PM	--	Folder

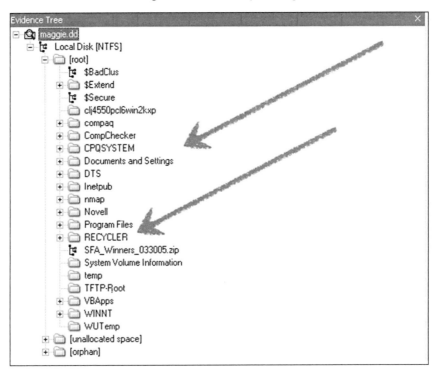

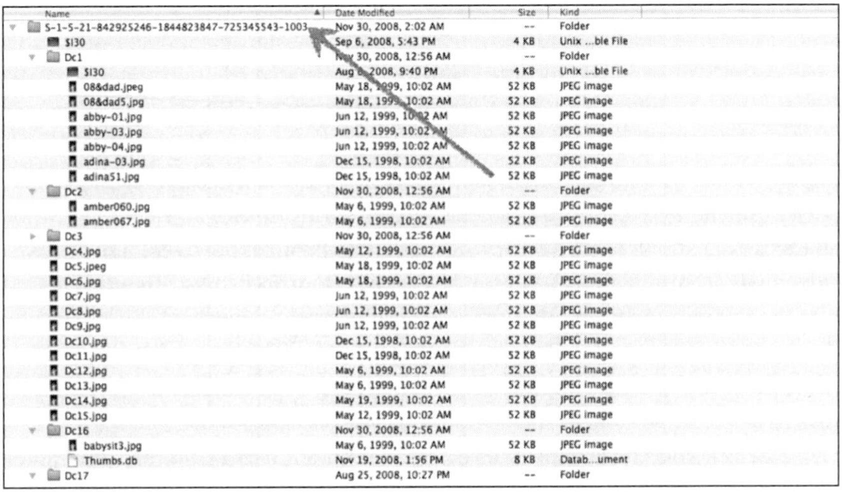

Figure 5.4 User Accounts

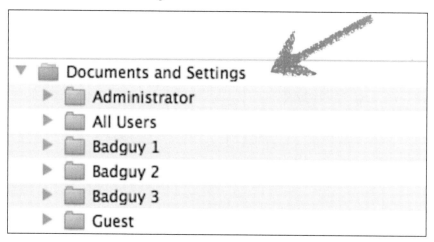

Figure 5.5 shows the location of the cookies folder belonging to the user Badguy 1. This folder contains cookie information related to activity of someone logged into the Badguy 1 account. Box 6 shows the content of the cookies folder. These cookie files are produced when a user visits a particular web page. They are generated by the external web page but stored locally on the users system. The cookies give an indication of the web pages that have been visited by the suspect, and provide information used for marketing purposes.

The Internet history folder shown in Figure 5.7 contains information related to websites visited, the dates and times of the visit and depending on the browser, the number of times visited by the user (see Figure 5.8).

We end our case study at this point as it should be clear how the model is used. In an actual case, the investigator would continue to locate the remaining system artifacts as listed in the model.

Conclusions

To say that the Internet poses the largest threat to our children is a gross exaggeration (Skenazy 2009; Wolak, Finkelhor, and Mitchell 2009; Wolak et al. 2008). However, we cannot be blind to the fact that sexual deviants, pedophiles, and other predatory offenders are using technology to find victims, trade pictures, and evolve their criminal tradecraft. In order to effectively deal with online child pornography, we must better understand the technology and those

Figure 5.5 Cookies Folder

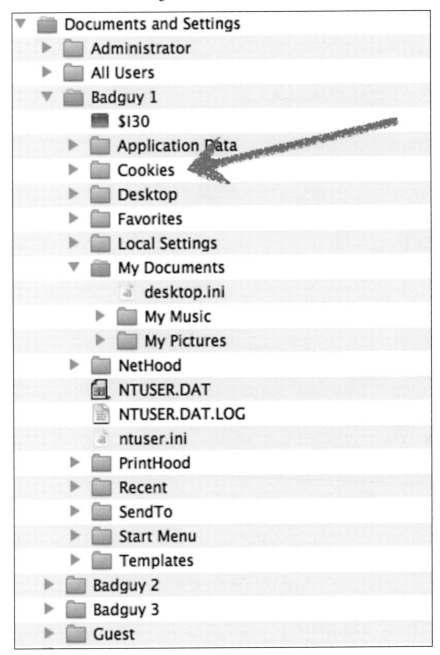

Figure 5.6 Cookie Content Information

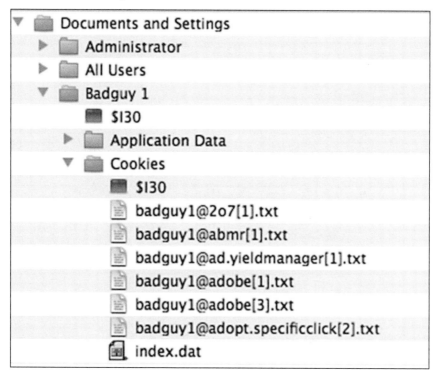

using it (Beech et al. 2008; Holt et al. 2010; Rogers and Seigfried-Spellar 2009; Schell et al. 2007; Taylor and Quayle 2003; Wolak, Finkelhor, and Mitchell 2005; Wolak, Finkelhor, and Mitchell 2009).

We need to continue our efforts to harmonize international law related to child pornography and eliminate any so called safe havens for these offenders. But as Taylor et al. (2003) indicated, simply locking these offenders up partially treats a symptom; it does not go after the root cause of the problem. Identifying the root cause of pedophilia or other deviant sexual behaviors is extremely difficult and requires funding and focused research.

In this chapter, we have attempted to provide an over view of the current models related to the offenders and the types of offenses they commit. We introduced the work in Europe on COPINE and how a modification of this could be integrated into the United States legal justice system as a better approach for sentencing guidelines. We also looked at the investigative typologies of Lanning and Krone, and how these typologies could be used to assist investigators in the form of the Rogers-Seigfried-Spellar Model.

Figure 5.7 Browser History

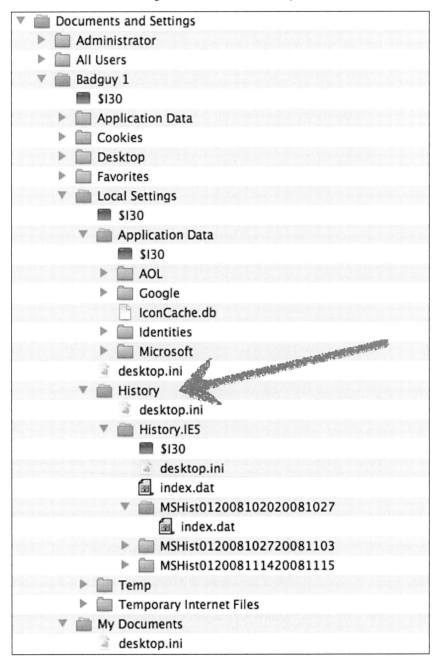

Figure 5.8 Browser History

URL	Title	Hits	Modified Date	Expiration Date	User Name
http://www.youtube.com/watch?v=o27BMewdsN0	YouTube - Yoga Weight Loss Exercises : Yoga for Weight Loss: Fish Pose	10	10/27/2008 11:51:15 PM	11/22/2008 11:44:08 PM	Abigail Sloan
http://www.youtube.com/watch?v=o27BMewdsN0	YouTube - Yoga Weight Loss Exercises : Yoga for Weight Loss: Fish Pose	11	10/27/2008 11:51:15 PM	11/22/2008 11:44:08 PM	Abigail Sloan
http://www.youtube.com/watch?v=o27BMewdsN0	YouTube - Yoga Weight Loss Exercises : Yoga for Weight Loss: Fish Pose	7	10/27/2008 11:51:15 PM	11/22/2008 11:44:06 PM	Abigail Sloan
http://www.youtube.com/rss	YouTube - [RSS]	5	10/27/2008 11:51:12 PM	11/22/2008 11:44:04 PM	Abigail Sloan
http://www.youtube.com/watch?v=o27BMewdsN0		4	10/27/2008 11:51:09 PM	11/22/2008 11:44:00 PM	Abigail Sloan
http://www.youtube.com/results?search_query=yoga+for+weight+loss&search_type...	YouTube - Broadcast Yourself.	16	10/27/2008 11:51:04 PM	11/22/2008 11:43:56 PM	Abigail Sloan
http://www.youtube.com/rss	YouTube - [RSS]	4	10/27/2008 11:51:01 PM	11/22/2008 11:43:54 PM	Abigail Sloan
http://www.youtube.com/watch?v=rpZKOHROnpCQ	YouTube - YOGA FOR WEIGHT LOSS, with Esther Ekhart.	11	10/27/2008 11:49:53 PM	11/22/2008 11:49:54 PM	Abigail Sloan
http://www.youtube.com/results		1	10/27/2008 11:49:39 PM	11/22/2008 11:49:40 PM	Abigail Sloan
http://www.youtube.com	YouTube - Broadcast Yourself.	11	10/27/2008 11:49:24 PM	11/22/2008 11:49:26 PM	Abigail Sloan
http://www.google.com/search?sourceid=navclient&aq=t&ie=UTF-8&rlz=1T...	youtube - Google Search	7	10/27/2008 11:49:03 PM	11/22/2008 11:49:04 PM	Abigail Sloan
http://mail.google.com/mail/?shva=&ui=2	Gmail	99	10/27/2008 11:48:46 PM	11/22/2008 11:48:48 PM	Abigail Sloan
http://mail.google.com/mail/feed/atom	Gmail Atom Feed	59	10/27/2008 11:48:43 PM	11/22/2008 11:48:44 PM	Abigail Sloan
http://client.web.aol.com/toolbar/client/signin.htm?lang=en&locale=en&u...	Untitled Document	49	10/27/2008 11:48:38 PM	11/22/2008 11:48:40 PM	Abigail Sloan
http://www.google.com	Google	493	10/27/2008 11:48:38 PM	11/22/2008 11:48:40 PM	Abigail Sloan
http://mail.google.com/mail/?shva=&ui=2	Gmail	85	10/23/2008 11:32:08 PM	11/18/2008 11:32:10 PM	Abigail Sloan
http://mail.google.com/mail/feed/atom	Gmail Atom Feed	58	10/23/2008 11:32:04 PM	11/18/2008 11:32:06 PM	Abigail Sloan
http://client.web.aol.com/toolbar/client/signin.htm?lang=en&locale=en&u...	Untitled Document	48	10/23/2008 11:32:01 PM	11/18/2008 11:32:02 PM	Abigail Sloan
http://www.cnn.com/2008/CRIME/11/06/spitzer.no.charges/index.html	Spitzer won't be charged in prostitution scandal - CNN.com	11	10/20/2008 11:37:28 PM	11/15/2008 11:30:20 PM	Abigail Sloan
http://www.cnn.com	CNN.com - Breaking News, U.S., World, Weather, Entertainment & Video News	156	10/20/2008 11:37:05 PM	11/15/2008 11:37:06 PM	Abigail Sloan
http://rss.cnn.com/rss/cnn_topstories.rss	CNN - Top Stories [RSS]	50	10/20/2008 11:37:03 PM	11/15/2008 11:37:04 PM	Abigail Sloan
http://rss.cnn.com/rss/cnn_latest.rss	CNN - Recent Stories [RSS]	57	10/20/2008 11:37:03 PM	11/15/2008 11:37:04 PM	Abigail Sloan
http://www.google.com/search?sourceid=navclient&ie=UTF-8&rlz=1T4ADBF_enU...	cnn - Google Search	97	10/20/2008 11:36:59 PM	11/15/2008 11:37:00 PM	Abigail Sloan
http://www.google.com/search?hl=en&q=civic+events+big+city	civic events big city - Google Search	7	10/19/2008 11:31:43 PM	11/14/2008 11:24:34 PM	Abigail Sloan

It is important to consider child pornography as a wide range of images involving different levels of victimization, rather than pictures that are defined as either legal or illegal. After all, images of children may be collected for sexual purposes despite the purity or lack of sexuality in the materials (Howitt 1995). In the end, the preferred type of images selected by the users may provide clues in understanding their personality traits and psychological characteristics. For instance, by understanding the types of images in the collection, we may be able to improve the criminal courts ability to assess an offender's risk of recidivism. In addition, a modified version of COPINE in the U.S. criminal courts may assist judges who must determine the appropriate level of punishment through sentencing guidelines. Despite legislative attempts at regulating and criminalizing the pornographic materials, technological advances (e.g., computer-generated images) will continue to occur making research an important part of society's attempt to better understand not only the consumer but the collection of images as well.

The proposed investigative model can greatly assist investigators working on online child pornography cases by providing some direction and consistency to the investigative process. Obviously the model needs to be further developed and refined in order to further validate the offender categories, identify overlapping offender characteristics, and ensure the file system artifacts and paths are correct. As the criminal category of online child pornography offenders becomes better understood and studied, it is anticipated that more precise offender categories will become apparent. These typology changes will be reflected in the revised model. The bigger challenge consists of keeping the model current as the technology being used by the offender changes rapidly. Newer software and operating systems (e.g., Windows 7) can have subtle and not so subtle changes to their files system, resulting in different artifacts being created (e.g., Web history, cookies) and different storage locations for this type of evidence (Carrier 2005).

As we struggle to deal with such emotional and politically charged topics, such as child pornography, we need to keep in mind that the problem by all accounts is not going away, and technology is becoming ever more integrated into the lives of our children. Therefore, any assistance that can be provided to the courts (in dealing with offenders), to the behavioral sciences community (in treating these individuals), and to the investigators (in collecting better evidence) is sorely needed. As a corollary, this assistance should also provide parents and care givers with a better understanding of the risk to children, and how to identify potentially dangerous situations.

References

Akdeniz, Yaman. 2008. *Internet child pornography and the law: National and international responses.* Burlington, VT: Ashgate Publishing Co.

Beech, Anthony, Ian Elliott, Astrid Birgden, and Donald Findlater. 2008. The Internet and child sexual offending: A criminological review. *Aggression and Violent Behavior* 13: 217–228.

Breeden, Bob and Judie Mulholland. 2006. Investigating internet crimes against children (ICAC) cases in the state of Florida. In *SAC'06*. Dijon, France: ACM.

Carr, Angela. 2004. Internet traders of child pornography and other censorship offenders in New Zealand. (June 21, 2005), http://www.dia.govt.nz/diaweb site.nsf/wpg_URL/Resource-material-Our-Research-and-Reports-Internet-Traders-of-Child-Pornography-and other-Censorship-Offenders-in-New-Zealand?OpenDocument.

Carrier, Brian. 2005. *File system forensic analysis.* New York, NY: Addison-Wesley.

Enough. 2009. *Enough is enough: Protecting our children online* 2009 (November 1, 2009), Available from http://enough.org/inside.php?id=2UXKJWRY8.

Finkelhor, David, Kimberly Mitchell, and Janis Wolak. 2000. Online victimization: A report on the nation's youth. Crimes Against Children Research Center.

Ferraro, Monique and Eoghan Casey. 2005. *Investigating child exploitation and pornography: The internet, the law and forensic science.* New York, NY: Elsevier Academic Press.

Frei, Andreas, Nuray Erenay, Voker Dittmann, and Marc Graf. 2005. Paedophilia on the internet—A study of 33 convicted offenders in the canton of lucerne. *Swiss Medical Review* 135: 488–494.

Friendman, Ian and Kristiana Supler. 2008, December. Child pornography sentencing: The road here and the road ahead. *Federal Sentencing Reporter* 21 (2): 83–89.

Furnell, Steven. 2002. *Cybercrime: Vandalizing the information society.* Boston, MA: Addison-Wesley.

Hagy, David. 2007. Investigations involving the internet and computer networks. Washington: Department of Justice.

Holt, Thomas J., Kristie R. Blevins, and Natasha Burkert. 2010. Considering the pedophile subculture on-line. *Sexual Abuse: Journal of Research and Treatment* 22: 3–24.

Holt, Thomas J. and Danielle C. Graves. 2007. A qualitative analysis of advanced fee fraud schemes. *The International Journal of Cyber-Criminology* 1: 137–154.

Holt, Thomas J. and Eric Lampke. 2010. Exploring stolen data markets online: Products and market forces. *Criminal Justice Studies* 23: 33–50.

Keith, Durkin and Clifton Bryant. 1999. Propagandizing pederasty: A thematic analysis of the on-line exculpatory accounts of unrepentant pedophiles. *Deviant Behavior* 20 (2): 103–127.

Hart, Sarah. 2004. Forensic examination of digital evidence: A guide for law enforcement. Washington: National Institute of Justice.

Healthymind. 2009. *Internet pornography statistics* 2009. (November 1 2009), http://www.healthymind.com/s-porn-stats.html.

Howitt, Dennis. 1995. Pornography and the paedophile: Is it criminogenic? *British Journal of Medical Psychiatric* 68: 15–27.

Jenkins, Philip. 2001. *Beyond tolerance: Child pornography online.* New York: New York University Press.

Krone, Tony. 2004. A typology of online child pornography offending. Canberra: Australian Institute of Criminology.

Lanning, Kenneth. 1992. Child sex rings: A behavioral analysis for criminal justice professionals handling cases of child sexual exploitation, 2nd Edition: National Center for Missing and Exploited Children. (October 1, 2009), http://www.skeptictank.org/nc72.pdf.

Lanning, Kenneth. 2001. Child molesters: A behavioral analysis 4th Edition.

Lanning, Kenneth and Ann Burgess. 1984. Child Pornography and sex rings. *FBI Law Enforcement Bulletin* January, 1984.

Marks, Kathy. *Art or abuse? Fury over image of naked girl.* The Independent 2008, July 8 (August 1, 2009), http://www.independent.co.uk/news/world/australasia/art-or-abuse-fury-over-image-girl-862068.html.

Media, Family Safe. 2009. *Pornography statistics.* (November 1, 2009), http://www.familysafemedia.com/pornography_statistics.html.

Newman, Grame, and Ronald Clarke. 2003. *Superhighway robbery: Preventing e-commerce crime.* Cullompton: Willan Press.

Quayle, Ethel. 2008, September. The COPINE project. *Irish Probation Journal* 5: 65–83.

Quayle, Ethel and Max Taylor. 2005. *Viewing child pornography on the internet: Understanding the offense, managing the offender, helping victims.* Dorset: Russell House Publishing.

R v. Oliver and others. 2003. EWCA Crim 2766 (Court of Criminal Appeal Division 2002).

R v. Thompson. 2004. EWCA Crim 699.

Rogers, Marcus and Sean Leshney. 2009. Virtualization and digital investigations. In *Information Security Management Handbook*, edited by H. Tipton and M. Krause. New York, NY: Auerbach.

Rogers, Marcus and Kathryn Seigfried. 2004. The future of computer forensics: A needs analysis survey. *Computers and Security* 23: 12–16.

Rogers, Marcus. 2005. DCSA: Digital crime scene analysis. In *Handbook of information security management*, edited by H. Tipton and M. Krause. Dunedin, FL: Auerbach.

Rogers, Marcus and Kathryn Seigfried-Spellar. 2009. Investigating online consumers of child Pornography. In *1st Annual ACM Northeast Digital Forensics Exchange*. John Jay College of Criminal Justice, City University of New York, New York.

Rogers, Marcus, Kate Seigfried, and Kirte Tidke. 2006. Self-reported computer criminal behavior: A psychological analysis. *Digital Investigation* 3: 116–120.

Schell, Bernadette, Miguel Martin, Patrick Hung, and Luis Rueda. 2007. Cyber child pornography: A review paper of the social and legal issues and remedies—and a proposed technical solution. *Aggression and Violent Behavior* 12: 45–63.

Seigfried-Spellar, Kathryn, Richard Lovely, and Marcus Rogers. 2010. *Personality assessment of self-reported Internet child pornography consumers using bandura's theory of reciprocal determinism*. Edited by K. Jaishankar, *Cyber Criminology*. Boca Raton, FL: CRC Press.

Skenazy, Lenore. 2009. The myth of online predators. In *The daily beast*, edited by L. Skenazy.

Slade, Robert M. 2004. *Software forensics : Collecting evidence from the scene of a digital crime*. New York, NY: McGraw-Hill.

Stambaugh, Hollis, David S. Beaupre, David J. Icove, Richard Baker, Wayne Cassaday, and Wayne P. Williams. 2001. Electronic crime needs assessment for state and local law enforcement. National Institute of Justice.

Taylor, Max. 1999, September. The nature and dimensions of child pornography on the Internet. In *US/EU International Conference, Combating Child Pornography on the Internet*. Vienna, Austria.

Taylor, Max, Gemma Holland, and Ethel Quayle, E. 2001. Typology of paedophile picture collections. *The Police Journal* 74: 97–107.

Taylor, Max and Ethel Quayle. 2003. *Child pornography an Internet crime*. New York, NY: Routledge.

U.S.S.C. 2009. *U.S. Sentencing Guidelines Manual* §2G2.2.

Wolak, Janis, David Finkelhor, and Kimberley Mitchell. 2005. Child pornography possessors arrested in Internet-related crimes: Findings from the national online victimization study. (October 5, 2008), http://www.missing kids.com/en_US/publications/NC144.pdf.

Wolak, Janis, David Finkelhor, Kimberley Mitchell, and Michele Ybarra. 2008. Online predators and the victims: Myth, realities and implications for prevention and treatment. *American Psychologist* 63 (2): 111–128.

Wolak, Janis, David Finkelhor, and Kimberly Mitchell. 2009. Trends in the arrests of "online predators." (December 20, 2009), http://unh.edu/ccrc/pdf/N-JOV2_methodology_report.pdf.

6

Sex for Sale: Online Commerce in the World's Oldest Profession

Scott Cunningham and Todd D. Kendall

Given the revolutionary effects of the Internet on marketing and commerce in other industries, it should come as no surprise that the web has also had a large impact on the world's oldest profession: prostitution. In August of 1997, the first fee-based advertising site catering to the escort market appeared on the World Wide Web (Brooks 2009). Online prostitution activity is therefore almost as old as the web itself, but seems to have reached a critical mass in the public eye in recent years. In April, 2009, Phillip Markoff was arrested for murdering a prostitute he contacted [via] an advertisement on craigslist.org, a major classified ad site. Tom Dart, sheriff of Cook County, Illinois sued craigslist that same year for allegedly facilitating prostitution, claiming the site drained police resources to monitor content and referring to it as "the largest source of prostitution in the nation." (U.S. District Court 2009) Recent movies (Stephen Soderburgh's *The Girlfriend Experience*) and television shows (*Diary of a Call Girl*) have also focused on prostitutes who operate online.

Prostitution involves serious costs, not only to those who participate in the market as buyers or sellers, but also to society. Such social costs include the transmission of sexually transmitted infections, the creation of public nuisance, marital disruption, exploitation, as well as human trafficking, rape, assault, drug abuse and other problems frequently associated with prostitution (Weitzer 2005). Hence, it is critical that policymakers and law enforcement officials understand the rapidly changing nature of prostitution in order to effectively reduce these harms to society.

This chapter reviews some of the means by which sex is bought and sold on the Internet, and the various market institutions which have developed to facilitate online prostitution. Additionally, this chapter analyzes available data to describe the characteristics and business practices of sex workers who solicit online, how they differ from streetwalking prostitutes and from traditional stereotypes of prostitutes. Empirical research on online prostitution is sparse (Weitzer 2005), so we employ data from a wide range of sources to present the most comprehensive view of the sex trade on-line. We conclude with some preliminary evidence on the effectiveness (and limitations) of attempts to disrupt the Internet-based prostitution market, including evidence on two specific legal interventions in 2008 and 2009 aimed at online prostitution advertising.

Institutions Facilitating Prostitution Online

Prostitution can be considered as a labor market where workers provide a service demanded by customers, much like that which exists for lawyers, teachers, or building contractors. The purchase and sale of sex obviously involves deeper moral issues and social concerns than does that of these other services, though there is pragmatic value for policymakers and law enforcement agents in understanding prostitution as a labor market in order to respond to it most effectively. As in other markets, various marketing, retailing, and ancillary practices and institutions have developed to facilitate the complex processes by which customers with diverse preferences are matched to sellers offering services of varying quality. We describe some of the chief such institutions in this section.

Information is the most valuable commodity to buyers of sexual services. Customers want to know and compare the prices; services offered; locations; physical characteristics; and "quality" of service (such as willingness to satisfy client requests and freedom from sexually transmitted infections) offered by a wide range of different sex workers. In this aspect, customers of prostitutes are like customers for any other product or service. The ability to obtain such information through advertising, business reputation, word-of-mouth and other means is, however, seriously restricted in the market for prostitution because of the regulations and statutory prohibitions associated with the industry in most locations.[1] These laws restrict the flow of information on prostitution and reduce buyers' willingness to participate in the market.

---

1. In the United States, the exceptions are a few rural counties in Nevada, and up until very recently, Rhode Island, where indoor prostitution was legal between 2003 and November, 2009. In all other states, prostitution (defined usually as sexual intercourse involving compensation) is a misdemeanor (Posner and Silbaugh 1996). In many other countries, prostitution is either prohibited, or severely restricted, particularly with respect to advertisement.

The Internet has substantially increased the ability of market participants to circumvent these limitations, leading to a virtual flood of prostitution advertising and other information being made available. This has had the effect of creating a virtual "red light" district, where prostitutes and their clients operate with relatively low risk of detection and arrest (Blevins and Holt 2009; Holt and Blevins 2007; Holt, Blevins, and Kuhns 2008; Hughes 2003; Sanders 2008; Sharpe and Earle 2003; Soothhill and Sanders 2005). There are a number of websites that offer free or low-cost advertising to prostitutes. Customers can quickly browse extraordinarily detailed and colorful ads and photographs of large numbers of sex workers on several national and regional sites (Blevins and Holt 2009; Holt and Blevins 2007; Holt et al., 2008; Sharpe and Earle 2003). Although the formats for advertisements vary across these services, most offer advertisers the opportunity to post large amounts of text and multiple color photographs, including sexually-explicit images. Ads frequently include information regarding the advertiser's race, age, location, telephone number and email address, willingness to travel to a client, as well as information about services offered and prices. A typical ad posted in the Chicago "escorts" section of a national advertising website was posted on November 29, 2009, accompanied by a photograph of a young, attractive woman of Asian descent, reading:[2]

Sexy Asian Pacific **GFE** Up Late and Downtown – 24
How would you like to be spoiled by a sexy and very tasty Vixxen????
I am the perfect lady that will treat you like a king..I have an amazing 34c-25
34 figure and I know how to use it. I love to please as well as be pleased, are
the guy that can please me.... ... I can be at your location in 20 mins or
less..I guarantee satisfaction

Jade
312*4*3*7*12*3*4
Outcalls only in Chicago
Doantion is $250 hr $200 half
Location: downtown Chicago

The ad provides the poster's age (24), prices (for 30 and 60 minute sessions), location, contact information, and willingness to travel to meet a customer ("outcall"). The many spelling and grammatical errors suggest the author is likely either poorly educated, or does not speak English as a first

---

2. For the purposes of anonymity, the telephone number has been changed from that in the original ad.

language. It is also notable that the advertiser uses the code word "GFE", which is part of an intricate lingo widely used and understood among online prostitution market participants (Blevins and Holt 2009; Holt and Blevins 2007; Sharpe and Earle 2003).[3] GFE is an abbreviation for "girlfriend experience," indicating that "Jade" offers emotional intimacy in the course of an encounter including kissing and cuddling (Bernstein 2007; Blevins and Holt 2009; Holt and Blevins 2007; Lever and Dolnick 2010). In an attempt to avoid attention from law enforcement, the author of the post also refers to her payment as a "donation."[4]

Advertisements like these offer rich and valuable information to clients who eagerly demand such details, but they also highlight a fundamental problem in criminal communication, what Gambetta (2009) refers to as "the problem of identification." Nobel Prize-winning economist Thomas Schelling (1960) provides an example in another criminal context:

> The bank employee who would like to rob the bank if he could only find an outside collaborator and the bank robber who would like to rob the bank if only he could find an inside accomplice may find it difficult to collaborate because they are unable to identify each other, there being severe penalties in the event that either should declare his intentions to someone who proved not to have identical interests.

The challenge in commercial sex markets is no different—prostitutes seek clients and clients seek prostitutes, and to the degree that information about each side is available, transactions can be completed successfully. But in an underground economy, advertising and other signals are costly due to the risks they impose on both parties of being detected by law enforcement.

Before the rise of Internet technology, identification of sex workers primarily occurred via word-of-mouth exchanges among market participants and signaling in risky open-air street market "strolls." In street markets, clients drive by (called "crawling" or "cruising") and observe pedestrians on the street (Holt and Blevins 2007; Holzman and Pines 1982). Streetwalkers wear certain revealing clothing and make catcalls in an attempt to signal to potential clients, though at considerable risk of arrest (Reynolds 1985). Law enforcement attempts to employ decoy streetwalkers and clients represent a direct attempt to

---

3. Brooks (2009) provides other examples: "CBJ" and "BBBJ" and "CBJ" represent fellatio with and without a condom, respectively, "DATY" is cunnilingus, "DFK" is deep french kissing, "FS" is vaginal sex, and "Greek" is anal receptive intercourse (see also Blevins and Holt 2009 for discussion).

4. Other slang for payment include "roses," "kisses," etc.

disrupt the flow of information in street markets, and ultimately lead participants to engage in more nuanced approaches to solve the problem of identification (Holt and Blevins 2007; Holt et al. 2008, 2009).

The Internet's effect on street prostitution markets has been profound, including shifting some of the transactions indoors and out of public sight entirely (Cunningham and Kendall 2010a). Anecdotal evidence of this phenomenon has also been acknowledged by law enforcement: "[Riverside, California police detective Woolley] noticed a spike in the number of ads on Craigslist three years ago and at the same the number of prostitutes walking University Avenue, a once-popular strip for streetwalkers, had been whittled down to a handful of prostitutes" (Logan 2008).

Aside from changing the location of transactions, the Internet has helped solve the problem of identification by strengthening and broadening certain methods that had been used prior to the Internet. For instance, online advertising allows prostitutes to publish detailed information anonymously using encrypted email addresses at very low cost, a vast improvement over catcalls on the street. Because of the scale of such advertising sites in most cities, clients are able to search over hundreds of different women to identify prostitutes with valued characteristics (Holt and Blevins 2007; Holt et al. 2008).

Another institution intended to solve the problem of identification is reflected in so-called "ratings" sites, where customers of prostitutes leave detailed "reviews" of sex workers they have met (Sharpe and Earle 2003; Soothhill and Sanders 2005). These sites operate on principles similar to that of customer review sites in other industries, such as hotels, books, restaurants, and electronic products. Both published sources and our own ethnographic interviews with sex workers indicate that reviews are widely recognized as a critical tool for business success among independently-operating workers (Brooks 2009; Cunningham and Kendall 2010b; Dellarocas 2006). In fact, prostitutes with positive reviews will frequently make a point to mention this fact in advertisements, providing hyperlinks to their reviews.

There are a number of websites that allow clients to review the services of prostitutes. In fact, one of the most well known sites for North America receives between 500,000 and 1,000,000 unique visitors each month (Richtel 2008).[5] As of August, 2008, there were over 500,000 reviews of more than 94,000 sex workers reviewed on the site. In order to understand the utility of review sites, we will briefly describe the process of posting content on one very large national

---

5. The names of the websites and addresses have been withheld in this analysis in an effort to maintain some confidentiality for the providers and customers.

review site. After an assignation, a customer may fill out an online review form demanding very detailed information on physical characteristics, prices, and services offered, as well as ratings (on a ten-point scale) of the worker's over-all appearance and "performance." The site requires that all workers reviewed must solicit for customers online, such as through an advertisement on a public classified ads site or a personal website.

Reviewing sites allow customers to easily compare characteristics and prices among a large number of providers of sexual services along uniform dimensions (Sanders 2008; Sharp and Earle 2005; Soothhill and Sanders 2003). A worker who has many reviews over a long period of time is unlikely to be an undercover law enforcement agent, thief, or robber. Thus, these sites also allow customers to reduce their risk of arrest or victimization by an advertiser. The potential for arrest and social embarrassment is a major deterrent for many prospective customers, so reviewing sites potentially expand participation in the market for prostitution, particularly among individuals with strong reputations in their community (Guista et al 2009; Holt et al. 2008, 2009; Holzman and Pines 1982). This may partially be the cause of so many recent scandals involving high-profile men caught with prostitutes.[6]

In addition to reviewing sites, there are also a number of more informal posting boards for the customers of prostitutes, where information is shared about available sellers, as well as tips for avoiding violence from prostitutes and pimps and even advice regarding law enforcement sting operations. One well-known site includes separate posting "threads" in each city, some focusing on online prostitution and others on street prostitution. Blevins and Holt (2009) summarize the conversations on this and other such sites. Typically, these forums operate as online message boards where users register (usually using anonymous profiles) and participate in discussions posted in public forums. Members of the forum can read and respond to each other, creating conversations delineated by subject (Blevins and Holt 2009; Holt and Blevins 2007). Over time, the individuals who respond will develop public reputations that help inform other readers about the quality of their advice, which can help address the aforementioned problem of identification in commercial sex markets (Blevins and Holt 2009).

In much the same fashion, prostitutes seek information about their prospective clients in an attempt to distinguish them from law enforcement agents, those with violent tendencies, indiscreet actors, or those who carry a sexually transmitted infection. One common method used by online prostitutes to

---

6. In recent years, Eliot Spitzer, former New York governor, and Ted Haggard, an important evangelical Christian leader, were both caught using prostitutes they met online.

"screen" clients is through a system of "references." Specifically, a given prostitute will refuse to see a customer unless he can provide the names of one or two other sex workers he has seen recently. The Internet facilitates this system by allowing prostitutes to quickly find and contact the prospective references via email or other means. In this way, it becomes extremely difficult for law enforcement to arrange a "sting" on a prostitute who consistently demands references. The findings from survey evidence presented below suggest that roughly 59% of sex workers who operate online regularly demand references.

Despite the fact that the use of references can substantially reduce the likelihood of discovery and/or arrest, they are not used by all sex workers. There are at least three potential reasons for the variation in the use of references. First, a demand for references screens out police officers and dangerous clients, but can also eliminate potentially acceptable clients who may be new to the industry or who do not frequently purchase sexual services. Thus, prostitutes who are in need of quick cash are much less likely to demand references than those with more patience. Second, the reduction in advertising costs as a result of the Internet enables many sellers in the online market today to act as "moonlighters" who enter the market to cover short-term expenditures or as a part-time job (Cunningham and Kendall 2010c). These workers may not be aware of these reference systems, or may not feel comfortable contacting other sex workers. Finally, in many interviews with prostitutes who solicit online, workers told the authors that they frequently can sense a client's validity through the tenor of pre-assignation discussion. Depending on the discussion, a worker may sometimes feel comfortable substituting their impressions of safety for a formal reference (see also Holt et al. 2009).

Another set of market institutions that facilitates the transmission of information about potential customers are anonymous background check services. One of the most popular of these is Room Service 2000 ("RS2K"); an independent company where customers pay a fee to have the company perform a background check on them. If the customer is deemed acceptable (presumably with no criminal record or background in law enforcement), they receive a code that can be provided to a prostitute they wish to see. The prostitute can then use the code to verify the safety of the client, who remains anonymous, through RS2K. This service helps prostitutes to screen their clients, and also provides a service to clients who do not then need to provide personal information to a prostitute which potentially could be used as blackmail. As one sex worker wrote on a prostitution-themed online posting board, "It is a great service. It allows us providers to verify without intruding too much on a gents [sic] privacy."

Finally, prostitutes who solicit online also maintain private posting boards where they discuss customers among themselves. Blogs, Facebook accounts, Twitter messaging and other social media have also become increasingly popular ways of communicating with clients (Brooks 2009). Prostitutes may post information on a blog, for instance, about their whereabouts over a given week, stating that they will be touring a group of cities in an effort to set up appointments. Workers also frequently use local "white lists" and "black lists" to inform other sex workers about good and bad clients. These sites further serve to provide information about market institutions to those new to sex work.

All of the market institutions and practices that aid in the identification and exchange of information between sellers and buyers of sexual services has likely expanded participation in the sex market. The negative social ramifications can, however, be contrasted by the benefits of free-flowing information. Many of the social harms associated with prostitution, such as public nuisance, the transmission of sexually-transmitted infections, violence, and ancillary crimes are perpetuated by a lack of market information about participants and processes in the sex trade. Online institutions increase the availability of information, and may ameliorate some of these harms for both client and provider (see Blevins and Holt 2009; Holt and Blevins 2007; Holt et al. 2008, 2009). For instance, online advertising undoubtedly serves to reduce the cost of participation in the market for prostitution for both customers and sellers. It also potentially moves some of the sex trade off street corners and alleys where it presents a visible nuisance (see Holt and Blevins 2007; Holt et al. 2008). Similarly, reviewing sites and the reference systems serve to screen out those who would perpetrate violence. Reviewing sites may even incentivize prostitutes to practice safer sex practices to reduce the likelihood of sexually transmitted infection (Cunningham and Kendall 2009a; 2010b). For these reasons, policymakers and law enforcement agencies should tread carefully in dealing with the new market institutions and practices that have developed online so as to minimize the social costs of prostitution.

Characteristics and Practices of Prostitutes Who Solicit Online

We now turn to a description of the types of women who engage in prostitution online. For brevity, we focus on female prostitutes, but see Logan (2009) and Logan and Shah (2009) for information on the highly-developed online market for male prostitution services. Male prostitution is primarily homosexual, and thus potentially impacts a relatively small share of the overall population (Laumann, Gagnon, Michael, and Michaels 2000). Relative to male prostitution, female prostitution also plays a larger role in the spread of

STIs throughout the heterosexual network in both developing and developed countries (Courtinho, van Andel, and Rijsdijk 1988; Gil, Wang, Anderson, Lin, and Wu 1996; Rosenbert and Weinberg 1988). Finally, the important problem of sex trafficking is largely associated with females, particularly in foreign nations (Kara 2008). The major themes of this section are the characteristics of online sex workers, the substantial differences between these women and street-based workers, as well as traditional prostitute stereotypes, and the changes in the types of women offering sex for sale over the Internet over time.

Comparison of Online Prostitutes with Persons Arrested for Prostitution

Despite increasing awareness of online prostitution solicitation and some advances in attacking it, the vast majority of prostitutes who come into contact with law enforcement are street-based workers (Scott 2001; Weidner 2001). The set of prostitutes who are arrested is not a random sample of all street-based prostitutes, since presumably the more discrete and successful prostitutes avoid arrest. It is likely, however, that this set of sex workers informs the beliefs and practices of law enforcement agencies, so it is valuable to compare them with online workers.

The best consistent information available on prostitutes who come into contact with law enforcement comes from Federal Bureau of Investigation administrative data known as the *Uniform Crime Reports* (UCR). UCR data is quite comprehensive, reflecting information voluntarily reported by law enforcement agencies throughout the U.S., and provides information on race and ages of arrested persons. In the FBI's classification, prostitution is a "part II" crime, for which only arrests, not actual crimes committed. The FBI defines prostitution as "the unlawful promotion of or participation in sexual activities for profit," and includes in its counts not only those arrested for prostituting themselves, but also keepers of houses of prostitution, panders, and pimps (Federal Bureau of Investigation 2004).[7]

To gauge the typical characteristics of prostitutes soliciting online, we collected data on more than 94,000 individuals listed on the largest and oldest sex worker review website for North America, described in the previous section. Table 6.1 illustrates the distribution of ages and races among prostitution arrests from UCR, and among reviewed sex workers during 2007 and 2008. The top panel of Table 6.1 shows that women arrested for prostitution

---

7. Those arrested for attempted prostitution are included as well.

Table 6.1 Comparison of Prostitutes Between Online and UCR
(Law Enforcement) Datasets

		Review Site (2007/2008) Full Sample	UCR Female Arrests (2007)
Age Group	18–20	12.9%	13.2%
	21–25	44.8%	18.3%
	26–30	24.3%	14.6%
	31–35	10.2%	13.2%
	36–40	4.6%	14.6%
	41–45	2.2%	12.8%
	46+	1.2%	11.0%
Race	Asian	13.9%	2.2%
	Black	13.2%	39.2%
	White	50.6%	57.6%
	Hispanic	15.5%	N/A
	Unknown/Other	6.9%	0.9%

Notes: Age and race are as estimated by the reviewing client for the review site data, and as recorded by arresting agency for UCR data.

span a wide range of ages; by comparison, Table 6.1 suggests that most women who solicit online are relatively young, with 82% in their teens or twenties. The review website examined does not accept reviews of sex workers under age 18, so we are unable to compare the frequency of underage prostitution online and offline. These substantial age differences suggest that women who solicit online include a higher share of those in their "prime" years for prostitution demand, while women arrested for prostitution are relatively older. While only 8% of women on the review website were 36 or older, 38.4% of women arrested at street locations were in this age range. Reynolds (1985) has argued that as women age, their prostitution wages decline, causing them to either leave the market entirely or to concentrate in street-based environments where clients have lower willingness to pay for services.

The lower panel of Table 6.1 shows the frequency of various racial/ethnic groups among the two datasets. UCR data does not distinguish those of Hispanic origin separate from other groups; however, since most Americans of Hispanic ethnicity are racially white (U.S. Census 2008), this is likely also the case among prostitutes. If so, then it is clear that workers who solicit online are substantially more likely to be white or Hispanic (66.1% total), in comparison with those who work on the street (57.6%). Moreover, Asian sex workers compose a large share (13.9%) of online workers, but a trivial percentage of arrests. Black sex workers are much more common in the street environment than online. These racial differences may partially stem from the documented slower growth of home Internet access, especially broadband connectivity, among African-Americans (Prieger and Hu 2008). Hence, these racial frequencies may converge at some point in the future as inequalities in Internet access diminish.

Characteristics and Business and Sexual Practices of Online Sex Workers

As previously stated, the reviews provided online for the site we examine are extremely detailed, and give significant additional information on the typical characteristics and business and sexual practices of prostitutes who solicit for customers online. Table 6.2 summarizes some of these dynamics as discussed through the on-line reviews. We calculate averages separately for 1999–2002, 2003–2005, and 2006–2008 in order to demonstrate how sex workers who solicit online have changed over the past decade. Table 6.2 shows that hourly wages (deflated to constant 2003 dollars in order to eliminate the effects of general inflation) are quite high. In fact, the rates near or surpass $300 per hour in all years, and are consistent with a long history of very high wages for prostitutes (Edlund and Korn 2002). Wages among online workers appear to have risen nearly 20% over the last ten years, suggesting increasing demand for their services. Alternatively, this may reflect a relative increase in the supply of prostitutes able to charge higher prices to the online market (e.g., more attractive, better quality women).

Turning to the next segment of Table 6.2 focusing on the services offered by online prostitutes, sessions involving a combination of vaginal and oral sex are the most common. In fact, this combination was offered by over 81% of online prostitutes during 2006 and 2008. The second most common service is manual stimulation and massage, given by 9.3% of the sample. In comparison with surveys of street-based prostitutes (e.g., Levitt and Venkatesh 2007), vaginal sex is much more common relative to manual stimulation among online prostitutes. This may reflect the greater perceived desirability of the women who solicit online by clients, or a lower likelihood of sexually transmitted infection. Table 6.2 also implies that the provision of less-risky sexual services, such as manual stimulation, has declined relative to vaginal, oral, and group sex involving multiple sex workers.

Under the "business practices" segment, the review site data shows that a typical assignation lasts around an hour. Roughly half of workers are "independent" of third-party management, such as an agency or pimp. Since one of

Table 6.2 Mean Values of Key Variables for Sex Workers Reviewed On-line 1999–2002, 2003–2005, and 2006–2008

Category	Variable	1999–2002	2003–2005	2006–2008
Wage	Avg. real hourly wage ($2003)	$263.13	$281.80	$313.35
Advertised Service	Vaginal sex and fellatio	71.4%	77.1%	81.3%
	Anal sex	2.0%	2.0%	2.5%
	Massage with manual stimulation	19.5%	13.1%	9.3%
	Massage with fellatio	3.3%	2.4%	1.6%
	Bondage/S&M	1.8%	2.0%	1.4%
	Group sex	1.5%	3.0%	3.7%
Business Practices	Avg. length of session in minutes	64.2	64.5	61.0
	Independent of third-party manager	53.1%	45.3%	58.4%
	Incall only (worker provides location)	38.0%	35.0%	31.0%
	Outcall only (client provides location)	20.9%	16.5%	12.9%
	Offers both incall and outcall	40.6%	48.3%	56.0%
	Showed up on time	93.1%	93.8%	94.3%
	Rushed service	26.6%	26.3%	23.7%
Sexual Practices	Does not kiss	42.0%	35.7%	38.2%
	Kisses, no tongue	23.8%	22.8%	21.7%
	Kisses with tongue	34.2%	41.5%	40.2%
	Offers no oral sex	16.3%	13.7%	11.0%
	Offers oral sex with condom	48.8%	42.8%	45.5%
	Offers oral sex without condom	34.8%	43.5%	43.6%
	Offers cunnilingus	55.8%	58.2%	57.1%
Age (As Estimated by Client)	18–20	8.2%	10.4%	13.2%
	21–25	38.8%	44.4%	44.8%
	26–30	28.7%	25.6%	23.8%
	31–35	14.8%	11.3%	10.1%
	36–40	5.8%	5.2%	4.7%
	41–45	2.5%	2.2%	2.2%
	46+	1.3%	0.9%	1.1%
Race/ Ethnicity	White	54.0%	52.0%	51.7%
	Black	7.3%	8.7%	12.3%
	Asian	16.4%	17.4%	14.8%
	Hispanic	12.8%	13.5%	14.2%
	Foreign	7.9%	6.9%	5.2%
	Other	1.6%	1.6%	1.8%
Reviews	Avg. appearance review (1–10)	7.0	7.3	7.4
	Avg. performance review (1–10)	6.7	7.1	7.1
N	Number of observations	15,008	30,257	34,042

Notes: All values in table are sample means. Date ranges refer to the year a worker was first reviewed.

the main functions of such managers is to screen prostitution customers, the Internet may allow prostitutes to perform these screening functions on their own and increase their overall independence. The share of workers reviewed on the site that were independent declined between 1999–2002 and 2003–2005, before rising substantially in 2006–2008.

The other variables associated with business practices generally indicate that clients perceive services to be of high quality and improve over time. For instance, the share of workers who offered clients an option of either incall (assignation at the worker's location) or outcall (assignation at the client's location) rose over the sample period, as did the share of workers appearing on time for their assignations. The share of workers who "rushed" through their service from the perspective of the client has declined over the last decade.

Focusing next on sexual practices, the online data indicate that women who solicit online appear to kiss their clients quite frequently. In fact, 61.9% of the reviews suggest workers offered some form of kissing. The share of sex workers who are willing to kiss with tongue contact, a measure of perceived emotional attachment, has increased over the last decade from 34% to 40%. The share of online prostitutes who offer unprotected oral sex is quite high, up to 43.6% over the 2006–2008 period, and has increased over time. Similarly, 57.1% of online prostitutes also offer cunnilingus. The site does not allow reviewers to indicate whether the prostitute offered unprotected vaginal or anal sex, though this issue will be explored further below using survey data.

Table 6.2 indicates that the age distribution of sex workers has trended toward young women over the last decade. The share of women reviewed who were age 25 and under grew from 47% to 58% over the entire period of study. The racial/ethnic distribution indicates growth among Black and Hispanic workers relative to White workers over time. Nevertheless, Whites continue to be the majority followed by Asian workers. Finally, as suggested by the business practice variables above, it appears that most clients are generally satisfied with the services they receive from online prostitutes. The mean overall client review, on a scale of one to ten, was around seven, both on "appearance" and "performance" dimensions. This average score has risen over time in both categories

Additional Characteristics and Practices from Survey Data

In order to learn more about the business and sexual practices of sex workers who solicit online, the authors implemented a survey of sex workers between August 2008 and June 2009, known as the Survey of Adult Service Providers

("SASP"). This survey represents the most comprehensive sampling of online workers to date, and is unique in the literature in its efforts to address selection bias by correcting for the inverse probability of appearing in the survey. Cunningham and Kendall (2009b) describe the survey procedure in more detail and give the full text of the questionnaire. To briefly summarize, SASP was implemented by sending requests to all valid email addresses among workers reviewed on the largest and oldest sex worker review site in North America, supplemented with all sex workers who advertise on a popular national site for escort ads. In the email, respondents were asked to click on a link that led them to the survey hosted on Baylor University servers. Each email sent was associated with a randomly-generated string of characters, which allowed us to prevent multiple responses from the same email, while at the same time maintaining the anonymity of the survey.[8] There were 685 valid responses received from this solicitation.

In order to facilitate extrapolations to the population of sex workers who solicit online, SASP responses were adjusted using probability weights constructed from the distribution of age and race characteristics of all workers reviewed on the site and SASP respondents. To the extent that the review website information represents the best available portrait of the population of sex workers who solicit online in North America, this procedure allows the SASP data to make general statements about the population. As a check on the validity of this assumption, we examined comparable questions between SASP and other surveys of sex workers (e.g., Church, Henderson, Barnard, and Hart 2001, Milrod 2008), and found a close correspondence in sample averages.

The SASP data is organized into two files: a worker-level file based on responses to questions about personal characteristics and general practices; and a transaction-level file with data on the respondent's five most recent client-session transactions. Table 6.3 presents population-weighted averages and frequencies from SASP. The top panel summarizes variables from the worker-level file, while the bottom panel focuses on variables derived from the transaction-level file. The findings confirm that sex work is highly compensated, with the average worker receiving $1,711 per week. Around 25% of online prostitutes saw no customers during the last week, whether by choice or some other factor. Additionally, the average prostitute saw 4.1 different clients during the last week, of which 2.2 were "regulars," that is, repeat customers. New clients rep-

---

8. Respondents were also allowed to answer survey questions by telephone with the authors or their research assistants.

Table 6.3 Population-Weighted Means of Key Characteristics and Practices among Sex Workers Based on 2008–2009 Survey of Adult Service Providers

Variable	Mean	Observations
Worker-Level Characteristics		
Avg. weekly earnings (all)	$1,710.84	593
Any clients last week	75.5%	601
Avg. # clients last week	4.1	598
Avg. # "regular" clients last week	2.2	595
Avg. # new clients last week	1.9	595
Avg. years since entry into prostitution	5.5	599
Have health insurance	52.7%	597
Have second job	43.7%	597
College graduate	41.4%	602
Married/Cohabitating with partner	13.0%	603
Demands references from clients	58.6%	608
Uses other screening methods with clients	67.0%	608
Transaction-Level Characteristics		
Fellatio with condom	50.2%	2,426
Fellatio without condom	31.2%	2,426
Vaginal sex with condom	69.0%	2,457
Vaginal sex without condom	5.2%	2,457
Anal sex with condom	4.9%	2,480
Anal sex without condom	1.1%	2,480
Group sex	5.5%	2,519
Avg. age of client	43.0	2,399
Client white race	80.2%	2,443
Client black race	5.0%	2,443
Client Hispanic race	3.5%	2,443
Client Asian race	7.4%	2,443

Notes: Data are drawn from Survey of Adult Service Providers (SASP). Survey responses are weighted by population means within each age-race cell, taking all reviewed workers as the population.

resent potential risks for prostitutes, and may be considered less desirable as customers.

Careers appear to be relatively lengthy among workers who solicit online, with the average respondent indicating around 5.5 years since her first entry into sex work. In addition, our sample indicates that these sex workers are likely to hold private health insurance (53%), be college graduates (41%), married (13%), and have children (38%). These results may be a reflection of the fact that many respondents appear to be "moonlighters": 43% indicated they hold a second job outside of sex work. Nearly 59% of online prostitutes demand references from other sex workers before seeing a potential customer, while 67% use other forms of screening, such as Room Service 2000.

Turning to the bottom panel of Table 3, SASP confirms both the general level and trend of unprotected oral sex in the review site data explored above. The SASP data reflects online prostitution in late 2008 and early 2009 and finds 51% of transactions involved unprotected oral sex compared with 44% for 2006–2008 in the online data (see Table 6.2). Unprotected vaginal and anal sex appears to be relatively uncommon, taking place in just 5.2% and 1.1% of all transactions respectively. Group sex transactions occurred in 5.7% of all exchanges, either with multiple sex workers or multiple clients. Table 6.3 also shows that the average age of clients was around 43 years old, and 80% of these clients are white. Over-all, these data indicate that prostitutes who solicit online are quite different from those who operate on the street and come into contact frequently with law enforcement. They are younger, more likely to be white, and appear to break the mold of typical prostitute stereotypes.

Cross-City Differences in Prostitution Markets

There appear to be significant differences across cities in online prostitu-tion markets, suggesting that regulatory and law enforcement agencies in these cities may wish to take different approaches. This finding is similarly supported in research by Holt and Blevins (2007), Soothhill and Sanders (2005) and Sharpe and Earle (2003). Table 6.4 summarizes some key variables from the re-viewing site for a set of 44 cities/regions identifiable on the site (the site some-times identifies areas by city, e.g., Reno or Houston, and sometimes by region, such as "Carolinas" or "New England"). All of the cities/regions are in North America, except London.

Hourly wages vary substantially across locations, with average prices in the most expensive city, London, being more than 2.5 times higher than those in the least expensive city, Tijuana (wages not denominated in U.S. dollars are converted to constant 2003 U.S. dollars using the contemporaneous exchange rate). Examining U.S. cities only reveals a similar trend, as wages in the most expensive city (Reno) are 1.8 times more than those in the least expensive area, Indiana. In general, larger cities have higher wages, which may represent higher cost of assignation locations, such as hotel rooms, or simply a higher overall cost-of-living. The fact that two cities in Nevada have the highest wages in the

Table 6.4 Wages and Selected Characteristics of On-line Reviewed Workers, by City

	Obs.	Hourly Wage		Independent	Body Thin	White	Black	Hispanic	Age 18–20
		Level	Index						
London	1,932	$477.35	100.00	25.31%	38.51%	39.29%	2.74%	8.28%	11.23%
Reno	274	$445.20	93.26	53.28%	30.66%	74.82%	5.47%	8.39%	7.66%
Las Vegas	1,772	$417.29	87.42	73.42%	31.26%	64.40%	6.66%	9.65%	10.05%
Atlanta	3,503	$376.30	78.83	54.67%	32.54%	46.33%	24.55%	18.07%	10.48%
Salt Lake City	316	$328.73	68.87	56.01%	34.18%	68.35%	12.66%	10.13%	23.10%
Chicago	3,562	$325.88	68.27	52.16%	32.93%	56.20%	12.07%	11.76%	13.50%
Toronto	1,735	$322.72	67.61	29.91%	37.06%	51.24%	3.75%	7.38%	12.85%
New York City	7,145	$322.26	67.51	36.67%	37.87%	34.28%	7.66%	18.74%	7.26%
Phoenix	2,240	$309.02	64.74	64.78%	31.52%	65.94%	7.90%	14.15%	12.59%
New Orleans	234	$304.01	63.69	52.99%	34.19%	78.63%	9.40%	3.85%	9.40%
Columbus	339	$302.99	63.47	61.65%	29.79%	87.02%	6.19%	2.36%	10.62%
Tampa	991	$301.91	63.25	70.03%	29.77%	73.26%	7.06%	8.68%	9.08%
Palm Springs	71	$298.65	62.56	71.83%	25.35%	54.93%	7.04%	16.90%	8.45%
Boston	2,554	$298.43	62.52	37.51%	36.37%	63.19%	7.48%	13.27%	10.06%
Philadelphia	1,272	$293.05	61.39	46.93%	33.81%	51.42%	14.94%	12.42%	10.93%
Miami	2,499	$292.34	61.24	40.26%	34.37%	45.50%	7.63%	36.13%	12.04%
Los Angeles	8,615	$291.74	61.12	63.77%	32.83%	36.39%	10.44%	14.27%	8.79%
Orlando	290	$290.89	60.94	78.28%	24.83%	55.86%	12.07%	20.69%	20.00%
San Diego	1,881	$288.84	60.51	78.79%	30.57%	52.74%	13.40%	15.68%	21.11%
New Mexico	53	$288.28	60.39	81.13%	32.08%	64.15%	11.32%	11.32%	5.66%
Orange County	1,611	$287.99	60.33	62.69%	32.34%	40.84%	8.13%	12.79%	14.84%
Tucson	121	$287.54	60.24	90.08%	29.75%	75.21%	4.13%	8.26%	14.05%

Table 6.4 Wages and Selected Characteristics of On-line Reviewed Workers, by City, *continued*

	Obs.	Hourly Wage		Independent	Body Thin	White	Black	Hispanic	Age 18–20
		Level	Index						
Austin	372	$284.05	59.51	66.94%	31.18%	66.40%	6.45%	14.25%	10.75%
Washington, DC	4,647	$283.88	59.47	47.04%	31.93%	38.84%	18.76%	18.61%	9.83%
Jacksonville	11	$282.62	59.21	81.82%	27.27%	72.73%	9.09%	18.18%	9.09%
Hawaii	303	$280.67	58.80	54.46%	30.03%	53.80%	5.28%	4.29%	12.54%
Nashville	193	$280.29	58.72	80.31%	27.98%	81.35%	13.47%	1.55%	12.95%
Detroit	1,026	$277.17	58.06	63.26%	27.39%	67.45%	17.64%	8.58%	11.89%
Vancouver	805	$271.43	56.86	48.70%	32.67%	73.17%	1.12%	4.84%	12.42%
Dallas	2,045	$271.19	56.81	69.34%	30.22%	70.42%	10.27%	7.73%	10.32%
Minnesota	1,681	$268.85	56.32	70.55%	30.64%	65.08%	15.23%	7.61%	14.87%
San Francisco	5,740	$265.86	55.69	58.21%	36.36%	38.89%	7.72%	10.12%	12.40%
Montreal	774	$264.44	55.40	16.54%	43.93%	63.95%	2.45%	4.78%	24.16%
Denver	1,366	$264.24	55.36	51.83%	34.77%	68.96%	5.34%	11.13%	8.93%
Houston	1,588	$263.20	55.14	37.91%	31.49%	59.07%	8.63%	21.54%	9.07%
Cleveland	692	$261.55	54.79	70.52%	34.25%	69.36%	16.91%	7.51%	11.71%
Seattle	1,527	$260.73	54.62	51.60%	34.25%	71.19%	6.09%	6.75%	13.00%
Gold Coast, Cal.	191	$260.52	54.58	54.97%	29.32%	45.03%	5.76%	10.99%	13.61%
Portland	673	$254.75	53.37	87.07%	26.60%	76.97%	7.88%	4.90%	11.29%
New England	678	$253.19	53.04	54.28%	35.10%	53.54%	7.96%	9.00%	8.55%
New Jersey	2,491	$252.59	52.92	27.90%	32.80%	42.60%	8.19%	24.93%	11.64%
Carolinas	1,584	$252.09	52.81	49.05%	29.29%	76.33%	12.37%	4.73%	11.36%
Indiana	282	$251.94	52.78	55.32%	29.43%	86.17%	3.55%	3.19%	6.74%
Tijuana	222	$170.97	35.82	30.18%	35.14%	1.35%	0.45%	95.95%	27.48%

U.S. may represent higher demand for sexual services associated with tourism in those locations. This may also reflect the presence of legal brothels in nearby rural counties where sex workers are able to charge high prices due to the perception of safety among customers.

The share of online prostitutes who operate "independently" also varies widely across locations in ways that are difficult to classify. In Montreal, only 16.5% of online sex workers operate independently, while in Tucson the share is 90.1%. These differences may reflect varying law enforcement approaches to prostitution across cities, since one of the purposes of third-party management is to assist in protecting prostitutes from arrest. The aggressiveness with which law enforcement agencies attack escort agencies and pimps relative to prostitutes and their clients is also likely an important factor.

We also display the share of online workers in each location with "thin" body type, as noted by the customer reviewer. Differences in this variable may correspond to general patterns in population obesity across cities since women in non-U.S. locations are generally thinner, but also the prevalence of drug use among prostitutes (Church et al. 2001; Goldstein 1979; Potterat, Rothenberg, Muth, Darrow, and Phillips-Plummer 1998). Focusing on U.S. locations, New York and Boston have a substantially higher share of thin online prostitutes than do Orlando and Palm Springs.

The racial distribution of online prostitutes also varies across locations, largely but not entirely corresponding to population differences (note, e.g., the high share of Hispanic sex workers in Tijuana). The last column of Table 6.3 indicates the share of reviewed workers who are teenagers. Since this site does not allow reviewers to indicate an age below 18, this figure may reflect underage prostitution if sex workers lie to customers about their age, or if reviewers lie to the site about the ages of prostitutes they have visited. Tijuana, Montreal, Salt Lake City, San Diego and Orlando all have more than 20% of online prostitutes under age 21, while Indiana, New York, Reno have very small shares of teenage online prostitutes in their local markets.

Effects of Interventions against Advertising

Law enforcement agencies have responded in a variety of ways to the rise of online prostitution. Most police departments in major cities now apply at least some resources to tracking and combating prostitution online, including the use of sting operations and mobile arrest facilities (Dodge, Starr-Gimeno, and Williams 2005; Hay 2005). In a previous section, we discussed the various market institutions and practices facilitated by the Internet that increase the flow of information between and among prostitutes and their clients. These resources have made police efforts to fight prostitution quite costly. An analysis by the Cook County Sheriff's Office found that each arrest of an online prostitute involved three police officers and 20 man-hours of time. The accounting indicated that arrests associated with persons advertising on craigslist.org alone cost the agency $105,081 in 2008 (U.S. District Court 2009).

A potentially more economical approach that has found some success is to place legal and political pressure on sites that allow advertisements for prostitutes. In this section, we describe the effects of two such interventions in 2008 and 2009. In 2008, the attorneys general of 40 states approached craigslist.org regarding its "erotic services" section, which in most cities is the largest website focused on prostitution advertisements (U.S. District Court 2009). Craigslist has traditionally operated the site in a "laissez faire" manner, with only a skeleton crew staff and little or no purview over ads posted. Many ads, therefore, were extremely explicit, displaying pornographic photos and listing prices and detailed descriptions of sexual services offered (Kennedy and Taylor 2010).[9] As the site grew, this led to substantial community protest, leading the state attorneys general to place increasing pressure on craigslist to do more to limit the use of the site for the purposes of prostitution.

Craigslist's first attempt to self-regulate posts was implemented on November 8, 2008. The site no longer allowed advertisers to post ads for free, but charged $5 to $10 per post (Fowler 2009a).[10] Given that typical hourly wages in the industry surpass $300 in many cities, one might not expect a substantial effect from such a small fee. Figure 6.1 displays the number of daily postings on the site in four cities, chosen for illustrative purposes: Denver, Minnesota, Philadelphia, and Seattle.[11]

As Figure 6.1 shows, the fee appears to have had a surprisingly dramatic effect, reducing the number of advertisements in at least three of the four cities.

---

9. Kennedy and Taylor (2010) reviewed manually over 12,000 individual advertisements made to Craigslist and found:

> Over a third (34.3%) of those advertising in "Erotic Services" provided a "disclaimer" which stated that they were not participating in prostitution and that they were advertising for a legal act between consenting adults. Despite this, 80% of those who provided a disclaimer also provided a cost. Providing a cost for a sexual service indicates that the act is in fact prostitution in direct contradiction to the disclaimer that it is not.

10. Some localities saw a $10 increase, while others had only a $5 increase.

11. These four cities were selected as part of a separate project (Cunningham and Kendall 2009c). The timing of the fee increase occurred fortuitously during the time period we were collecting data.

Figure 6.1 Effect of Price Increase at Craigslist
"Erotic Services" for Four U.S. Cities

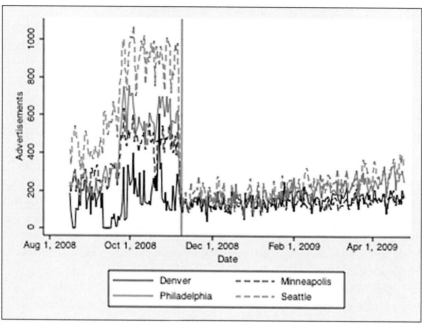

We speculate that it was not so much the size of the fee, but the manner in which it was necessary to pay that was the cause of the dramatic effect. After November 8, 2008, advertisers on craigslist had to use a credit card to post ads. While the fee is small, the credit card potentially identifies the payer, leaving traceable information that police may be able to subpoena in criminal cases. The results of this intervention suggest that the requirement that advertisers identify themselves in some way may be an effective disruption of the market.

Despite the apparent success of the $5–10 fee, there were continued protests against the use of craigslist for prostitution, and some state officials continued to press the site for further regulation. Several high-profile violent crimes associated with craigslist ads, including the Markoff murder case, kept the site in the public spotlight. The attorney general of South Carolina demanded that craigslist shut down its local erotic services posting boards in the state, or else face arrest of its management team (Fowler 2009b).

Craigslist has claimed immunity from prosecution under the Communications Decency Act of 1996, which holds that websites are not legally responsible for material contributed by users. When faced with the increasing likelihood of serious legal liabilities and costs, craigslist closed down the erotic services sites on May 13, 2009, and replaced them with a new set of posting boards, known as "adult services" (Fowler 2009b). The company also hired a staff to monitor ads on the site more closely and work with law enforcement to identify and target offenders. Even a cursory review of the advertisements on the "adult services" sites indicates that craigslist is still being used to solicit prostitution (Kennedy and Taylor 2010). However, most ads are now less explicit, prices are rarely mentioned, and images generally do not contain pornography, though they are suggestive in more subtle ways. Many ads contain only a photograph and a telephone number. Nevertheless, the disruption in service and the degree of attention given to craigslist have had a clear and immediate impact on prostitution advertising.

From April 29 to June 29, 2009, we collected daily advertisements in Craigslist's "erotic services" and "adult services" sites across 31 U.S. cities.[12] Figure 2 shows the number of daily ads nationally on craigslist's erotic services before its closure and on the adult services sites afterwards. A comparison between the number of advertisements on erotic services and the number on adult services indicates more than a 50% national decline in the immediate weeks after the change.

Figure 6.2 also suggests a major potential limitation associated with legal attacks on sites like craigslist. In the Figure, we plot number of advertisements on a rival advertising site operated by Village Voice which also caters to sex work-related classified ads known as Backpage.com. The Figure suggests that before the closure of the erotic services sites on craigslist, Backpage.com was not widely used. However, the closure of the craigslist sites apparently had the effect of stimulating an immediate increase in usage of Backpage, as well as "jumpstarting" the site's longer term growth. Overall, the total amount of advertising on the two sites combined just a few of months after the end of craigslist's erotic services sites was only slightly below the level reached before the closure. While criminologists have long noted the displacement effect that law enforcement strategies can have on the location decisions of street prostitution markets (Holt et al. 2008; Lowman 1992; Matthews 19990; Weidner 2001), we are unaware of any evidence before this of displacement in a digital context.

---

12. The 31 cities were Albuquerque, Atlanta, Austin, Boston, Chicago, Cleveland, Columbus, Dallas, Denver, Detroit, Hawaiian Islands, Houston, Las Vegas, Los Angeles, Miami, Minneapolis, Nashville, New Jersey, New Orleans, New York City, Orlando, Philadelphia, Portland, Reno, Salt Lake City, San Diego, San Diego, San Francisco, Seattle, Tampa, Tucson, and Washington DC.

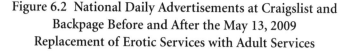

Figure 6.2 National Daily Advertisements at Craigslist and Backpage Before and After the May 13, 2009 Replacement of Erotic Services with Adult Services

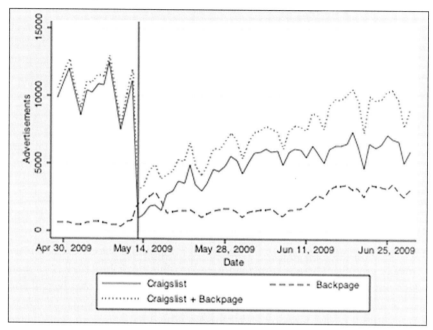

While Figure 6.2 plots the total national trends in advertising, Table 6.5 disaggregates the effect of the closure of craigslist's erotic services on the combined number of ads posted on the two sites by city. While a general pattern appears to holds across all cities, reflecting an immediate decline in prostitution advertising with a rebound soon following, there is also substantial variation suggesting the importance of tailoring regulatory and policing responses to local markets.

The findings in Figure 6.2 and Table 6.5 point to one of the greatest challenges law enforcement agencies face in dealing with online prostitution: after police target one site, market participants appear to be able to quickly converge on a new site. In order to cover the market, law enforcement must now monitor two separate sites. Therefore, it is possible that the creation of additional sites to monitor may ultimately increase law enforcement costs without significant long-term declines in prostitution transactions. The process of moving the market from one location to another online is reminiscent of the way street-based prostitution markets may be displaced—but rarely extinguished —by police efforts (Holt et al. 2008; Weidner 2001).

Table 6.5 Average Daily Sex Work-Related Advertisements on Two Websites Before and After Closure of Craigslist "Erotic Services" Sections, by City

City	2 Weeks Before Change Avg. daily ads	2 Weeks Following Change		2–6 Weeks Following Change	
		Avg. daily ads	% diff. with before change	Avg. daily ads	% diff. with before change
New York	2,813.9	1,167.1	-58.5%	2,123.6	-24.5%
San Francisco	1,316.3	436.9	-66.8%	844.4	-35.9%
Los Angeles	1,075.1	442.4	-58.8%	790.9	-26.4%
Washington DC	617.7	225.3	-63.5%	446.7	-27.7%
Chicago	549.9	230.3	-58.1%	412.0	-25.1%
Las Vegas	495.3	242.0	-51.1%	412.9	-16.6%
Dallas	470.6	237.6	-49.5%	315.1	-33.0%
Atlanta	469.6	192.6	-59.0%	348.4	-25.8%
New Jersey	438.5	185.1	-57.8%	367.6	-16.2%
Seattle	331.0	133.6	-59.6%	202.9	-38.7%
Boston	273.1	103.8	-62.0%	180.1	-34.0%
Philadelphia	252.2	108.9	-56.8%	232.5	-7.8%
Houston	227.4	110.6	-51.4%	202.1	-11.1%
Denver	213.4	118.6	-44.4%	177.9	-16.6%
Minneapolis	205.4	93.9	-54.3%	150.7	-26.6%
Miami	190.3	165.4	-13.1%	277.2	+45.6%
Orlando	174.0	100.7	-42.1%	143.2	-17.7%
Tampa	158.6	71.0	-55.2%	117.6	-25.9%
Portland	143.3	65.3	-54.4%	98.0	-31.6%
Austin	113.2	49.9	-56.0%	100.5	-11.2%
Detroit	98.6	30.9	-68.7%	72.6	-26.4%
New Orleans	58.9	28.1	-52.2%	52.0	-11.7%
Salt Lake City	49.7	26.9	-45.8%	45.6	-8.3%
Tucson	48.9	21.9	-55.1%	36.7	-25.0%
Columbus	34.4	13.8	-59.9%	22.9	-33.4%
Cleveland	34.1	26.9	-21.3%	44.5	+30.4%
Nashville	32.7	18.6	-42.9%	32.8	+0.4%
Reno	31.2	8.9	-71.6%	14.4	-53.9%
Hawaii	25.6	12.6	-50.7%	22.2	-13.6%
New Mexico	17.9	8.3	-53.8%	15.8	-11.9%
TOTAL	10,960.9	4,677.9	-57.3%	8,304.7	-24.2%

Notes: Craigslist closed its "erotic services" advertising sections on May 13, 2009, replacing them with a more closely-monitored "adult services" section. Counts of advertisements from both "erotic services" and "adult services" are included in these totals.

Another potential limitation of interventions targeting prostitution advertisements is the lack of clarity in the impact of advertising regulation on the profitability of sellers. In other industries where advertising expenditures have been limited by regulation, such as cigarette sales, there is some evidence that sellers profited by reducing the intensity of competition (Farr, et al., 2001). In the case of online prostitution advertising, many sites place the most recently posted ads at the top of the page, occupying the most valuable "real estate" on the site. When advertising is free and unregulated, sellers spend much time repeatedly re-posting ads in order to remain near the top. Limitations on advertising may actually benefit prostitutes by reducing the effort they spend in re-posting. In other words, the interventions discussed above may have led to a reduction in ads, though they may have largely done so by reducing some of the "noise" in these markets by discouraging multiple postings, and improved the efficiency of these advertising sites.[13]

A third problem with interventions like those attempted with craigslist in 2008 and 2009 is that, to the extent they are successful, they reduce the flow of information between and among sellers and buyers of prostitution services. This has the effect of disrupting the market and potentially limiting participation. The institutions and practices that facilitate the flow of information in the market also serve to reduce some of the harms associated with prostitution by limiting the ability of violent individuals to participate, and by incentivizing more care in preventing the spread of sexually transmitted infections. For instance, the Internet-facilitated word-of-mouth mechanisms that help enforce contracts (Cunningham and Kendall 2010b; Dellarocas 2006) provide incentives to prostitutes to satisfy customers, which in turn could reduce violence and STI transmission. Police and regulatory interventions that reduce market information are, therefore, a double-edged sword.

Finally, many police agencies have actually found advertising sites like craigslist to be valuable complements for their efforts to weed out the most serious cases of exploitation and child prostitution.[14] By monitoring such sites, police have been able to track lost children and heinous criminals in ways that

---

13. This also suggests one possibly effective disruption method law enforcement agencies may wish to consider: flooding online advertisement markets with "shill" posts on a regular basis. We are unaware of any attempts by police to do so.

14. Connecticut State Attorney General Richard Blumenthal has been particularly aggressive in shutting down online prostitution classified advertising like Craigslist, but Connecticut police have also noted the fact that craigslist and other sites offer the ability to monitor prostitution and ultimately make arrests (Chambers 2009).

would have been impossible otherwise. In the "Craigslist Killer" case, this is precisely how the suspect was caught. Thus, one benefit of Internet-facilitated prostitution is that advertising sites like craigslist amass thousands of advertisements in one place. Insofar as these sites have displaced other forms of prostitution advertising such as streetwalking, then law enforcement may be better able to focus their monitoring efforts. With more eyes on a single location, law enforcement may have better chances of observing evidence of kidnapping and trafficking than if their efforts were to displace those activities even further underground.

Conclusion

The Internet has proved invaluable in reducing the time and expense of consumer searches for all sorts of consumer goods and services. Since such "search costs" are an especially large burden for consumers of prohibited goods, it is not surprising that the Internet has impacted the market for prostitution services so substantially (see also Holt and Blevins 2007; Holt et al. 2008, 2009; Sanders 2008; Sharpe and Earle 2003; Soothhill and Sanders 2005). In this chapter, we have described the growth of the online prostitution market and some of the institutions and market practices that have facilitated that growth, primarily by increasing the flow of information between sellers and buyers. New participants in the market appear to be different in important ways than those involved in prostitution before the Internet when buyers and sellers more frequently met each other on the street or through other offline means. The new entrants to the sex trade are younger, more likely to operate independently of an agency or pimp, and have characteristics less like those associated with the traditional prostitution stereotypes, and more like average members of society.

Law enforcement agencies face serious challenges in responding to the rise of online prostitution. The free flow of information associated with the Internet hinders traditional police work, and increases staffing and administrative costs. Legal and regulatory interventions show promise but may have important unintended consequences. Overall, we tentatively suggest that the best approach may be to take limited steps towards direct restrictions on online prostitution activity, while partnering with the market institutions that facilitate it in order to identify and target the most serious and problematic cases involving trafficked or exploited individuals, and children. There are also important differences in prostitution markets across cities, implying that whatever approach is taken to the rise in online prostitution it should be carefully tailored to the local market environment. Ultimately, there is likely no complete solution to the problem of prostitution. By better understanding the market, policymakers and law enforcement agencies can more effectively direct limited resources to best benefit the community as a whole.

References

Brooks, Amanda. 2009. *The Internet Escort's Handbook: Advertising and Marketing (Book 2)*. Golden Girl Press, LLC.

Blevins, Kristie R., and Thomas J. Holt. 2009. Examining the Virtual Subculture of Johns. *Journal of Contemporary Ethnography* 8 (5): 619–648.

Chambers, Marsha. 2009. Branford Cops Use Craigslist for Prostitution Stings. *New Haven Independent*. (November 13, 2009), http://newhavenindependent.org/archives/2009/11/branford_cops_u.php

Church, Stephanie, Marion Henderson, Marina Barnard and Graham Hart. 2001. Violence by Clients Towards Female Prostitutes in Different Work Settings: Questionnaire Survey. *British Medical Journal* 322: 524–525.

Coutinho, Roel A., Ruud L. van Andel, and Toine J. Rijsdijk. 1988. Role of Male Prostitution in Spread of Sexually Transmitted Diseases and Human Immunodeficiency Virus. *Genitourin Medicine* 64: 207–208.

Cunningham, Scott and Todd D. Kendall. 2009a. Changing Practices and Characteristics among Internet-Facilitated Sex Workers in North America. *Unpublished manuscript*.

Cunningham, Scott and Todd D. Kendall. 2009b. "Prostitution, Technology, and the Law: New Data and Directions." In *Handbook on Family Law and Economics*, ed. Edward Elgar, forthcoming. Portland OR; Elsevier.

Cunningham, Scott and Todd D. Kendall. 2009c. Using Political Conventions to Test the Relationship Between Men-in-Transit and Prostitution. *Unpublished Manuscript*.

Cunningham, Scott and Todd D. Kendall. 2010a. Prostitution 2.0: The Changing Face of Sex Work. *Unpublished Manuscript*.

Cunningham, Scott and Todd D. Kendall. 2010b. Reputation and Contract Enforcement: The Case of Professional Escorts. *Unpublished Manuscript*.

Cunningham, Scott and Todd D. Kendall. 2010c. Moonlighting: Skill Premia in the Commercialized Sex Market. *Unpublished Manuscript*.

Dellarocas, Chrysanthos. 2006. "Reputation Mechanisms." In *The Handbook of Economics and Information Systems*, ed. Thomas Hendershott, 629–660. Portland OR: Elsevier Science.

Dodge, Mary, Donna Starr-Gimeno, and Thomas Williams. 2005. Puttin' on the Sting: Women Police Officers' Perspectives on Reverse Prostitution Assignments. *International Journal of Police Science & Management* 7(2): 71–85.

Edlund, Lena, and Evelyn Korn. 2002. A Theory of Prostitution,. *Journal of Political Economy* 110 (1): 181–214.

Farley, Melissa. 2004. "Bad for the body, bad for the heart": Prostitution harms women even if legalized or decriminalized. *Violence Against Women* 10(10): 1087–1135.

Farr, Stephen J., Carol Horton Trembla, and Victor J. Tremblay. 2001. The Welfare Effect of Advertising Restrictions in the U.S. Cigarette Industry. *Review of Industrial Organization* 8: 147–160.

Federal Bureau of Investigation. 2004. *Uniform Crime Reporting Handbook*, Washington, DC: U.S. Department of Justice.

Fowler, Geoffrey A. 2009a. Craigslist abandons its erotic category. *Wall Street Journal*, May 13, 2009.

Fowler, Geoffrey A. 2009b. Craigslist sues critic of its adult ads. *Wall Street Journal*, May 23, 2009.

Gil, Vincent E., Marco S. Wang, Allen F. Anderson, Guo Matthew Lin, and Zongjian Oliver Wu. 1996. Prostitutes, Prostitution and STD/HIV Transmission in Mainland China. *Social Science & Medicine* 42(1): 141–152.

Goldstein, Paul J. 1979. *Prostitution and Drugs*. Lexington, MA: Lexington Books.

Hay, Bruce. 2005. Sting Operations, Undercover Agents, and Entrapment. *Missouri Law Review* 70: 387–432.

Holt, Thomas J., and Kristie R. Blevins. 2007. Examining Sex Work from the Client's Perspective: Assessing Johns Using Online Data. *Deviant Behavior* 28: 333–354.

Holt, Thomas J., Kristie R. Blevins, and Joseph B. Kuhns, III. 2008. Examining the Displacement Practices of Johns with On-Line Data. *Journal of Criminal Justice* 36: 522–528.

Holt, Thomas J., Kristie R. Blevins, and Joseph B. Kuhns, III. 2009. Examining Diffusion and Arrest Avoidance Practices Among Johns. *Crime & Delinquency*: 1–24.

Holzman, Harold, and Sharon Pines. 1982. Buying Sex: The Phenomenology of Being a John. *Deviant Behavior* 4: 89–116.

Kara, Siddharth. 2008. *Sex Trafficking: Inside the Modern Business of Slavery*. Columbia University Press.

Kenndy, M. Alexis, and Melanie A. Taylor. 2010. Prostitution on Craigslist. *Unpublished Manuscript*.

Laumann, Edward O., John H. Gagnon, Robert T. Michael, and Stuart Michaels. 2000. *The Social Organization of Sexuality: Sexual Practices in the United States*. Chicago, IL: University of Chicago Press.

Levitt, Steven, and Sudhir Alladi Venkatesh. 2007. *An Empirical Analysis of Street-Level Prostitution.* University of Chicago Working Paper.

Logan, Jessica. 2008. Internet Replacing Streetwalking for Inland Prostitution. *The Press-Enterprise* January 1, 2008.

Logan, Trevon. 2009. Personal Characteristics, Sexual Behaviors, and Male Sex Work: A Quantitative Approach. *Unpublished Manuscript.*

Logan, Trevon, and Manisha Shah. 2009. Face Value: Information and Signaling in an Illegal Market. *NBER Working Paper 14841.*

Lowman, John. 1992. Street Prostitution Control: Some Canadian Reflections on the Finsbury Park Experience. *British Journal of Criminology* 32: 1–17.

Matthews, Roger. 1990. Developing More Effective Strategies for Curbing Prostitution. *Security Journal* 1: 182–187.

Milrod, Christine. 2008. Sexual Attitudes and Experiences. *Unpublished Manuscript.*

Prieger, James E., and Wei-Min Hu. 2008. The Broadband Digital Divide and the Nexus of Race, Competition and Quality. *Information Economics and Policy* 20(2): 150–167.

Potterat, John J., Richard B. Rothenberg, Stephen Q. Muth, William W. Darrow, and Lyanne Phillips-Plummer. 1998. Pathways to Prostitution: The Chronology of Sexual and Drug Abuse Milestones. *The Journal of Sex Research* 35 (4): 333–340.

Richtel, Matt. 2008. Sex trade monitors a key figure's woes. *New York Times,* June 17, 2008.

Rosenberg, Michael J., and Jodie M. Weiner. 1988. Prostitutes and AIDS: A Health Department Priority? *American Journal of Public Health* 78(4): 418–423.

Sanders, Teela. 2008. *Paying for Pleasure: Men Who Buy Sex.* Portland, OR: Willan.

Schelling, Thomas. 1960. *The Strategy of Conflict.* Cambridge, MA: Harvard University Press.

Scott, Michael. 2001. Street Prostitution. *Problem-Oriented Guides for Police Series,* No. 2.

Sharpe, Keith, and Sarah Earle. 2003. "Cyberpunters and cyberwhores: prostitution on the Internet." In *Dot Cons. Crime, Deviance and Identity on the Internet,* ed. Yvonne Jewkes, 36–52. Portland, OR: Willan Publishing.

Soothhill, Keith, and Teela Sanders. 2005. The geographical mobility, preferences and pleasures of prolific punters: A demonstration study of the activities of prostitutes' clients. *Sociological Research On-Line* 10(1). http://www.socresonline.org.uk/10/1/soothhill.html (October 10, 2005).

U.S. Census. 2008. *Hispanic or Latino origins by race—Universe: total population: Table B03002.* (April 15, 2010), http://factfinder.census.gov/

servlet/DTTable?_bm=y&-context=dt&-ds_name=ACS_2008_1YR_G00_&-CONTEXT=dt&-mt_name=ACS_2008_1YR_G2000_B03002&-tree_id=306&-redoLog=false&- all_geo_types=N&-geo_id=01000US&-format=&-_lang=en.

U.S. District Court for the Northern District of Illinois Eastern Division. 2009. *Thomas Dart, Sheriff of Cook County, Plaintiff, v. Craigslist Inc., Defendant.* "Complaint," filed March 5, 2009.

Weidner, Robert. 2001. *I Won't Do Manhattan: Causes and Consequences of a Decline in Street Prostitution.* El Paso, TX: LFB Scholarly Publishing.

Weitzer, Ronald. 2005. New Directions in Research on Prostitution. *Crime, Law & Social Change* 43: 211–235.

7

Examining Cyberstalking and Bullying: Causes, Context, and Control

Catherine Marcum

In the early 1960s, J.C.R. Licklider of the Massachusetts Institute of Technology created the idea of an electronic global communication system (Licklider and Clark 1962, as cited in Leiner, et al. 2003). His "Galactic Network" idea entailed an internationally connected set of computers that allowed for easy accessibility to information. His idea developed into what we now know as the Internet. This intercontinental information highway has enabled people of all ages, especially youth, to drastically expand their social circles and improve their ability to communicate with friends and family (Roberts, Foehr, Rideout, and Brodie 1999; Rosenbaum, Altman, Brodie, Flournoy, Blendon, and Benson 2000). Besides communication and socialization, users are able to participate easily in other activities, such as research, shopping, and online gaming.

Unfortunately, individuals are often unable to participate in online activities without the annoyance of uninvited communication and harassment from other online users. Illegal activities occurring with the Internet as the location of these crimes are becoming more and more prevalent for users. While online victimization can range from identity theft to child pornography, two of the more prevalent classifications of cybercrime are cyberbullying and cyberstalking. These crimes are also mirrored in the physical world, but due to the complexity of the Internet, are often more difficult to define and prosecute.

This chapter will attempt to clarify issues related to cyberbullying and cyberstalking, as well as legislative and legal challenges that have arisen because of these complex crimes. First, cyberbullying and cyberstalking will be separately defined, as well as explored in regard to behaviors of offenders and victims. Legislation and prevention techniques for each type of victimization will also be discussed. Finally, the effect of prosecution of these behaviors will be discussed in regard to the free speech rights of youth and adults.

Cyberbullying

Bullying in the physical world is defined as intentional, aggressive behavior that involves an imbalance of power (Nansel et al. 2001, 2094); therefore, cyberbullying is intentional, aggressive behavior that is performed through electronic means (Hinduja and Patchin 2008, 129; Reeckman and Cannard 2009, 41). Cyberbullying can take place in various forms of computer-mediated communication (CMCs), such as instant messaging, email, or chat room. Additionally, text messages are becoming a common method for cyberbullying as more young people use cellular telephones. For example, repetitive and harassing text messages can be sent continuously to a recipient.

Perhaps one of the most sensational examples of cyberbullying is the story of Megan Meier. Megan was a young teenager who faced the same develop mental and emotional challenges experienced by most adolescent females. She befriended another teenager named Josh via her MySpace account, but after several weeks, the messages from Josh became hostile and demeaning. Megan became confused by Josh's aggressions and became devastated when he told her the world would be a better place without her. Sadly, Megan committed suicide as a result of these conversations and was completely unaware of the true identity of Josh. Her parents later discovered that Josh was actually the middle-aged mother of a former friend of Megan, Lori Drew. Drew was convicted in federal court of three counts of "accessing a computer without authorization via interstate commerce to obtain information to inflict emotional distress," but the conviction was later overturned based on the terms of use of MySpace. However, prosecutors and parents considered the case a victory as it paved the way for the criminalization of cyberbullying (Beckstrom 2008, 283).

Cyberbullying can occur in several forms of electronic communication (Hinduja and Patchin 2008, 129). The following forms of cyberbullying are listed and defined as the following:

- Harassment in the cyber form entails repetitive messages, generally offensive to the recipient (Kowalski, Limber, and Agatston 2008, 47);
- Outing and trickery refers to the unintended sharing of personal information with others (Beckstrom 2008, 290);

- Flaming occurs in a public setting, such as a chat room or discussion board, and is a brief exchange of insults between two or more parties (Adams 2007; Bauman 2007; Willard 2006);
- Denigration involves posting information about another that is disparaging and untrue; and
- Exclusion/ostracism is the perception of feeling in or out (Kowalski et al. 2008, 48–49).

According to Wolak, Mitchell and Finkelhor (2007), while physical bullying occurs over multiple incidents, cyberbullying generally does not involve repeated aggression. However, the threats or offensive behavior performed online may only involve a single post, but that post could be passed on to many recipients. This challenges the notion of the repetition missing from cyberbullying, as the information could be posted in multiple places online. For example, YouTube is a website that anyone can post anything to be viewed by all other online users. This website has made homemade viral videos, such as the Star Wars kid and the Chocolate Rain singer, extremely popular. However, if someone takes a home video (whether it be on a video camera, digital camera, or cellular telephone) of another person performing an embarrassing act and posts it YouTube without his or her permission, it can be viewed by thousands of online users. Moreover, the website link could also be emailed to thousands of other online users, continuing the cycle.

Cyberbullying can be both direct and indirect. Direct cyberbullying involves messages sent specifically to the victim, such as insults, demeaning words, or threats. On the other hand, indirect cyberbullying (also known as cyberbullying by proxy) occurs when the perpetrators poses as the victim by hacking into his or her account and sending out hateful and inappropriate messages (Aftab 2006). For example, sending harassing emails to a friend from your sister's email account and signing the emails with your sister's name instead of your own would be indirect cyberbullying.

There is a disagreement among some researchers regarding the age group that can be cyberbullied. According to Aftab (2006), the term "cyberbullying" only occurs between minors. If an adult becomes involved in the exchange, the behavior is then termed cyber harassment or cyberstalking. However, Kowalski et al. (2008, 44) disagree with that assertion and believe that adults can be victims of cyberbullying as well. For instance, there have been instances of students superimposing teachers' heads on nude bodies, or harassing teachers online.

Persons who participate in cyberbullying generally exhibit one or more of the same characteristics. For example, they have a temper and are easily frustrated. Second, they may have dominant personalities and relate to others in aggressive ways (proactively and reactively). Finally, they may show little compassion for victims of bullying (Camodeca and Goossens 2005, 186–197). This lack of empathy by offenders presents concern for school administrators, as this form of victimization can cause physical, psychological, and emotional harm to its victims (Hinduja and Satchin 2007, 89).

There have been several notable studies performed regarding the prevalence of cyberbullying and the overall findings have been consistent. In a study of Internet behavior of high school seniors, Marcum (2009, 356) found that approximately 31% of the respondents had experienced some form of harassment online. The National Children's Home study (NCH 2002) found that almost 30% of youth (ages 11 to 19 years old) polled had been cyberbullied in some form, while O'Connell (2004, 4) found that 20% of children aged 9–16 were harassed specifically in chat rooms. Moreover, Patchin and Hinduja (2006, 148) found that among their respondents under the age of 18, 30% reported being a victim of cyberbullying and 11% confessed to perpetrating cyberbullying.

Findings regarding the separation of the sexes are not consistent, as males and females are shown to experience harassment differently depending on the study. Marcum (forthcoming) found that 35.2% of male college freshmen had experienced some form of cyberbullying, compared to 16.0% of female college freshmen. Conversely, the National Children's Home (NCH 2002) found that females were more likely to be cyberbullied via text messaging compared to males (21% vs. 12%); however, females (3%) and males (5%) were quite comparable in regard to victimization via email. (Holt and Bossler 2009; Marcum. Forthcoming).

Males and females also display aggression and perpetrate harassment in different ways. Males generally engage in more direct aggression, such as physical violence, while females use indirect forms of aggression, such as gossiping or spreading false rumors (Bjorkqvist, Lagerspetz, and Osterman 1992, 51); therefore, females should participate more in cyberbullying as offenders compared to males. As support for this assumption, a study of middle school students by Kowalski and Limber (2006, as cited in Kowalski et al. 2008, 78) found that 13% of females and 9% of males had perpetrated cyberbullying.

Cyberbullying can have varying effects on the victim and perpetrator, often mirroring reactions to physical bullying. Victims of cyberbullying can exhibit feelings of depression, stress, anxiety, and suicidal thoughts (Ybarra and Mitchell 2004, 1308). Kowalski et al. (2008) argue that the effects of cyberbullying can even be worse than physical altercations as the bullying messages can continue to reappear on the Internet in multiple places. Targets of cyberbullying often do not report incidences of abuse as they are afraid of losing the mediums where the bullying is occurring (cellular telephones and the Internet), as they are valued commodities (Campbell 2005; Li 2006). There has even been an assertion that social networking websites cause a "suicide contagion effect" (Zayas 2006), a term that indicates individuals who are contemplating suicide are more likely to act if they see others have published their suicide on social networking websites.

Conversely, perpetrators of cyberbullying often feel vindicated, pleased, and proud of their behavior (Kowalski and Witte 2006). By abusing someone else and feeling dominant, they feel compensated for wrongs done to them at one time. Patchin and Hinduja (forthcoming) found that offenders of cyberbullying are often fueled by various forms of strain, as well as peer aggression. Moreover, in a separate study, Hinduja and Patchin (2008, 1) found that computer proficiency and time spent online were both positively related to committing the offense of cyberbullying.

Prevention of Cyberbullying

Other than formal legislation, there are steps that can be taken to prevent cyberbullying. For example, there are tips parents can use to protect their children while using the Internet online. Kowalski et al. (2008, 113–114) held focus groups with high school students and obtained the following suggestions:

- Set age-appropriate guidelines;
- Communicate about appropriate ways to deal with conflict;
- Monitor use of the Internet;
- Supervise, but do not violate privacy;
- Watch for warning signs;
- Do not punish the victim for the online offender's behavior; and
- Educate yourself.

Furthermore, organizations such as NetSmartz (www.netsmartz.org) and i-SAFE (www.isafe.org) provide resources for parents to educate themselves of the dangers online and how to be prepared for their children.

There are also steps that educators can take to better prepare themselves for incidences of cyberbullyling in their schools. First, educators need to be given a definition of cyberbullying and instructed on how to assess potential problems in the classroom and with students. This can be accomplished through regular staff training. As the Internet changes by the second, it is imperative to keep abreast of new technology and its functioning. Next, educators should spend class time covering cyberbullying, proper and safe Internet use, as well as encouraging students to report incidences they encounter. Finally, educators not only teach children, but also parents. While there are steps parents should take to educate themselves, they are not always motivated to be proactive; therefore, teachers should send home literature to parents instructing them on what to watch for during Internet use (Kowalski et al. 2008, 128–138).

Cyberstalking

The term stalking is defined as behavior that involves one individual repeatedly intruding on another in a manner that produces fear or distress (McEwan, Mullen, MacKenzie, and Ogloff 2009, 1469). There is a blurred line between the difference, if any, of harassment and stalking, as harassment is also categorized as behavior that annoys or distresses the victim. Often, the level of stress, fear and disturbance is considered when determining if a person is being harassed or stalked (Turmanis and Brown 2006, 184). However, according to Sinclair and Frieze (2000, 23), it is not possible to make a clear distinction of what behaviors should be labeled as harassment or stalking, and therefore it is beneficial to refer to the terms interchangeably.

Typical methods of physical stalking involve consistent, unwanted monitoring of a person, arriving at homes or workplaces uninvited, and participating in intimidating behavior. Much like the term cyberbullying, the term cyberstalking refers to stalking in an electronic format. While cyberstalking can occur in a multitude of ways (much like stalking in the physical sense), methods include, but are not limited to the following: gathering personal information to threaten or intimidate the victim; unwanted, repetitious emailing or instant messaging; sending hostile messages or threats; and impersonation of another person (Sheridan and Grant 2007, 627). Although Bocij (2004, 78) found that cyberstalking is experienced slightly more by females than males, it is still an issue for both sexes. Furthermore, Sheridan and Grant (2007) asserted that cyberstalking is perpetrated less by ex-intimate partners, and more by acquaintances or strangers.

Multiple studies have indicated that Internet users of a wide age range have reported being victimized by a cyberstalker. In regard to the younger adolescent population (17 years and younger) a direct example comes from evidence derived from the Youth Internet Safety Survey, a nationally representative study (sponsored by the National Center for Missing and Exploited Children) of 1,501 adolescents, 10 to 17 years old, who participated in regular use of the Internet. The two administrations of the Youth Internet Safety Survey [the first (YISS-1) occurred between August 1999 and February 2000 and the second (YISS-2) between March and June 2005] showed an increase in Internet victimization between the two time periods. First, the proportion of youth who reported online harassment grew from 6% to 9%. A larger amount percentage of youth received unwanted sexual solicitation compared to the first survey (13% in 2001 versus 19% in 2006) (Mitchell, Finkelhor, and Wolak 2003; Wolak, Mitchell and Finkelhor 2006).

Although adolescent populations often fall prey to cyberstalking, adults are also experiencing various forms of cyberstalking. Fisher, Cullen, and Turner (2000) questioned approximately 4500 female undergraduates and found that 13.1% had reported cyberstalking in some form. Alexy, Burgess, Baker, and Smoyak (2005) and Finn (2004) both found that 5–10% of male and female undergraduates reported cyberstalking online, generally in email form, and offline. Moreover, Spitzberg and Hoobler (2002) utilized the Cyber-Obsessional Pursuit scale to measure stalking and harassment online. Eighteen percent of respondents confirmed that someone had obsessively communicated with them in a sexually harassing way, while 3% had threatened them. While there is a limited amount of literature utilizing theory to explain online victimization, especially between sexes, Holt and Bossler (2009) found support for Routine Activity Theory as an explanation for this form of victimization. They found that females were more likely to be victimized due to their target suitability, and hypothesized that this may be a result of their communication patterns online that allow them to be easily identified as women (Holt and Bossler 2009).

Since the concept of cyberstalking is fairly new, there is a division amongst researchers if it truly is a social problem (Bocij and McFarlane 2002, 204). Some theorists believe that cyberstalking is a gateway to physical stalking. Lee (1998) stated that "electronic stalking often leads to, or is accompanied by, physical stalking, and explicitly or implicitly threatens physical stalking" (p. 407). Furthermore, McGrath and Casey (2002, 85) affirm that the anonymous availability of the Internet can turn a low-risk victim to a high-risk victim. As the Internet allows for masked or changed identity, the opportunities for deception are increased and offenders can better depersonalize their victims (Bocij and McFarlane 2003, 204).

Motivators of cyberstalking can vary for each offender. However, according to Bocji (2004, 92–106), they can be grouped into two categories: technological and social factors. Technological factors, such as easier access to technology and the ability to hide one's identity, allow for easier deceptive practices online. For example, many social networking websites do not validate the identity of their users, so it is easy to create false identities online. Social factors, such as disinhibition (based on the anonymity available online) and the perception of power and control, can increase the likelihood of the stalking behaviors. Furthermore, difficulty policing this behavior online increases the ability for a person to participate in the behavior, as well as become victims of it. An example of this can also be found in Holt and Bossler's (2009) study of college students and online victimization. Utilizing Routine Activity Theory to examine the behavior, they found a positive relationship between students who reported involvement in computer-based deviance and their likelihood of victimization. In other words, involvement in deviant and/or illegal behaviors online as an offender increased the likelihood that the student would also become a victim.

Along with the controversy of its detriment to the criminal justice system, there is also dispute of its uniqueness compared to offline stalking. Bocij (2004, 21–29) argued that the following fallacies about cyberstalking confirm it is a unique form of deviant behavior compared to offline stalking:

- Cyberstalking is an extension of offline stalking;
- Cyberstalkers are "obsessional";
- Cyberstalkers know their victims;
- Cyberstalkers cause less harm than offline stalkers;
- Cyberstalkers seldom use stalking-by-proxy;
- Cyberstalkers do not make "credible threats"; and
- Cyberstalkers share the same motivations as offline stalkers.

Bocij (2004, 21–29) disproves these fallacies by providing empirical research, as well as confirmation by Congress, that affirms the uniqueness of this deviant behavior and the potential danger that results from it. Moreover, the reaction victims experience from cyberstalking can mimic those of offline stalking and be just as serious (Bocij 2004, 66).

Bocij (2004, 66) asserted that victims of cyberstalking can be categorized into three groups based on their computer literacy: novice, intermediate, or expert. He reported that while novice users were more likely to receive threats, expert users were more likely to experience sophisticated attacks on their hardware and software. Despite the type of cyberstalking, the reaction of the victim can include: powerlessness, shame, feelings of isolation, anxiety/depression, and substance abuse (Ashcroft 2001, 24; Blaauw et al. 2002, 50). Furthermore, Pathe (2002, 48) asserted that friends and relatives of stalking victims may also become secondary victims, as the stalker may use them as a tool to control the primary target.

Prevention of Cyberstalking

According to the organization "Working to Halt Online Abuse (W.H.O.A)," there are several steps a person can take to decrease the likelihood of experiencing cyberstalking (Bureau of Justice Assistance, 2009). For instance, it is suggested that a person use a free email account, such as Hotmail or Yahoo!, along with a gender neutral email address. Secondly, do not give out email addresses or personal information to people not known or trusted. Marcum (2009) found that people who provide personal information to online contacts are more likely to be victimized compared to those who keep personal information private. Therefore, release of personal information to strangers or people met online can be risky behavior. Finally, and most importantly, do not trust new online friends or acquaintances. Other sources also recommend installing a virus scanner on personal computers, as well as refusing file attachments from unknown sources to cut back on viruses and Trojans (Bocij et al. 2002, 628). Hinduja and Patchin (2007) also recommend installation of protective software, but warn that technically-savvy individuals are always finding ways around these measures and are not surefire means of protection.

Most large businesses have security specialists who control cyber security issues. However, there are steps smaller organizations can take to protect themselves. For instance, implement an acceptable use policy for all employees, as well as place controls on employee computers with regard to browsing and email use. Performing regular software audits is also a good way to make sure illegal content is not being stored on company computers (Blacharksi 2000; Lee 2001).

Emergence of Legislation

As mentioned previously, the issue of bullying and stalking in the electronic realm is a fairly new concept. As a result, few attempts at preventing and prosecuting the problem through legislation have been made. While states and the federal government recognize these forms of online victimization as a true problem, many technical issues, as well as constitutional issues, are present. While the constitutional problems will be addressed in the next section, this section will provide information on the current state of legislation that has been implemented to fight cyberbullying and cyberstalking.

The issue of bullying has increasingly become of concern in the public school system, especially since the shootings at Columbine High School. By the year 2000, over half the states in America had passed anti-bullying legislation. Along with other school shootings and publicized incidents, there has been widespread media coverage addressing the issue of bullying. Yet, as Internet use has become more prevalent (especially by adolescents), the concept of electronic harassment and stalking has placed school officials in a realm of uncertainty of how to control this behavior without infringing on constitutional rights.

Currently, approximately ten states have enacted some form of legislation requiring schools to create preventative cyberbullying policies, and other states are considering amendments to their current legislation. Generally, these states have extended their definition of bullying to include those of the electronic and physical form. Arkansas (Act 115 2007) defines bullying as "... intentional harassment, intimidation, humiliation, ridicule, defamation, or threat or incitement of violence by a student against another student or public school employee by written, verbal, electronic or physical act ..."

When referring to bullying that occurs at "school," the majority of states have extended that term to various locations related to school. For example, Iowa law asserts that policies against bullying will be enforced in the school building, on the outside property, and at any school function at any location. Furthermore, South Carolina asserted that "school" also includes any school-related vehicle or the school bus stop (Kowalski et al. 2008, 163).

With regard to cyberstalking, Alaska, California, Oklahoma, and Wyoming have added electronic communication to their anti-stalking laws. Furthermore, in 2000, the federal government passed the Violence Against Women Act, which made cyberstalking a part of the federal interstate stalking statute (National Center for Victims of Crime 2003).

There has also been international efforts to prosecute cyberbullying and cyberstalking. For example, Singapore law is currently in the process of amending its stalking statutes to include those made in electronic arenas (Chik 2008, 13). The United Kingdom passed the Malicious Communications Act of 2003, which allows for up to six months of imprisonment for a person participating in obscene or menacing communication online (Gillespie 2006, 125). Due to the innovation of this piece of legislation, cyberbullying and cyberstalking can now be prosecuted in Britain, Ireland, Scotland, and Wales.

Addressing Free Speech Issues

As cyberbullying and cyberstalking has become more prevalent among adolescents, the issue of censorship and free speech rights for students is often scrutinized. While the First Amendment guarantees the right to freedom of speech, there are always exceptions to the rule, especially when it involves infringing on the rights of others. The United States Supreme Court has examined these exceptions in a few notable cases.

The United States Supreme Court first considered these rights with the case *Tinker v. Des Moines School District* (393 U.S. 403, 507 (1969)). Students were demonstrating their opposition of the Vietnam War and wore armbands to school as a form of protest. The school enacted a policy to discipline any of the students who wore the armbands, and the lawsuit ensued as students insisted their right to free speech was violated through the restriction of their clothing. Under *Tinker,* the Court ruled that student speech may be censored if it causes a substantial disruption or invades the rights of other students. *Tinker* has recently been applied regarding off-campus cyberspeech by students. In cases such as *J.S.* ex rel. *H.S. v. Bethlehem Area School District* (807 A.2d 847, 850–51 (Pa. 2002)) and *Layshock v. Hermitage School District* (412 F.Supp. 2d 502, 504 (W.D. PA. 2006)), the Court ruled that certain types of cyber speech caused a substantial disruption on campus, affecting both staff and students, and was justifiably removed.

Thirty years after *Tinker,* the Supreme Court again weighed on the issue of student speech with the case *Bethel School District No. 403 v. Fraser* (478 U.S. 675 (1986)). Fraser, a student, nominated a fellow student for an office and delivered a speech that included explicit, sexual language. Shortly thereafter, Fraser was suspended for his language and his name was removed from the list of graduation speakers. The Supreme Court veered away from *Tinker,* and stated that students are entitled to the same First Amendment protections as adults and that if the student was attempting to make a political point, offensive language was allowed. However, the Court did state that it is up to the determination of school boards to determine what is offensive and prohibited in the school arena.

Lastly, *Hazelwood School District v. Kuhlmeier* (484 U.S. 260 (1988)) examined restrictions placed on student speech by school administration. The administration deleted portions of a school newspaper they believed to be inappropriate without the students' approval. The Supreme Court supported the decision of the administration, and stated that the First Amendment rights were not violated as the newspaper was funded by the school district and part of school curriculum.

There are other standards that have been used as an alternative to the *Tinker* substantial disruption test. Some courts use the "true threat" doctrine, as applied in *Watts v. United States* (394 U.S. 705 (1969)), in which threats made inside or outside the classroom are not constitutionally protected if designated a true threat. This "true threat" doctrine was applied via the "reasonable recipient" or "reasonable speaker" standard (as ruled in the Eighth and Ninth Circuit respectively), in which an objective person could interpret the communication as a true threat of intent to harm or assault (Beckstrom 2008, 306–308).

In summary, the Supreme Court has stated that there are certain circumstances in which school personnel can intervene on student speech without violating their First Amendment rights. First, according to *Watts v. United States* (1969), true threats are not protected. Furthermore, according to *Rogers v. United States* (1975), even statements that are intended to be threatening but not carried out are considered true threats. Second, according to the previously mentioned *Bethel School District* case, speech that is lewd, vulgar and profane can be regulated at the very least if it is used on school grounds (Kowalski et al. 2008, 171).

There are other types of speech not protected by the First Amendment. Speech that is school sponsored, such as newspapers or theatrical productions, are subject to school intervention. Also, as was defined in *Tinker*, speech that disrupts the rights of others can be censored. Furthermore, although it is difficult to address the censorship of off-campus speech, the *Tinker* standard often applies if it involves "disruption of classwork, substantial disorder, or invasion of others' rights" (Kowalski et al. 2008, 172). For example, in *Coy v. Board of Education of the North Canton City Schools* (2002) and *J.S. v. Bethlehem Area School District* (2001), the Court ruled that although the websites were created off-campus by students, the access on school property and derogatory effect it had on students and teachers indicated it was not Constitutionally protected speech.

Conclusion

Daily use of the Internet is a customary behavior for many Americans, whether for socialization, research, or various other activities. Though the idea of the Internet was not conceived until 1962 (Leiner et al. 2003) and just became a familiar facet of businesses and homes in the early 1990s (Sanger et al. 2004), this new commodity of communication that has become a mainstay in American homes. Due to its easy accessibility and availability, the frequency of

Internet use has increased in all age groups; however, Internet use by adolescents has had the largest increase compared to any other age group (Addison 2001).

Today's adolescents grew up using the Internet, and are extremely familiar with the opportunities available online. Youth and younger adults are especially involved in online socialization with various methods of computer-mediated communication (CMC), such as email, chat rooms, instant messaging, and social networking websites. Not only are they using the Internet to socialize, they are also spending more time online (Nie and Erbring 2000; United States Department of Commerce 2002). Unfortunately, while the use of CMCs can produce positive interaction and enjoyable relationships for users, people spending extensive amounts of time online are also placing themselves at risk for victimization. Cyberbullying and cyberstalking are two main ways people can be victimized.

There needs to be a continued effort to research cyberbullying and cyberstalking so that credibility is given to these crimes as true threats of victimization for Internet users. Explanatory studies that provide better insight into the behaviors that increase these forms of victimization would be extremely beneficial, especially for younger Internet users who may engage in more risky online behaviors. Furthermore, these studies can help shape safety programs and policies to ensure a safer Internet experience for users. Another gap in the literature is research examining the effectiveness of legislation currently in place to prosecute cyberbullying and cyberstalking. First, studies investigating the amount of effort used to prosecute these crimes compared to bullying and stalking in the physical world would be beneficial. Secondly, the actual effectiveness of these pieces of legislation in regard to a deterrent factor for offenders should be explored as well.

While everyone is entitled to certain rights under the First Amendment regarding free speech, this does not give us the right to victimize others. There are certain things we can do to protect ourselves while online, such as use of protective software and protection of personal information. However, the most important step to take in this process is to educate ourselves and others of the dangers online and what can be done to decrease the likelihood of victimization.

References

Alexy, Eileen M., Ann W. Burgess, Timothy Baker, and Shirley A. Smoyak. 2005. Perceptions of cyberstalking among college students. *Brief Treatment and Crisis Intervention* 5: 279–289.

Ashcroft, John. 2001. *Stalking and domestic violence.* NCJ 186157. Washington, DC: U.S. Department of Justice.

Beckstrom, Darryn C. 2008. State legislation mandating school cyberbullying policies and the potential threat to students' free speech rights. *Vermont Law Review* 33: 283–321.

Bethel School District No. 403 v. Fraser, 478 U.S. 675 (1986).

Blacharski, Dan. 2000. Emerging technology: Create order with a strong security policy. S.l.: Network Magazine. http://www.networkmagazine.com/shared/article/showArticle.jhtml?articleId=8702862

Blauuw, Eric, Frans W. Winkel, Ella Arensman, Lorraine Sheridan, and Adrienne Freeve. 2002. *The toll of stalking:* The relationship between features of stalking and psychopathology of victims. *Journal of Interpersonal Violence* 17(1): 50–63.

Bocij, Paul. 2004. *Cyberstalking: Harassment in the Internet age and how to protect your family.* Westport, CT: Praeger Publishers.

Bocij, Paul, and Leroy McFarlane. 2002. Online harassment: Towards a definition of cyberstalking. *Prison Service Journal* 39: 31–38.

Bocij, Paul, and Leroy McFarlane. 2003. Cyberstalking: The technology of hate. *Police Journal* 76: 204–221.

Bureau of Justice Assistance. 2009. *2008 Internet crime report.* Department of Justice: Office of Justice Programs. Washington DC.

Chik, Warren. 2008. Harassment through the digital medium: A cross-jurisdictional comparative analysis on the law of cyberstalking. *Journal of International Law & Technology* 3(1): 13–44.

Coy v. Board of Education of the North Canton City Schools, 205 F Supp. 2d 791 (2002).

Finn, Jerry. 2004. A survey of online harassment at a university camps. *Journal of Interpersonal Violence* 19: 468–483.

Fisher, Bonnie, Francis Cullen, and Michael G. Turner. 2000. *The sexual victimization of college women.* National Institute of Justice Publication No. NCJ 182369. Washington: Department of Justice.

Gillespie, Alisdair. 2006. Cyberbullying and harassment of teenagers: The legal response. *Journal of Social Welfare and Family Law* 28(2): 123–136.

Hazelwood School District v. Kuhlmeier, 484 U.S. 260, (1988).

Hinduja, Sameer, and Justin Patchin. 2007. Offline consequences of online victimization: School violence and delinquency. *Journal of School Violence* 6(3): 89–112.

Hinduja, Sameer, and Justin Patchin. 2008. Cyberbullying: An exploratory analysis of factors related to offending and victimization. *Deviant Behavior* 29(2): 1–29.

Holt, Thomas, and Adam Bossler. 2009. Examining the applicability of Lifestyle-Routine Activities Theory for cybercrime victimization. *Deviant Behavior* 30(1): 1–25.

J.S. ex rel. H.S. v. Bethlehem Area School District, 807 A.2d 847, 850–51, (Pa. 2002).

Kowalski, Robin M, and James C. Witte. 2006. *Youth Internet Survey.* Available: http://www.camss.clemson.edu/KowalskiSurvey/servelet/Page1.

Kowalski, Robim M., Susan P. Limber, and Patricia W. Agatston. 2008. *Cyberbullying: Bullying in the digital age.* Maldon, MA: Blackwell Publishing.

Layshock v. Hermitage School District, 412 F.Supp. 2d 502, 504 (W.D. PA. 2006).

Lee, Doris. 2001. *Developing effective information systems security policies.* Bethesda, MD: SANS Institute. http://www.sans.org/rr/policy/effective.php.

Lee, Rebecca. 1998. Romantic and electronic stalking in a college context. *William and Mary Journal of Women and the Law* 4: 373–466.

Leiner, Barry M., Vinton G. Cerf, David D. Clark, Robert E. Kahn, Leonard Kleinrock, Daniel C. Lynch, Jon Postel, Larry G. Roberts, and Stephen Wolff. 2003. "A Brief History of the Internet." *Internet Society.* (June 7, 2007), http://www.isoc.org/internet/history/brief.shtml.

Marcum, Catherine D. 2009. Identifying potential factors of adolescent online victimization in high school seniors. *International Journal of Cyber Criminology* 2(2): 346–367.

Marcum, Catherine D. forthcoming 2010. Assessing sex experiences of online victimization: An examination of adolescent online behaviors utilizing Routine Activity Theory. *Criminal Justice Review.*

McEwan, Troy, Paul Mullen, Richard MacKenzie, and James Ogloff. 2009. Violence in stalking situations. *Psychological Medicine* 39: 1469–1478.

McGrath, Michael G., and Egohan Casey. 2002. Forensic psychiatry and the Internet: Practical perspectives on sexual predators and obsessional harassers in cyberspace. *Journal of the American Academy of Psychiatry and the Law* 30: 81–94.

Mitchell, Kimberly, David Finkelhor, and Janice Wolak. 2003. The exposure of youth to unwanted sexual material on the Internet: A national survey of risk, impact and prevention. *Youth & Society 34(3):* 3300–3358.

Nansel, Tonja R., Mary Overpeck, Ramani S. Pilla, W. June Ruan, Bruce Simmons-Morton, and Peter Scheidt. 2001. Bullying behavior among U.S. youth: Prevalence and association with psychosocial adjustment. *Journal of the American Medical Association* 285: 2094–2100.

National Center for Victims of Crime. 2003. *Cyberstalking.* Available: http://www.victimbar.org/ncvc/main.aspx?dbName=DocumentViewer& DocumentID=32458.

Nie, Norman, and Lutz Erbring. 2000. *Internet and Society: A Preliminary Report*. Stanford: Stanford Institute for the Quantitative Study of Society.

O'Connell, Rachel, Joanna Price, and Charlotte Barrow. 2004. *Cyberstalking, abusive cyber sex, and online grooming*. Centre for Cyberspace Research, Preston.

Patchin, Justin, and Sameer Hinduja. 2006. Bullies move beyond the schoolyard: A preliminary look at cyberbullying. *Youth Violence and Juvenile Justice 4(2)*: 148–169.

Patchin, Justin, and Sameer Hinduja. Forthcoming. Traditional and nontraditional bullying among youth: A test of General Strain Theory. *Youth and Society.*

Pathe, Michele. 2002. *Surviving stalking*. Cambridge: Cambridge University Press.

Reekman, Barbara, and Laine Cannard. 2009. Cyberbullying: A TAFE perspective. *Youth Studies Australia* 28: 41–49.

Roberts, Donald F., Ulla G. Foehr, Victoria J. Rideout, and Mollyann Brodie. 1999. Kids and media @ the new millennium: A comprehensive analysis of children's media se. The Henry J. Kaiser Family Foundation.

Rogers v. United States, 422 U.S. 35 (1975).

Rosenbaum, Michele J., Drew Altman, Mollyann Brodie, Rebecca Flournoy, Robert J. Blendon, and John Benson. 2000. NPR/Kaiser/Kennedy school kids and technology survey. (June 21, 2008), http://www.npr.org/programs/specials/pool/technology/technology.kids.html

Sanger, Dixie, Amie Long, Mitzi Ritzman, Keri Stofer, and Candy Davis. 2004. Opinions of Female Juvenile Delinquents about their Interactions in Chat Rooms. *Journal of Correctional Education* 55: 120–131.

Sheridan, L, and T. Grant. 2007. Is cyberstalking different? *Psychology, Crime & Law* 13(6): 627–640.

Sinclair, H Colleen, and Irene Hanson Frieze. 2000. Initial courtship behavior and stalking: How should we draw the line? *Violence and Participants* 15: 23–40.

Spitzburg, Brian H., and Gregory Hoobler. 2002. Cyberstalking and the technologies of interpersonal terrorism. *New Media & Society* 4: 71–92.

Tinker v. Des Moines School District, 393 U.S. 403, 507 (1969).

Turmanis, Simon A., and Robert I. Brown. 2006. The stalking and harassment behavior scale: Measuring the incidence, nature, and severity of stalking and relational harassment and their psychological effects. *Psychology and Psychotherapy: Theory, Research and Practice* 79: 183–198.

United States Department of Commerce. 2002. Computer and Internet usage by Age and Disability Status: 2002. Washington, DC: United States Department of Commerce. Available: http://www.census.gov/hhes/www/disability/sipp/disab02/ds02f6.pdf.

Watts v. United States, 394 U.S. 705 (1969).

Wolak, Janice, Kimberly Mitchell, and David Finkelhor. 2006. *Online victimization of children: Five years later.* Washington, DC: National Center for Missing & Exploited Children.

Zayas, Alexandra. 2006. Online death dialogues prompt suicide? *St. Petersburg Times.* (April 20, 2007), http://www.sptimes.com/2006/08/27/Tampabay/_Online_death_dialogu.shtml.

8

Terrorism and Technology: Operationalizing Cyberterrorism and Identifying Concepts

Marjie T. Britz

The lack of a universal, or even generalizable, definition of terrorism has complicated both academic and government inquiries into the phenomenon. Obfuscated by ideological, cultural, or political agendas, conceptualizations of terrorism or terrorist activities may be characterized as localized reactions to situational or historical cultural events. In the wake of the Terror Attacks of 9/11, a plethora of discussions, publications, and legislation was evidenced in the United States, including the passage of the *Uniting and Strengthening America by Providing Appropriate Tools Required to Intercept and Obstruct Terrorism Act of 2001*. Commonly known as the U.S.A. Patriot Act, the legislation was originally introduced by Representative Frank Sensenbrenner (R—Wisconsin), and incorporated provisions of two earlier anti-terrorism bills (Public Law 107–56). While the Act brought together disparate House committees (e.g., Education and the Workforce; Transportation and Infrastructure; Armed Services; Financial Services; International Relations; Energy and Commerce; and, the Permanent Select Committee on Intelligence), it neither led to a universally accepted definition nor a greater understanding of the potential of the Internet as a terrorist tool. Even those that acknowledged the emerging threat associated with technology concentrated too heavily on the web as a mechanism of destruction. Such characterizations were both implausible and fantastical, presenting scenarios equivalent to a cyber-apocalypse or a digital Pearl Harbor.

Theoretically, the globalization of commerce, information, and communications has created a technological house of cards. As those in legitimate society increasingly employ the Internet as a medium to conduct business, disseminate research findings, store sensitive information, and communicate with others; those in illegitimate society will exploit the vulnerabilities associated with such interconnectivity. For individuals and corporation, such threats largely include disruption of commerce or communication; extortion; theft or destruction of intellectual property or personal identifying information; and, theft or destruction of funds or commodities. The threats to government and the society at large are much more significant, and include the theft, disruption, or destruction of information or systems critical to the nation's security, infrastructure, or military. While traditional definitions of cyberterror specifically addressed such threats, contemporary conceptualizations must also recognize that the greatest utility of the Internet for terrorists is as a facilitator not a trigger. The interconnectivity of the Internet perfectly complements the amorphous structure and media-centric nature of contemporary terrorist organizations which use the medium for propaganda, recruitment, fund-raising, dissemination of information, and justification. In this way, the Internet may be most appropriately characterized as a force multiplier and agility enabler that connect geographically disparate individuals by affecting situational awareness.

Defining Terrorism

While most contemporary scholars trace the term *terrorism* to the Latin *terrere* which is defined *as to arouse fear*, the modern etymology of the term is most commonly attributed to Robespierre's "The Terror" which immediately followed the French Revolution (Tsfati and Weimann 2002). However, the notion that the fear of a populace could result in political, ideological, or social change is more deeply rooted. In fact, the justification of attacks on noncombatants and institutionalized reactions to same may be as old as society itself (Britz 2009; Garrison 2003; Tsfati and Weimann 2002). While the parameters of this chapter preclude a comprehensive discussion of the history of such actions, it is sufficient and appropriate to recognize that *terrorism*, as both a notion and a reality, is neither a recent contrivance nor a novel field of academic inquiry or government scrutiny. At the same time, an examination of the extant literature reveals a marked absence of a singular definition which has been universally employed by either community. Rather, operationalization of the phenomenon tends to be localized and entirely dependent upon both the individual and social characteristics affecting the defining body. These include cultural norms; religious ideology; institutional history; political or organizational agenda; stability of government institutions; status of economic superstructure; situational placement or vulnerability; and, historical stratification or marginalization.

Regardless of social, cultural, or political agenda, definitions of terrorism by government entities have traditionally required the demonstration of three common elements: 1) the use of violence against noncombatants; 2) political objectives; and, 3) the use of fear as a coercive tactic. For example,

- (1930)—International Conferences for the Unification of Criminal Law (3rd Conference, Brussels)—the intentional use of means capable of producing a common danger that represents an act of terrorism on the part of anyone making use of crimes against life, liberty or physical integrity of persons or directed against private or state property with the purpose of expressing or executing political or social ideas will be punished.(Saul, 2005: 59)
- (1931)—International Conferences for the Unification of Criminal Law (4th Conference, Paris)—whoever, for the purpose of terrorizing the population, uses against persons or property bombs, mines, incendiary or explosive devices or products, fire arms or other deadly or deleterious devices, or who provokes or attempts to provoke, spreads or attempts to spread an epidemy, a contagious disease or other disaster, or who interrupts or attempts to interrupt a public service or public utility will be punished (Saul, 2005: 59).
- (1937)—League of Nations Convention—all criminal acts directed against a State and intended or calculated to create a state of terror in the minds of particular persons or a group of persons or the general public.
- (1991)—Turkish Anti-Terrorism Act—all kinds of activities attempted by a member or members of an organization for the purpose of changing the characteristics of the Republic which is stated in the constitution, and the political, jurisdictional, social, secular, economic system, destroying the territorial integrity of the state and the government and its people, weakening or ruining or invading the authority of the government, demolishing the rights and freedom, jeopardizing the existence of Turkish government and Republic, destroying the public order or peace and security.
- (1994)—United Nations Resolution Language—criminal acts intended or calculated to provoke a state of terror in the general public, a group of persons or particular persons for political purposes are in any circumstance unjustifiable, whatever the considerations of a political, philosophical, ideological, racial, ethnic, religious or other nature that may be invoked to justify them.

- (2007) — United States Department of Defense — the calculated use of unlawful violence or threat of unlawful violence to inculcate fear; intended to coerce or to intimidate governments or societies in the pursuit of goals that are generally political, religious, or ideological.

The lack of international consensus on cultural, religious, and expressive expectations has further complicated attempts at elucidation. Questions regarding the appropriate placement and treatment of "politically motivated" actions, delineation of *state sponsored* versus *individual* motivations, and legal clarification of sovereignty and extradition have rendered international consortium ineffectual (Britz 2009).

An analysis of the extant academic literature reveals a similar pattern of discord with a variety of scholars noting the impossibility of consensus (see Altheide Merari 1993; Rice 2009; Reid and Chen 2006; Ruby 2002; Saul 2005; Schmid and Jongman 1988; Tsfati and Weimann 2002, 2006). At the same time, articulated commonalities suggest that a working definition of terrorism may best be approached as a compilation of characteristics. To wit, the following definitional elements were found: the presence of violence (83.5%); political (65%); fear or terror (51%); threats (47%); anticipated psychological reactions (41.5%); premeditation or system operation (32%); and, tactical, strategic, or combative methodology (30.5%) (Schmid and Jongman 1988). A synthesis of the academic and political entomologies reveals that traditional acts characterized as *terrorism* may be conceptualized as a sum of the following components:

- Violence
- The victimization of innocents
- Methodical or serial operations
- Advance planning
- Criminal character
- Absence of moral restraint
- Political, social, or ideological motivation
- Attempt to garner attention
- Performed for an audience
- Unpredictable and/or unexpected
- Intended to instill fear (Britz 2009)

However, it must be noted that across all landscapes *fear* and *violence* are necessary definitional elements, and ends and means are often used interchangeably with academic definitions concentrating exclusively on the ends while government definitions further obfuscate the discussion by focusing entirely on the means employed (i.e., violence). Violence, for example, is often treated as both the ends and the means to both physical and hypothetical scenarios. Subsequently, government policies, legislative actions, and academic inquiry are founded upon approaches which unavoidably overlook the potentiality of technologically facilitated terrorist actions. Thus, dissection of traditional definitions of terrorism and other sorts of criminal behavior is not simply an intellectual exercise; rather, it is an essential component for the evolution of social constructions of reality which are not necessarily defined by situational characteristics.

Operationalizing Cyberterrorism[1]

Although discussions of "cyberterrorism" as a concept have exploded in recent years, a universal operationalization of the phenomenon has not. Rather, the dissonance surrounding notions of traditional terrorism has been exacerbated by the introduction of new approaches, constructs, and theaters in a borderless, intangible environment. In fact, definitions are widely disparate and range from the general to the specific. The term has been used to include actions as varied as: attacks on information systems; incitement to violence; theft of data; and, the planning of terrorist attacks (Foltz 2004). For the most part, however, definitions maintain foundational elements which require attacks on computer systems that result in physical violence. To wit, Denning's (2000) Testimony before Congress stated:

> Cyberterrorism is the convergence of terrorism and cyberspace. It is generally understood to mean unlawful attacks and threats of attack against computers, networks, and the information stored therein when done to intimidate or coerce a government or its people in furtherance of political or social objectives. Further, to qualify as cyberterrorism, an attack should result in violence against persons or property, or at least cause enough harm to generate fear. Attacks that lead to death or bodily injury, explosions, plane crashes, water contamination, or se-

---

1. It must be noted that the operationalization of other technologically facilitated political or social action has been equally disparate. While space and time constraints preclude a comprehensive discussion of such here, it is sufficient to state that *hacktivism* may be defined as *the act of computer trespass to achieve or advance political causes* (Britz 2009); and *netwar* may be defined as *conflict (and crime) at societal levels where the protagonists rely on network forms of organization, and related doctrines, strategies, and technologies* (Ronfeldt and Martinez 1997). Neither may be considered *cyberterrorism* as the former involves peaceful, social resistance and the latter involves actions by government entities.

vere economic loss would be examples. Serious attacks against critical infrastructures could be acts of cyberterrorism, depending on their
impact. Attacks that disrupt nonessential services or that are mainly
a costly nuisance would not.

Similarly, Pollitt (1998) defined cyberterrorism as the *premeditated, politically
motivated attack against information, computer systems, and data which result
in violence against noncombatant targets by subnational groups.* The identification of particular target populations necessarily precluded government entities
as terrorist actors. As a result, Foltz (2004) concluded that:

> Cyberterrorism is an attack or threat of an attack, politically moti
> vated, intended to: interfere with the political, social, or economic
> functioning of a group, organization, or country; or induce either
> physical violence or the unjust use of power; or in conju8ctions with
> a more traditional terrorist action.

While Foltz (2004) effectively synthesized traditional notions of *cyberterrorism,* it must be noted that neither *fear* nor *violence* should be preponderant in
the conceptualization of *cyberterrorism.* In fact, both are equally important, worthy of discourse, and must be incorporated into emergent terminology or inquiry.
For operationalization purposes, *fear* may be defined as a strong emotion caused
by an awareness of vulnerability or an anticipation of danger. It is individually
perceived and continent upon situational characteristics. *Violence,* on the other
hand, may be characterized as an intentional force which is exerted to inflict
damage or abuse on living things or physical objects. While terrorists may use
violence to affect fear within a population, their primary objective remains political, ideological, or social change. In fact, both concepts are necessarily dependent upon the cultural expectations and values of the selected audience.

Generally speaking, terrorism may be characterized as a theater—a stage
in which the audience is far more important than the actors. While it was originally conceptualized that the invocation of fear was best achieved through displays of catastrophic physical destruction to human life, it must be recognized
that the impact of such demonstrations are necessarily related to the particular target's prioritization and sensitization of same. It can be argued that in
some societies, perception of situational or potential victimization may significantly lessen or even negate the impact of a particular event. In addition,
cultural values or beliefs may heighten fear or perceptions of vulnerability in
the aftermath of a terrorist incident which might otherwise be characterized as
insignificant or having minimal impact on another society. Consequently, a
violent act causing significant loss of life in one culture may result in an equiv-

alent level of fear as a disruption in the communications or economic system of another. In both scenarios, actions taken to facilitate either scenario are appropriately designated as terrorism. Thus, *cyberterrorism* may be conceptualized as a technological extension of traditional definitions of terrorism which recognizes that fear and violence are neither interchangeable nor inevitable components.

Similar to the non-technological counterpart, traditional definitions of *cyberterrorism* required a demonstration of physical destruction or loss of human life facilitated by computer interconnectivity. Such characterizations necessarily portended cataclysmic events, and warned that a catastrophic disruption of communication, commerce, and government services and systems, or "digital Pearl Harbor" was imminent. Discussions of a "digital" or "electronic" Pearl Harbor began in earnest in 1998, when Richard A. Clarke, the National Security Council's Senior Director and National Coordinator for Security, Critical Infrastructure, and Counter-terrorism, presented a fantastical scenario where multiple system failures occur in a single day. These included: multiple computer failures at military bases across the world; a massive blackout in San Francisco; telephone outages across Miami and New York; and, widespread failure of personal pagers, airline reservation systems, and automatic teller machines. Such an occurrence, he stated, would be more catastrophic than Pearl Harbor. As such, he encouraged proactive measures to prepare for the *giant tsunami coming* (Madsen 1998). Although he was not the first to use the term (e.g., Bowman 1995; Washington 1995), he is often credited with its' origination. Since his remarks, the terms "digital" or "electronic" Pearl Harbor have become part of the verbiage associated with discussions of cyber-terrorism and cyber-warfare. There is little consensus in terms of the likelihood of such an event, but the discussion continues (see Britz 2009; Gable 2009; Lewis 2003).

While such attacks are conceivable, an analysis of web usage by terrorists suggest more insidious activities far removed from the Internet as an attack mechanism (Denning 2000; Kohlmann 2006). Thus, *cyberterrorism* may be defined as the premeditated, methodological, ideologically motivated dissemination of information, facilitation of communication, or, attack against physical targets, digital information, computer systems, and/or computer programs which is intended to cause social, financial, physical, or psychological harm to noncombatant targets and audiences for the purpose of affecting ideological, political, or social change; or any utilization of digital communication or information which facilitates such actions directly or indirectly (Britz 2009). Such actions include propaganda; information dissemination; recruitment; training; communication; research and planning; criminal activities and money laundering; and, of course, mechanism of attack.

Propaganda, Information Dissemination, and Recruitment

Without question, the introduction of the Internet has both globalized and revolutionized communication systems, knowledge acquisition, and commercial enterprise. In addition, the increasing accessibility and availability of the medium represents a method of empowerment in class-based systems in which information and commerce are regulated by formal structures. Such interconnectivity and anonymity has also resulted in a virtual renaissance in which intellectual and ideological discourse has flourished. At the same time, it has created a forum in which extremists communicate, conduct research, and promote their agendas.

The propagandizing of ideologies and activities has long been recognized as fundamental to both the maximization of fear among the target audience and the longevity and growth of the organization itself. Throughout much of the second half of the twentieth century, the mechanisms for dissemination have included self-published documents, word of mouth, and homemade videos. Such methods required significant financial expenditures, and posed considerable risk of identification. However, increases in technology have minimized both. Ideologues and jihadists have embraced the medium as the primary platform to stage their campaign of terror—effectively using it to enhance perceptions of vulnerability and to promote their rhetoric to a global community. In fact, the Internet has become a staple in jihadist training, and formally championed by terrorist leaders. A statement posted on www.azzam.com urged extremist to use the web to disseminate news and information about jihad, stating that *the more Web sites, the better it is for us. We must make the Internet our tool* (Weimann et al. 2008, 884). Ironically, al-Qaeda and other organizations are increasingly using American ISPs, and exploiting the protections afforded under both the 1st and 4th Amendments to the Constitution of the United States (Ahituv 2008).

The utilization of the technological medium for recruitment and propaganda is not new among religious zealots or political extremists. Leaders of neo-Nazi and supremacist groups in the United States, like Tom Metzger, embraced the medium in the 1980s to recruit college-aged members (Grennan et al. 2005). Using generational images, humor, and content, the White Aryan Resistance (WAR) effectively broadened its appeal and increased membership rolls. In fact, the increase in American hate groups in the 1990s was directly related to the use of online recruitment and propaganda (Crilley 2001). Today, all active terrorist groups maintain organizational websites irrespective of their ideological orientation or physical location (Weimann et al. 2008). These groups include, by global region: *Asia*—al-Qaeda, Aum Shinrikyo, the Japanese Red Army (JRA), the Islamic Movement of Uzbekistan, and the Liberation Tigers of Tamil Eelam (LTTE); *Europe*—the Basque ETA movement and Armata Corsa (the Corsican Army); *Latin America*—Shining Path, Colombia National Liberation Army (ELN), and the Armed Revolutionary Forces of Colombia (FARC); *Middle East*—Hamas, Lebanese Hezbollah, the Popular Front for the Liberation of Palestine (PLFP), the Kurdish Workers' Party (PKK), People's Mujahedin of Iran (PMOI), and Mujahedin-e-Khalq.

Many of the above listed groups maintain multiple sites and make them available in different languages. However, the prevalence or exact accounting of online terrorist/extremist sites does not lend itself to traditional empirical research for a variety of reasons. These include technological portability; filter configurations; alternative spellings or designations; absence of translational context; etc. This is true of research on both domestic and international groups. Prevalence notwithstanding, the mechanisms employed and the messages communicated may be evaluated for both content and consistency. Terrorists use the Internet to propagandize their actions and ideologies to recruit new members, justify their actions, and to evoke fear within a specific population.

Similar to their physical counterparts, online terrorist sites construct a rationalization frame through which their aggressive tactics are made palatable to a broad audience. While justifications range from patriotism to divinity, all include the vilification of a particular group, and, all demonstrate adaptability. Such bastardization characterizes the group's actions as self-defensive—a necessary byproduct in their campaign for universal principles and humanity. Thus, the insurgent becomes the purveyor of truth and justice, and the soldier or citizen becomes a representative of the malevolent warmongers. Ironically, these strategies often appeal to the very victims of their terrorist acts. To wit:

> This year, the Nobel Prize Committee in Sweden awarded the Peace Prize to Obama while he was in the White House for less than ten days before the nomination deadline. Ironically, the committee chose him among 205 candidates to win the prize—still less for any concrete accomplishments but for his inspirational words. It is a pity that he will now receive the prize after the announcement of the troop surge for Afghanistan. This year, USA launched vast military operations in Helmand in South Afghanistan. Ten thousand American troops and almost the same number of British troops participated in the operations named Sword and Panther's claws. They killed hundreds of innocent Afghans during the most trumpeted operations, the largest ever after the Vietnam War. As for the Afghans, they did not expect Obama, a Nobel peace prize winner, to flare up the war in the country. Nor would Alfred Nobel ever have agreed to give a peace prize to a person who is fanning the flames

of war rather than spreading fraternity and peace ... It seems, the peace prize winner Obama is trying to implement the expansionist policy left to him as a legacy by W. Bush.

The aim of the Mujahideen is to have a free and independent country and Islamic government which represents the aspirations of the Afghan people ... But the so-called advocates of democracy and human rights are not ready to give these natural rights to the Afghans ... Washington turns down the constructive proposal of the leadership of Mujahideen who ... will ensure that the next government of the Mujahideen will not meddle in the internal affairs of other countries, including the neighbors, if foreign troops pull out of Afghanistan ... Thousands of innocent Afghans have been killed ... the invading Americans have focused ... their conduct ... war seem(s) more like ... a cleansing campaign ... Those with free conscience living anywhere in the world should come forward and defend their shared values of humanity which are being violated by an imperialist power insatiably extending its tentacles over countries of the world.

This statement, issued by the Islamic Emirate of Afghanistan (i.e., the Taliban) and posted on a variety of sites sympathetic to the group, clearly characterizes the United States as an invading army. This statement and those similar in content have been published in a variety of venues, including, but not limited to: official organizational websites (e.g., www.alemarah.info/english); blog spots (e.g., http://al-tawbah.blogspot.com; http://supporttaliban.blogspot.com); media outlets (e.g., www.afghanvoice.com); social networking sites (e.g., www.facebook.com; www.myspace.com); and, community forums (e.g., www.scribd.com).

Statements of justification are often accompanied by visual aids which further the illusion of victimization. Depictions of dead children, destroyed villages, and weeping mothers are used to evoke a collective anger of the populace, an element which is essential to organizational longevity and growth. In April of 2004, anti-American extremists across the world were handed the equivalent of the golden ring when images from Abu Ghraib were aired on an American news program. Within hours, these images were posted on websites across the world. These photos appeared to show the use of torture and humiliation against Arabic prisoners. Without exception, the global community condemned both the soldiers involved and the Bush administration, arguing that such treatment was made more reprehensible due to the country's democratic foundations. While all of the images provided fodder for terrorist organizations across the globe, the images depicting piles of naked detainees and female soldiers with unclothed male inmates were used to demonstrate America's apathy to the cultural values and religious obligations of others. In fact, the photos were used to portray the United States as inherently anti-Middle Eastern and anti-Islamic. Thus, both political and religious terrorist organizations benefitted from the widely available images. Political groups employed the visual aids to further the illusion of victimization, and religious groups used them to solidify their divination as the chosen ones.

As previously stated, propaganda is a necessary component of any terrorist organization for both longevity and growth. The contextual presentation of such information is necessarily related to the intention of the poster. Lines of justification or rationales are more essential for the recruitment and retention of members within political terrorist organizations. Downplaying the harm suffered by innocents and making their rhetoric and propaganda available in multiple languages appeals to many in the global community, and increases the potential for cooperation between multinational individuals. Jihadists, on the other hand, openly embrace and promote human suffering of noncombatants. Depicting themselves not as victims but as martyrs, such organizations glorify violence as divine ordination. Two of al-Qaeda's most visible leaders, Abu Musab al-Zarqawi and Khalid Sheikh Mohammed, successfully used the medium to transmit the videotaped beheadings of contractor, Nick Berg, and journalist, Daniel Pearl (Gunaratna 2004; Heuston 2005). Both of these videos continue to have global implications outside the boundaries of the viewing audience, and continue to be used for recruitment and to induce terror.

The terrorist capital which is expended in the production and promotion of the recorded assassinations of both Americans is relatively insignificant compared to the impact on the global audience. Both films, designed to incite religious fervor among believers, were similarly intended to create terror among those identified as the enemy. This type of propaganda tactic is more effective than traditional methods as both the gruesomeness and the accessibility of the images conjoin to create an environment in which the film eludes containment and the viewing itself becomes irrelevant. Indeed, the psychological and cultural weight afforded these depictions are far greater than those displayed in traditional venues as they intrude upon those self-identified safe zones, such as private homes or areas shared with loved ones (Heuston 2006). Thus, the Internet as a means for inciting fear cannot be overlooked, as it reinforces perceptions of vulnerability through self-propagation.

Videos and creative images have also been employed to enhance recruitment practices. While traditional practices still exist, the introduction of the Internet has enabled terrorists to extend their organizational reach to diverse populations and geographically distant locales. This is especially true as these groups target younger generations. Similar to Metzger's use of music and popular culture in the development of WAR, contemporary jihadists have developed assorted videos which use rap music to communicate extremist ideology. *Dirty Kuffar*, released on the Internet in 2004 by Sheikh Terra and the Soul Salah Crew, was the first widely circulated video of this sort. The video opens with the Title, "Dirty Kuffar Murder Iraqi Civilian," prefacing what appears to be a CNN report of an American soldier bragging about killing an innocent Iraqi citizen. Although the majority of the rap is difficult to understand, clever editing and the superimposition of images clarify the meaning of the film. Various world leaders are vilified, and Vladimir Putin is characterized as George W. Bush's "lapdog." The power of the video cannot be overstated. The flow of images and the relationships inferred clearly justify the use of violence against the infidels. Although jihad is encouraged against assorted nations, including Great Britain and Russia, the video focuses on the killing of Americans, and ends with a listing of countries which they claim have been "Victims of U.S. Violence Since 1945."[2]

Since the release of *Dirty Kuffar*, "djihad" (i.e., digital jihad) has experienced exponential growth. While many of these videos may be viewed or downloaded from official terrorist sites, most have been uploaded to popular video sharing or social networking sites like www.islamicvideos.net, www.youtube.com, www.metacafe.com, www.myspace.com, www.orkut.com, and www.facebook.com. To further broaden their appeal, they are available in multiple languages and cultural contexts. By identifying unique social icons and historical tensions specific to a particular audience, propagandists can effectively target those social groups most predisposed to extremist ideology. A video of the song *By Any Means Necessary*[3] by Sheikh Terra and Soul Salah Crew targets young, black males in the United States. From the onset of the opening credits, it is apparent that the filmmakers wish to incite anger among this population by displaying images of racial hatred in the 1960s superimposed with the atrocities of Abu Graib. Unlike the messages in *Dirty Kuffar*, which include Sheihk Terra dancing with a gun, the presentation of images and the inference of relationships are more subtle. This approach is more palatable to Americans, as it enables them to perceive their actions as defensive and necessary as opposed to aggressive and hostile. Towards this end, the video is prefaced by a portion of Malcolm X's, *Grass Roots Speech*, from 1963:

---

2. Copies of the video may be found on a variety of popular sites like YouTube and GoogleVideos under the title *Dirty Kuffar*.

3. Copies of this video may also be found on YouTube and GoogleVideos under the title *By Any Means Necessary by Sheikh Terra*.

There's nothing in our book the qu'ran, as you call it Koran, that teaches us to suffer peacefully. Our religion teaches us to be intelligent. Be peaceful, be courteous, obey the law, respect everyone, but if someone puts his hand on you, send him to the cemetery. (Malcolm X, the Grass Roots, speech, November 1963, Detroit)

Verbalizations throughout the video remain consistent with the spectre of oppression and marginalization. This medium of communication is successful in the indoctrination of individuals, as it breaks down psychological barriers to involvement (O'Rourke 2007).

Summarily, the Internet is increasingly employed as the medium of choice for terrorist propaganda, information dissemination, and recruitment. As contemporary terrorist groups are increasingly defined by their amorphous or fluid networks, the use of technology provides an ideal environment for the globalization of extremist rhetoric. Logistical and financial impediments are minimized, and propaganda and recruitment strategies can be easily modified to include particularized social icons and cultural boundaries. The explosion of social networking and video sharing sites has further proliferated terrorist propaganda, and all but negated the need for a formal organizational website. This is critical to their continued development as official sites are often hacked or blocked by ISPs at the government's request. For example, Internet Service Providers in the United Kingdom are required to "take down" jihadist sites, so that they are no longer accessible (Goth 2008). While First Amendment considerations preclude such government censorship in the United States, many ISPs in the country voluntarily remove jihadist material.

The Internet as a Medium of Communication

In addition to using the Internet to disseminate propaganda, terrorist organizations are increasingly using the web as a means of communication. Online dialogue is cheaper, international in scope, more widely accessible, and poses far less risk of discovery or interception than traditional methods. In fact, the global interconnectivity of the Internet has proven invaluable to extremists, as was evidenced when al Qaeda members went into hiding in the wake of September 11. As Hamid Mir reported, laptops and Kalashnikovs were among the few possessions that individuals transported as they fled (Britz 2009). Ironically, the Taliban, who have traditionally eschewed such technology, are now embracing it as a means of communication (Giustozzi 2008).

As stated previously, terrorist organizations in the 21st Century have evolved from hierarchical structures to less centralized, cell based networks. This amorphous approach more effectively insulates members from detection and protects the organization as a whole, and is made plausible due to advancements in communication technology and the borderless nature of the Internet. In 2001, Krebs (2001a)[4] used social network metrics to establish that all nineteen of the 9/11 hijackers were within two degrees of two terrorist suspects identified more than a year prior to the attacks. Much of their communications in the final stages of planning were facilitated through online chat rooms.

In the days preceding his capture, Ramzi Binal-Shibh, the alleged 20th hijacker and former roommate of Mohammed Atta, granted an audiotaped interview to *al-Jazeera*. Throughout the interview, Binal-Shibh emphasized the importance of electronic communication and the decentralized nature of al-Qaeda operations. He also revealed contents of online chat between himself and Atta in which Atta communicated (CNN 2002):

> The first semester starts in three weeks. Nothing has changed. Everything is fine. There are good signs and encouraging ideas. Two high schools and two universities. Everything is going according to plan. This summer will surely be hot. I would like to talk to you about a few details. Nineteen certificates for private study and four exams. Regards to the professor. Goodbye.

Discussing the utility of Internet communications, Binal-Shibh recognized the impossibility of monitoring all electronic exchanges and identifying all participants in a cell based conspiracy (CNN 2002). Such weaknesses were further exploited by Younis Tsouli, a Pakistan-based terrorist who employed *Irhaby007* (i.e., Terrorist 007) as a screen name.

Arrested by Scotland Yard in 2007, Tsouli was responsible for the creation of a global virtual support network for terrorists in Bosnia, Denmark, Canada, and, the United States. Towards this end, Tsouli used the terrorist web forum, *Muntada al-Ansar*, to: 1) propagate the terror induced by assorted videotaped beheadings; 2) claim responsibility for assorted attacks; 3) promote the mission and ideologies of al-Qaeda leader Abu Musab al-Zarqawi; 4) provide a secure mechanism for online communication between operatives; and, 5) disseminate training videos. All of these methods were designed to facilitate situational awareness of Islamic extremists across the globe. As a propagandist,

---

4. Kreb's research on social networking may be found on his website, www.orgnet.com. In addition to his analysis on the hijackers of 9/11, Krebs has also used this approach to delineate relationships and networks of a variety of groups, including those in academia, politics, and sports.

recruiter, and webmaster, Tsouli effectively promoted the spread of violent jihad as evidenced by the convictions of two Atlanta men who were originally attracted to the extremist rhetoric in their teens (FBI 2009c). While both men, Ehsanul Sadequee and Syed Harris Ahmed, were arrested prior to the execution of a physical attack, their case illustrates the power of the Internet as a mechanism for computer mediated communication and information exchange. The decentralized, uncensored nature of the medium reaches across geographical boundaries, and is creating a community of radical jihadists within American borders.

In October, 2009, David Headley, a former drug trafficker and government informant, was arrested for conspiring to commit terrorist attacks in Denmark after the publication of cartoons offensive to many Muslims. A subsequent investigation revealed that Headley had used online communications to further the extremism of Lashkar e Tayyiba (LeT), a Kashmiri separatist group, who was responsible for the 2008 Mumbai terror attacks. Towards this end, Headley had conducted extensive surveillance and provided videos of various targeted locations in India, including, the Nariman House, the Taj Mahal hotel, government facilities, public transportation systems, and infrastructure facilities. Prior to his arrest, Headley had communicated his commitment to radical Islam on various open boards, in chat rooms, and electronic exchanges with friends. Such public posting is typically eschewed by operatives responsible for the collection and dissemination of mission-related information as the effectiveness of the proposed operation is necessarily contingent upon the level of secrecy maintained. Indeed, terrorists often employ methods involving electronic dead drops, social networking sites, anonymizer software and sophisticated encryption to hinder detection of their pre-mission activities.

As recently as September, 2009, federal authorities continued to find evidence of the use of electronic dead drops in the furtherance of terrorist acts. On 24 September 2009, the Department of Justice reported that Najibullah Zazi, an American resident, was conspiring with others to detonate explosives in New York City. Towards this end, he had received bomb-making training in Pakistan, conducted extensive research on the Internet, and, purchased components necessary to produce TATP (Triacetone Triperoxide) and other peroxide-based explosives similar to those used to attack London's subway system. He communicated with other conspirators through the use of shared e-mail accounts where he left documents in the "drafts" folder for retrieval by others. This technique, known as *dead dropping*, was also employed by both David Headley and the Madrid bombers. Theoretically, such methods facilitate asynchronous, anonymous communication and defeat electronic sniffers as the e-mails are never transmitted. Instead, co-conspirators use a single account and password to exchange information.[5]

Terrorists further insulate themselves from surveillance and undercover operations through the use of encryption. In fact, ranking al-Qaeda members have been employing this technology for more than sixteen years. For example, Ramzi Yousef, the mastermind behind the 1993 World Trade Center bombings employed encryption, as did the individuals who were responsible for the deaths of eighteen American soldiers in Somalia in the same year. Further examples of encrypted communications include, but are not limited to, the 1998 bombings in Africa and the attack on the U.S.S. Cole (Voors 2003). Such techniques can significantly hamper counter-terrorism efforts (Freeh 2001). As a result, federal authorities have petitioned the prohibition of sophisticated encryption software.[6] However, the practice continues unabated in both e-mail and social networking communications.

As stated, the use of social networking sites as a mechanism for propaganda dissemination has been increasingly recognized by government authorities. However, the utility of this medium reaches far beyond the parameters of recruitment or sensationalization. In fact, popular sites like Yahoo!, MySpace, SecondLife, Orkut, and Facebook provide for the use of invitation-only, online communities. While the majority of the resulting forums do not represent threats to national security, there exists a small minority which includes various groups comprised of terrorist sympathizers (Britz 2009). For example, there were at least ten communities which advocated jihad against the United States (Denning 2009). Additional information available to identified members includes, but is not limited to: videos of terror attack; photos of deceased American soldiers; recruitment solicitations; propaganda materials; and, most importantly in this discussion, secured means of communication.

The use of social networking sites by terrorists cannot be overstated. One of the first notable examples, *Orkut*, was originally established as an invitation-only social network, and was popular among terrorist sympathizers and deviant subcultures. While it is still a favorite in both Brazil and India, searches for "al-Qaeda" and "global jihad" returned thousands of hits on both *MySpace* and *Facebook*. In December, 2009, Howard University dental student Ramy

---

5. Confidential government sources indicate that such practices do not defeat electronic surveillance techniques as data is transmitted from a user (i.e., mbritz@hotmail.com) to a server account (i.e., hotmail) irrespective of transmission to a third party.

6. While the debate between privacy advocates and the federal government continues, it must be noted that encryption is not an effective tool of concealment in cases where electronic surveillance software, such as the FBI's Magic Lantern, is employed.

Zamzam was arrested with four other Americans for suspected terrorist associations. Along with other terror suspects, Zamzam was a member of Facebook, and had used the site to reach out to extremist groups in Pakistan. Such social networking sites provide extremists with a medium to identify and communicate with similarly inclined members. In the wake of his arrest, assorted Facebook groups and YouTube videos were posted which demonstrated their support.

Summarily, the Internet has proven invaluable to contemporary terrorists. Online dialogue is cheaper, international in scope, more widely accessible, and poses far less risk than traditional methods. Like other netizens, radical jihadists increasingly rely on the technology for both social networking and communication. Websites, e-mail, chat rooms, and virtual message boards are all employed to recruit new members, propagandize actions, provide an electronic auditorium for organizational rhetoric, and secure their communications. Recent arrests indicate that utilization of the medium has proven successful in spreading radical jihad within the borders of the United States.

Training, Research, and Facilitation

The globalization of information has revolutionized the manner in which terrorists conduct both training and research. Like their predecessors, contemporary terrorists have demonstrated an ability to adopt training modules appropriate to both the resources available and the current technological landscape. While effective, methods of instruction for most of the 20th Century were largely limited to jihadist encampments, training films, and text manuals. These approaches to training were expensive, and the impact of the subsequent attack was largely localized and small in scope. However, the globalization of communication, commerce, and information has provided an avenue for mass dissemination of rhetoric, propaganda, and instruction.

Just as corporations and organizations with legitimate goals have turned to web-based training to offset corporate downsizing and shrinking budgets, jihadists have maximized their available resources by employing the web and media enhancements to offer online tutorials to geographically distant participants. As such, web-based learning is presented in a variety of formats and languages. In keeping with the media-centric culture of contemporary society, much of this content is available in the form of AVI or MPEG files, however, textual communications, like checklists and outlines, are still available. Terrorist videos or documents cover topics ranging from tactical operations (e.g., bomb making, use of surface-to-air missiles, assembling a suicide vest, etc.) to research (e.g., data mining, public information sites, etc.) to hacking (e.g., social engineering, unauthorized access, Trojans, etc.) to facilitation (e.g., creation of fraudulent identification, transfer of funds, money laundering, etc.). Such materials and information are circulated in the same method as those previously discussed, but the synergy created by the marriage of extremist, social networking, and video sharing websites has created a self-propagating phenomenon.

A solo search of YouTube.com revealed a significant number of videos devoted to: "terrorist training" (n=3,340); "bomb making instructions" (n=743); "bomb making tutorials" (n=3,370); "make explosives" (n=13,600); and, "how to make explosives at home" (n=840). A random viewing of each category reveals an assortment of news reports, spoofs, and, instructional videos. The sheer volume of material presented and the dynamic nature of the medium render empirical analysis impractical. Thus, evaluation of alternative avenues, government actions, and court transcripts is increasingly important. Such sources indicate that the popularity of such searches suggests an unprecedented interest in such material, but that official training videos are most often located on organizational websites. However, the greatest utility of the Internet in terms of training may be found in the information contained on seemingly innocuous sites, such as those that were used by a variety of the individuals previously mentioned. In addition, Mohamed Atta used both flight simulator software and computer games via the Internet to prepare for flight training (Hamilton 2004).

A solo Google search for "how do I make TATP" returned over 25,000 hits from a variety of sites. Of the first ten hits returned, at least four (i.e., globalsecurity.org; en.wikipedia.org; wiki.answers.com; and, askville.amazon.com) of them gave detailed, easy-to-follow instructions. The same search on Bing returns over 17,000 hits. Of the first ten hits returned, three provided the same type of instructions, including two from en.wikipedia.org and one from scribd.com. A subsequent search for "how do I make cyanide" returned over two million hits on Google and 780,000 on Bing. Of the first 10 hits, detailed instructions were found on Google (5) and Bing (2). In addition, two of the first ten hits on Bing provided information on where to buy cyanide. In 2009, federal authorities revealed that Ali al-Marri had been conducting extensive research on the manufacturing of cyanide gas in an al-Qaeda plot to release the gas in dams, waterways, and tunnels in the United States (FBI 2009d). Additional evidence recovered from al-Marri's computer included anonymizer and wiping software programs. Finally, the government uncovered various fraudulent identities and credit card and social security numbers. Al-Marri played a pivotal support role in the Terror Attacks in NYC, and was actively involved in online communications with Khalid Sheikh Mohammed and other al-Qaeda leaders.

In addition to training and research, the Internet has also proven to be a critical component in pre-mission planning and coordination. For example, the al-Qaeda hijackers used the Internet to evaluate flight schedules and purchase at least nine of the plane tickets on 9/11. In December, 2008, Ahmed Ansari, a conspirator in the Mumbai attacks, claimed that he had been shown satellite images of targeted locations, including the Taj Mahal hotel. Downloaded from Google Earth, these images were employed in the attacks that killed more than 160 people. An India High Court is considering whether Google has a responsibility to censor such information. Other countries have also expressed concern, asking the company to blur certain images. A search of Google Earth for satellite images indicated that such information was available without exception and without obfuscation. Additional information provided by the site included: surrounding areas, labels, topical maps, and driving directions. These include, but are not limited to: *Executive Residences*: U.S. White House (U.S.); Camp David (U.S.); 10 Downing Street (Great Britain); Great Kremlin Palace (Russia); The Lodge (Australia); The Vatican. *Government Buildings*: U.S. Pentagon (U.S.); Northwood Headquarters (Great Britain). *Nuclear Facilities*: Paducah Gaseous Diffusion Plant (U.S.); Sandia National Laboratory (U.S.); and Siberian Chemical Combine (Russia).

Terrorist groups also use the Internet to commit criminal activities to further their mission and to supplement the funding they receive from organizational supporters. Identity fraud, money laundering, identity fraud, theft of proprietary data, narcotics trafficking and hacking are a few of the activities employed by jihadists. Identity theft and the creation of fraudulent forms of identification have been noted in all acts of recent terrorist activity directed at the United States. For example, each of the suicide bombers involved in the Terror Attacks had established fraudulent identities. The documentation included, but was not limited to: stolen credit cards, fictitious or temporary addresses, passports; and driver's licenses. Identity theft is beneficial to these organizations in a variety of ways as it may grant them access to protected data, travel to and within a particular geographic location, provides an environment free from government scrutiny. While there are a variety of ways to create fraudulent identification, much of this is done with information received from data mining or computer hacking, both of which are included in training curriculum (Hamilton 2004).

As a Mechanism

Traditionally, the notion that the Internet could be employed as a mechanism through which a terrorist act could be affected was repudiated by both the academic and practitioner communities. Based on the premise that the measure of effectiveness was necessarily contingent upon catastrophic loss of life, a collective rejection effectively chilled any inquiry into the possibility, creating a level of apathy in both communities. It must be noted that such conceptualizations are inherently flawed as they are based on the assumption that *fear* and *vulnerability* are universally constructed. As stated previously, re-actions to performances and events are defined by cultural values and expec-tations. In order to affect social change via a physical or cyber attack, terrorist groups must focus on those elements which define and sustain a given society.

While the Internet has become a conduit to globalize the impact of a geo-graphically distant act, it can be argued that the impact of any given event is affected by both the cultural expectations and the normalcy of the image to the targeted audience. Thus, the inducement of fear in some areas may require a more substantial or extraordinary demonstration of loss than others. For ex-ample, the Sbarro restaurant bombing in Jerusalem[7] and the Beslan massacre,[8] both of which occurred in areas accustomed to terrorist incidents, were con-sidered significant by observers primarily due to the selection of targets tradi-tionally deemed off limits. In Jerusalem, the bombing occurred at a popular intersection where teenagers and families were known to congregate. In Beslan, the seizing of School Number One was particularly significant as it occurred on First September, a day of great celebration where families accompanied their children to school. Both incidents resulted in immediate government ac-tions. In Jerusalem, Israeli authorities forced the closure of the PLO's east Jerusalem headquarters. In Russia, government reforms included the consol-idation of power within the Kremlin. The swift reaction of both governments is similar to that of federal authorities in the United States. In each case, it can be argued that the reaction of formal government structures demonstrates the abnormality of the terrorist act.

Founded on capitalist principals, there are critical complex networks which both define and sustain the United States. These include: financial markets, commerce and capitalism, transportation, and communications. The selec-tion of targets on 9/11 was based on knowledge of American culture, and was both deliberate and methodical. The attacks on the World Trade Center were a deliberate attempt to strike at the foundation of the country. Targeting the

---

7. Additional information regarding the Sbarro bombing and resulting government ac-tions may be located at the Israel Ministry of Foreign Affairs, http://www.mfa.gov.il/MFA/MFAArchive/2000_2009/2000/10/Suicide+bombing+at+the+Sbarro+pizzeria+in+Jerusale.htm.

8. For additional information on the Beslam massacre, see (Giduck 2005).

Pentagon and the White House, al-Qaeda attempted to display the vulnerability of both our government and our military. It can be argued that the group chose unwisely due to their superficial understanding of American culture. The symbolism of their targets was not entirely understood or appreciated by the intended audience. In addition, the existence of alternate facilities for data, information, and computer equipment minimized the damage to financial markets, and the physical security of future targets has been improved.

While the attacks of 9/11 were not successful in creating and maintaining perceptions of vulnerability, it is possible that a major disruption of the financial market or a significant threat to quality of life could create a sense of unrest or fear within a capitalist population. Such occurrences could be predicated on a compromise of digital systems in two areas: physical infrastructure and critical data. Digital threats to the physical infrastructure would be those that involve systems essential to physical infrastructures. These would include: power grids; water and sewer systems; dams; hospitals; communications; GPS; air traffic systems; etc. Critical data threats would be those that involved the compromise of critical databases including, but not limited to: Social Security; Centers for Disease Control; Department of Defense, etc. (Britz 2009). In fact, the tight coupling and feedback loops which characterize the architecture of the Internet result in an unsound and unsecure infrastructure. While projections that the Internet will replace traditional physical attacks have not been realized, recent events across the globe suggest that concentrated and/or protracted cyberattacks may result in significant disruptions to communication and financial networks.

In April of 2007, websites across Estonia were crippled as a result of a coordinated distributed denial of service (DDOS) attack. The attack, sparked by the relocation of a Soviet-era war memorial, was largely directed at government and financial sites. Although initial speculation blamed the Russian government for the attacks, there is no evidence to substantiate such claims. In fact, it appears more likely that a loosely structured cyber mob facilitated the attacks by following instructions posted in the Russian blogosphere (Vijayan 2007). In a country that is 97 percent dependent on Internet banking, the unsophisticated attacks were extremely effective, and were a clear indication that concentrated attacks on government and banking sites could be used to substantially disrupt a targeted population (Espiner 2008). Such strategies are similar to those historically employed by Zapatista supporters, like the Electronic Disturbance Theater, who have effectively shut down government sites through electronic "sit-ins." While social and economic impacts in such cases are not often articulated, such actions may result in elevated perceptions of vulnerability and millions of dollars of profitability (Ronfeldt and Martinez 1997).

Conclusions

Historically, the conceptualization of *terrorism* by both ideologues and observers necessitated physical displays of catastrophic destruction. Firmly rooted in the belief that evidence of damage to physical structures and the loss of human life were intrinsically related to the measure of operational effectiveness, discussions of and reactions to ideologically and/or politically motivated attacks have almost exclusively concentrated on the corporeal vulnerability of potential targets. While it must be noted that the protection of physical infrastructures remain of paramount importance, government authorities and academics alike must recognize the potential of the Internet in the furtherance of political, religious, or ideological extremism. Such implications for web utilization include, but are not limited to: medium of communication; dissemination of information; propagandizing of ideology; platform for recruitment; environment for fundraising; and, mechanism of both cyber and physical attacks. As such, *cyberterrorism* should be defined as the premeditated, methodological, ideologically motivated dissemination of information, facilitation of communication, or, attack against physical targets, digital information, computer systems, and/or computer programs which is intended to cause social, financial, physical, or psychological harm to noncombatant targets and audiences for the purpose of affecting ideological, political, or social change; or any utilization of digital communication or information which facilitates such actions directly or indirectly.

While the portended *digital apocalypse* has not been witnessed, evidence suggests that terrorist organizations are increasingly utilizing web-based technology to communicate, plan, propagandize, recruit, and finance their operations. Unfortunately, traditional definitions of the phenomenon, relying exclusively on the web as a mechanism, obfuscated these activities. As a result, both private and public awareness of the potential of web facilitation must be reconsidered. Policymakers must develop legislation that addresses all of these areas, and specifically recognizes the globalization of financial and communications systems. It is anticipated that such recognition will result in significant modifications to investigative strategies and prosecutions. Opportunities for academic inquiry are boundless, and will continue to grow in pace with technology. Some possible areas include: the evolution of organizational ideology and social framing of online rhetoric; level of indoctrination and/or individual commitment of online recruits; the nature and growth of grassroots organizations; operational effectiveness of netcentric versus physical cells; and, the architecture of terror via social networking analysis.

References

Ahituv, Niv. 2008. Old Threats, New Channels: the Internet as a tool for terrorists" NATO Workshop, Berlin.

Altheide, David L. 2006. Terrorism and the politics of fear. *Cultural Studies and Critical Methodologies* 6: 415–439.

Anti-Defamation League (ADL). 2000. Jihad Online: Islamic terrorists and the Internet. (August 20, 2008), www.adl.org/internet.jihad_online.pdf.

Banita, Georgiana. 2008. Decency, torture, and the words that tell us nothing. *Peace Review* 20(1): 58–66.

Bardis, Panos D. 2008. "Violence: Theory and Quantification." In *Political Readings in Research and Theory*, eds. George A. Kourvetaris and Betty A. Dobratz, 221–244. Amsterdam, New Holland: Transaction Books.

Bergen, Peter. 2006. *The Osama bin Laden I know: An oral history of al Qaeda's leader.* New York: Free Press.

Bowman, M.E. 1995. Is International Law Ready for the Information Age? *Fordham International Law Journal* 19: 1935.

Britz, Marjie T. 2009. *Computer Forensics and Cybercrime* (2nd edition). New Jersey: Prentice-Hall.

Britz, Marjie T. 2008. A new paradigm of organized crime in the United States: Criminal syndicates, cyber-gangs, and the worldwide web. *Sociology Focus* 2: 1750–1765.

Bunt, Gary. 2003. *Islam in the Digital Age: E-jihad, online fatwas and cyber Islamic environments.* London: Pluto Books.

Chiricos, Ted, Sarah Escholz, and Marc Gertz. 1997. Crime, news and fear of crime: Toward an identification of audience effects. *Social Problems* 44: 342–357.

Collin, Barry. 1997. Future of cyberterrorism: The physical and virtual worlds converge. *Crime and Justice International* 13: 15–18.

CNN. 2002. "Al-Jazeera offers accounts of 9/11 planning." (September 12, 2002), http://archives.cnn.com/2002/WORLD/meast/09/12/alqaeda.911.claim/index.html.

Crilley, Kathy. 2001. Information warfare: New battlefields, terrorists, propaganda and the Internet. *Aslib Proceedings: New Information Proceedings* 53: 250–264.

Denning, Dorothy E. 2000. *Cyberterrorism.* Testimony before the Special Oversight Panel on Terrorism Committee on Armed Services U.S. House of Representatives, May 23, 2000. (November 19, 2009), http://www.cs.george town.edu/~denning/infosec/cyberterror.html.

Denning, Dorothy E. 2009. "Terror's web: How the Internet is transforming terrorism." In *Handbook on Internet Crime*, eds., 194–213. Portland OR: Willan Publishing.

Denning, Dorothy E. 2003. "Information technology and security." In *Grave New World: Security challenges in the Twenty-First Century*, ed., Michael E. Brown, 91–112. Washington, D.C.: Georgetown University Press.

Espiner, Tom. 2008. "How Estonia's attacks shook the world." *ZDNet Australia.* (December 30, 2009), http://www.zdnet.com.au/insight/security/soa/How-Estonia-s-attacks-shook-the-world/0,139023764,339288625,00.htm.

Espiner, Tom. 2008. "Cyberattack caused multiple-city power failure." *ZDNet Australia.* (January 22, 2008), http://www.zdnet.com.au/news/security/soa/Cyberattack-caused-multiple-city-power-failure/0,130061744,339285286,00.htm.

Federal Bureau of Investigation. 2009a. "Najibullah Zazi indicted for conspiracy to use explosives against person or property in the United States." *Department of Justice Press Release.* (September 24, 2009), http://newyork.fbi.gov/dojpressrel/pressrel09/nyfo092409.htm.

Federal Bureau of Investigation. 2009b. "Two men charged in connection with alleged roles in foreign terror plot that focused on targets in Denmark." *Department of Justice Press Release*, (October 27, 2009), http://chicago.fbi.gov/dojpressrel/pressrel09/cg102709.htm.

Federal Bureau of Investigation. 2009c. "The path to terror: The jihadists of Georgia," *Department of Justice Headline Archives.* (December 15, 2009), http://www.fbi.gov/page2/dec09/jihadists_121509.html.

Federal Bureau of Investigation. 2009d. "Ali Al-Marri pleads guilty to conspiracy to provide material support to al Qaeda," *Department of Justice Press Release.* (April 30, 2009), http://www.justice.gov/opa/pr/2009/April/09-nsd-415.html.

Fellman, Philip Vos and Roxana Wright. 2003. Modeling Terrorist Networks: Complex systems at the mid-range. Paper presented at the Joint Complexity Conference, September 16–18, in London, England.

Foltz, C. Bryan. 2004. Cyberterrorism, computer crime, and reality. Information Management & Computer Security 12: 154–166.

Freeh, Louis J. 2001. Testimony of Louis J. Freeh, Director, FBI, Before the United States Senate, Committees on Appropriations, Armed Services, and Select Committee on Intelligence. *Threat of Terrorism to the United States*, Washington, D.C., United States, May 10, 2001.

Gable, Kelly. 2009. "Cyber-apocalypse now: Securing the Internet against cyberterrorism and using universal jurisdiction as a deterrent." (August 14, 2009), http://ssrn.com/abstract=1452803.

Ganor, Boaz. 2002. Defining terrorism: Is one man's terrorist another man's freedom fighter? *Police Practice and Research* 3: 287–304.

Garrison, Arthur H. 2003. Terrorism: The nature of its history. *Criminal Justice Studies* 16: 39–52.

Giacomello, Giampiero. 2004. Bangs for the buck: A cost-benefit analysis of cyberterrorism. *Studies in Conflict and Terrorism* 27: 387–408.

Giduck, John. 2005. *Terror at Beslan: A Russian tragedy with lessons for America's schools.* USA: Archangel Press.

Giroux, Henry A. 2006. *Beyond the Spectacle of Terrorism: Global uncertainty and the challenge of the new media.* New York: Paradigm Publishers.

Giustozzi, Antonio. 2008. *Koran, Kalashnikov and Laptop: The neo-Taliban insurgency in Afghanistan.* New York: Columbia University Press.

Goth, Greg. 2008. Terror on the Internet: A complex issue, and getting harder. *IEEE Distributed Systems Online* 9: 3.

Grennan, Sean, and Marjie T. Britz. 2005. *Organized Crime: A worldwide perspective.* New Jersey: Prentice-Hall.

Gunaratna, Rohan. 2004. "Abu Musab Al Zarqawi: A new generation terrorist leader," *IDSS Commentaries.* (September 15, 2006), http://dr.ntu.edu.sg/bitstream/handle/10220/4048/RSIS-COMMENT_212.pdf?sequence=1.

Heuston, Sean. 2005. Weapons of mass instruction: Terrorism, propaganda film, politics, and us. *Studies in Popular Culture* 27: 59–73.

Hoffman, Bruce. 2003. Al Qaeda, trends in terrorism, and future potentialities: An assessment. *Studies in Conflict and Terrorism* 26: 429–442.

Hoffman, Bruce. 2002. Rethinking terrorism and counterterrorism since 9/11. *Studies in Conflict and Terrorism* 25: 301–316.

Ito, Harumi, and Darin Lee. 2005. Assessing the impact of the September 11 terrorist attacks on U.S. airline demand. *Journal of Economics and Business* 51: 75–95.

Kaplan, Eben. 2009. Terrorists and the Internet. Council on Foreign Relations. (December 12, 2009). http://www.cfr.org/publication/10005.

Kohlman, Evan. 2006. Expert report on the ~AQCORPO website. Global Terror Alert. (August 20, 2006). http://nefafoundation.org/miscellaneous/FeaturedDocs/ekirhaby0108.pdf.

Krebs, Valdis. 2001a. Connecting the dots: Tracking two identified terrorists. (September 21, 2009), http://www.orgnet.com/tnet.html.

Krebs, Valdis. 2001b. Uncloaking terrorist networks. First Monday. (September 20, 2008), http://www.orgnet.com/hijackers.html.

Lewis, James. 2003. Cyber terror: Missing in action. *Knowledge, Technology & Policy* 16: 34–41.

Loza, Wagdy. 2007. The psychology of extremism and terrorism: A Middle-Eastern perspective. *Aggression and Violent Behavior* 12: 141–155.

Lynch, Marc. 2006. *Al-Qaeda's media strategies.* (March 17, 2006), http://ics.leeds. ac.uk/papers/vp01.cfm?outfit=pmt&folder=1087&paper=2662.

Madsen, Wayne. 1998. Critical Infrastructure Protection Gathering at the Supreme Court. *Computer Fraud and Security* 9: 12–15.

Merari, Ariel. 1993. Terrorism as a strategy of insurgency. *Terrorism and Political Violence* 5: 213–251.

Montalbano, Elizabeth. 2009. "Social networks link terrorists: A new breed of cyberterrorists are using online forums to recruit people who support Al-Qaeda, creating global networks of would-be terrorists," *PCWorld.* (1 August 2009), http://www.pcworld.idg.com.au/article/272364/social_networks_ link_terrorists.

Nacos, B. L. 2003. The terrorist calculus behind 9-11: A model for future terrorism? *Studies in Conflict and Terrorism* 26: 1–16.

Hamilton, Lee. 2004. *The 9/11 Commission Report: Final report of the National Commission on Terrorist Attacks upon the United States.* Washington, D.C.: National Commission on Terrorist Attacks upon the United States.

NEFA Foundation. 2009. *Taliban: "Obama, following in Bush's step."* Statement of the Islamic Emirate of Afghanistan. (December 8, 2009), http://www.nefa foundation.org/miscellaneous/nefaTaliObamaBush1209.pdf.

O'Rourke, Simon. 2007. Virtual radicalization: Challenges for police. *Proceedings of the 8th Australian Information Warfare and Security Conference*: 29–35.

Pollitt, Mark M. 1998. Cyberterrorism—fact or fancy? *Computer Fraud & Security* 2: 8–10.

Power, Richard. 2000. *Tangled Web: Tales of digital crime from the shadows of cyberspace.* Indianapolis, Indiana: Que.

Reid, Edna F. 1997. Evolution of a body of knowledge: An analysis of terrorism research. *Information Processing and Management* 33: 91–106.

Reid, Edna F. and Hsinchun Chen. 2006. Mapping the contemporary terrorism research domain. *International Journal of Human-Computer Studies* 65: 42–56.

Rice, Stephen K. 2009. Emotions and terrorism research: A case for a social-psychological agenda. *Journal of Criminal Justice* 37: 248–255.

Ronfeldt, David and Armando Martinez. 1997. "A comment on the Zapatista 'Netwar.'" In *In Athena's Camp: Preparing for Conflict in the Information Age,* eds. John Arquilla and David Ronfeldt, 369–391. California: RAND Corporation.

Ruby, Charles S. 2002. The definition of terrorism. *Analyses of Social Issues and Public Policy*: 9–14.

Saul, Ben. 2005. Attempts to define 'terrorism' in international law. *Netherlands International Law Review* L II: 57–83.

Schmid, Alex P. and Albert J. Jongman. 1988. *Political Terrorism*. Amsterdam, Holland; Transaction Books.

Sheffer, Matthew J. 2006. *Awareness through agility: Teenagers as a model for terrorist development of situational awareness.* (April 20, 2009), http://www.dtic.mil/cgibin/GetTRDoc?AD=ADA474177&Location=U2&doc =GetTRDoc.pdf.

Shelley, Louise I., and John T. Picarelli. 2002. Methods not motives: implications of the convergence of international organized crime and terrorism. *Police Practice and Research 3*: 305–318.

Stohl, Michael. 2008. Old myths, new fantasies and the enduring realities of terrorism. *Critical Studies on Terrorism* 1: 5–16.

Stohl, Michael. 2006. Cyberterrorism: A clear and present danger, the sum of all fears, breaking point or patriot games. *Crime, Law & Social Change* 46: 223–238.

Tsafati, Yariv, and Gabriel Weimann. 2002. Www.terrorism.com: Terror on the internet. *Studies in Conflict and Terrorism* 25: 317–322.

Turk, Robert J. 2005. *Cyber Incidents involving control systems.* INL/EXT-05-00671: Idaho National Laboratory for the U.S. Department of Homeland Security, contract DE-AC07-05ID14517.

U.S. v. Zazi, Memorandum of Law in Support of the Government's Motion for a Permanent Order of Detention, 09-CR-00663, (RJD, 2009).

Vijayan, Jaikumar. 2007. Hackers evaluate Estonia attacks. *PC World.*

Voors, Matthew Parker. 2003. Encryption regulation in the wake of September 11, 2001: Must we protect national security at the expense of the economy? *Federal Communications Law Journal* 55: 331–352.

Washington, Douglas Waller. 1995. Onward Cyber Soldiers. *Time Magazine* 146: 8 (April 21, 2005), http://www.csm.ornl.gov/~dunigan/timemag.html.

Weimann, Gabriel, 2005. Cyberterrorism: The sum of all fears? *Studies in Conflict and Terrorism* 28: 129–149.

Weimann, Gabriel and Katharina Von Knop. 2009. Applying the notion of noise to countering online terrorism. *Studies in Conflict and Terrorism* 23: 883–902.

Wilkinson, Paul. 1997. The media and terrorism: A reassessment. *Terrorism and Political Violence* 9, 2: 51–64.

X, Malcolm. 1969. *Malcolm X Speaks: Selected Speeches and Statements.* Chicago: Grove/ Atlantic.

Zulaika, Joseba and William A. Douglass. 1996. *Terror and Taboo: The Follies, Fables, and Faces of Terrorism.* New York: Routledge.

9

Examining State and Local Law Enforcement Perceptions of Computer Crime

Thomas J. Holt, Adam M. Bossler, and Sarah Fitzgerald

The impact of computer-mediated communications and the Internet on all facets of human life has been well documented across the social sciences (Jewkes and Sharp 2003; Mann and Sutton 1998; Quinn and Forsyth 2005). Not only have these technologies changed the way that business and personal communications take place, but they have radically altered the capacity of offenders to engage in a variety of crimes (see Brenner 2008; McQuade 2006; Wall 2007). Electronic communications and the Internet have augmented or facilitated most forms of illegal behavior, including prostitution (Holt and Blevins 2007; Sharpe and Earle 2003; Soothhill and Sanders 2005), pedophilia (Durkin 1997; Durkin and Bryant 1999; Holt, Blevins, and Burkert 2010; Quayle and Taylor 2002), fraud (Burns, Whitworth, & Thompson, 2004; Holt and Graves 2007; Holt and Lampke 2010; Newman and Clarke 2003) and piracy (see Higgins 2005; Higgins, Fell, and Wilson 2007; Hinduja 2001, 2003).

The economic impact of computer crimes is also substantial, affecting individuals and corporations alike. Businesses reported average losses of $500,000 in 2008 due to financial fraud incidents (Computer Security Institute 2008), while individual consumers lost an average of $575 to various types of fraud in 2009 (Internet Crime Complaint Center 2010). The music and movie industries also claim to have lost billions due to intellectual property theft and digital piracy (Higgins 2005; Higgins et al. 2007; Hinduja 2001, 2003; Motion Picture Association of America 2007). Furthermore, there are significant emotional and psychological consequences for victims of cyberstalking (Finn 2004; Holt and Bossler 2009) and children affected by pornography and pedophilia (see Berson 2003; Durkin and Bryant 1999).

In addition, computer-based terror attacks against all manner of targets have become an increasingly important issue for local law enforcement agencies across the nation (Aeilts 2005; Brenner 2008; Stambaugh et al. 2001). Many key resources in the public and private sector are linked to and depend on computer technology to function, including electrical grids, nuclear power plants, water, and financial systems (Aeilts 2005; Denning 2001; Taylor, Fritsch, Liederbach, and Holt 2010). As a consequence, local law enforcement agencies must recognize and collaborate with private sector partners to protect and secure threats to critical infrastructure (see Brenner 2008; Taylor et al. 2010). Thus, law enforcement must be prepared to investigate a diverse range of offenses and offenders.

There is, however, a significant gap in our knowledge of law enforcement agencies' awareness, preparation, and attitudes toward computer crimes. Statistics on computer crimes are rarely collected by law enforcement agencies or reported in outlets such as the Uniform Crime Report or National Crime Victimization Survey. There are several reasons for this lack of data, including victim confusion over appropriate reporting agencies, concern that the incident is not important enough to report, and victims' inabilities to recognize when crimes have occurred (see Holt 2003; Speer 2000). This lack of statistical information makes it is difficult to estimate the true prevalence of computer crimes and how local law enforcement has or can respond to it. The lack of data at the local level is particularly significant, as these law enforcement agencies serve as primary first responders at all crime scenes, and their knowledge and ability to properly initiate an investigation has a significant impact on the way that cases are handled and investigated (see Burns et al. 2004; Goodman 1997; Hinduja 2004; McQuade 2006; Senjo 2004; Stambaugh et al. 2001). Thus, it is critical that researchers consider local agencies' attitudes toward the severity, frequency, and importance of computer crime offenses in order to assess training and resource needs, as well as their overall ability to properly investigate these offenses (see Burns et al. 2004; Hinduja 2004; McQuade 2006; Senjo 2004; Stambaugh et al. 2001).

This study seeks to fill this gap in our knowledge in two ways. First, we use data collected from a sample of state and local law enforcement officers and agents to understand their departments' and agencies' staffing and training for computer crime investigations and the handling of digital evidence. Second, we consider their perceptions of computer crime, their severity relative to street crimes, and knowledge of basic technology terms. The findings give insight into the preparedness of state and local police agencies to handle computer crime and the ways that their attitudes toward these offenses may affect investigations and officer behavior. The implications of this research for policy and future investigation are also considered.

Policing Computer Crime

There have been relatively few studies documenting the capacity for state and local law enforcement to properly investigate computer crime. One of the main studies considering police responses to computer crime is the Electronic Crime Needs Assessment for State and Local Law Enforcement report, published by the National Institute of Justice, which utilized data collected from a sample of 126 individuals from 114 agencies in 1998 (Stambaugh et al. 2001). Before conducting this study, the researchers recognized the complex issues surrounding the measurement of computer-based offenses and the lack of a universal definition for computer crime. Thus, they worked in collaboration with state and local agencies to develop a definition of "electronic crime" that refers to:

> fraud, theft, forgery, child pornography or exploitation, stalking, traditional white-collar crimes, privacy violations, illegal drug transactions, espionage, computer intrusions, or any other offenses that occur in an electronic environment for the purpose of economic gain or with the intent to destroy or otherwise inflict harm on another person or institution (Stambaugh et al. 2001, 2).

A similarly broad definition of cyberterrorism was developed, recognizing any "premeditated, politically motivated attack against information systems, computer programs and data … to disrupt the political, social, or physical infrastructure of the target" (Stambaugh et al. 2001, 2). The wide range of offenses included in these definitions was meant to provide a frame of reference for respondents and some standard to assess computer-based crime.

Using these definitions, Stambaugh et al. (2001) found a significant increase in computer crimes reported to law enforcement. At the same time, the respondents suggested that a substantial proportion of offenses were not being reported to law enforcement. Computer crime cases were given low priority across most agencies, unless they were child pornography or pedophile cases. This may have been a consequence of unsuccessful prosecutions, as many agencies felt that management, officers, and prosecutors appeared to have little knowledge and resources to adequately carry out computer crime investigations and prosecutions. Furthermore, respondents indicated the need for assistance with tools and training to better investigate these crimes. In fact, only half of all agencies had a formal electronic crime unit, and less than one third belonged to an interagency crime task force (Stambaugh et al. 2001).

Based on these findings, Stambaugh et al. (2001) identified ten critical needs to improve the capability of local and state law enforcement agencies to combat computer crimes. Specifically, these needs included (Stambaugh et al. 2001, 31–36).

1) **Public Awareness:** The public and private sectors needed to be better educated on the growing threat of computer crimes to decrease the likelihood of victimization.

2) **Data and Reporting:** Statistics and data collection on computer crime were needed to better understand computer crime prevalence and trends.

3) **Uniform training and certification courses:** Justice system actors, including prosecutors and judges, needed better training and certifications to effectively deal with computer crimes at all levels of the system.

4) **Onsite management assistance for electronic crime units and task forces:** State and local law enforcement agencies needed to develop computer crime units, as well as collaborative task forces, to better investigate computer crime cases.

5) **Updated laws:** Continuously updated legislation against computer crimes was needed to effectively prosecute cutting edge criminal acts and those crimes that cross jurisdictional boundaries.

6) **Cooperation with the high-tech industry:** The need for greater collaboration and communication with private industry was needed to increase reports of criminal incidents and improve high-tech crime training for law enforcement.

7) **Special research and publications:** A guidebook with information on training and investigative resources was needed to improve communications between investigators, forensic experts, management, and practitioners to deal with computer crime.

8) **Management awareness and support:** Law enforcement management and administrators needed to recognize the severity of computer crime and better support the investigation of these offenses.

9) **Investigative and forensic tools:** Better technological resources were needed to improve the investigation of computer crime cases, including budget conscious equipment to engender forensic examinations.

10) **Structuring a computer crime unit:** Research was needed to explore the needs and staffing issues present in the development of computer crime and forensic investigation units to create a best practices guide for law enforcement agencies.

Although a number of years have passed since the publication of the Electronic Crime Needs Assessment study (Stambaugh et al. 2001), there has been no systematic exploration of the impact of its policy recommendations or the general awareness of computer crime in local police agencies. A limited number of studies have examined the preparedness of law enforcement to examine specific forms of cybercrime, such as fraud (Burns et al. 2004), or cybercrime in specific areas (Hinduja, 2004; Senjo, 2004).

Burns et al. (2004) assessed the preparedness of law local enforcement to investigate Internet fraud. They found that most of the individuals responsible for filling out the survey believed online fraud was a serious problem (76.5 percent), but that law enforcement agencies in general did not consider Internet fraud to be a significant societal problem (41.0 percent). Most of them did not believe that they had sufficient funds to address Internet fraud (only 15.3 percent believed they had the necessary resources). Almost half of the agencies did not even have a computer crime division (46.7 percent). In fact, they would prefer Internet fraud laws to be enforced by federal (93.0 percent) or state law enforcement (69.7 percent) rather than local law enforcement (52.1 percent).

Hinduja (2004) considered the needs and preparedness of local law enforcement agencies in Michigan to deal with computer crimes. His study found that approximately twenty percent of the agencies (n=275) reported that they had one or more individuals trained to investigate these cases. Most agencies (66 percent), however, investigated less than ten computer crime cases in the year 2000. Of the computer crimes reported, harassment was the most common offense, followed by child pornography, solicitation of minors, identity theft, e-commerce fraud, and forgery. Thirty-six percent, however, reported that computer crimes detract attention from traditional crimes (Hinduja 2004).

The findings from Hinduja's (2004) research suggest that there is a need for greater preparation among law enforcement agencies to deal with computer crime, especially since some officers perceive computer crime cases to be insignificant. There has been little empirical research on police officer perspectives regarding the severity of computer crime: whether they think it is fundamentally different from "traditional" crime; the ways that law enforcement agencies have changed in response; and what they think should be done about these offenses. Senjo (2004) conducted one of the few studies examining line officers' perceptions of computer crime. In his sample of officers in a Western state, he found that officers, particularly younger officers with less experience, viewed pedophilia as the most serious computer crime that is occurring (Senjo 2004). Furthermore, officers believed computer criminals to be older males rather than young offenders. The reported officer perspectives were somewhat inconsistent with the larger empirical literature on computer crime, suggesting that there may be a gap in law enforcement knowledge of computer crime (Senjo 2004).

Taken as a whole, there is a critical need for greater research on local law enforcement awareness and training to deal with computer crimes. Few researchers have considered how the significant needs identified by the Electronic Crime Needs Assessment study (Stambaugh et al. 2001) have been met or improved on in local law enforcement agencies. Considering that the primary responsibility of investigating new types of crime falls on local law enforcement, it is critical that we understand how prepared first responders are to deal with computer crime and their attitudes toward the severity, frequency, and importance of these offenses. Such information can provide key policy recommendations to improve the training and resources available for local law enforcement agencies and increase the capability of first responders to appropriately handle computer crime cases.

Data

The data for this study were collected through an electronic survey solicitation administered by the Federal Law Enforcement Training Center (FLETC). This solicitation was delivered via email to approximately ten thousand individuals in state and local law enforcement agencies across the country who attended training classes related to computer crime and digital forensic examination. The solicitation provided a detailed introduction to the study, the relationship between the researchers and FLETC, and included a hyperlink to the online survey instrument. This process solicited 437 responses, less than five percent of the overall total of solicitations. Despite utilizing multiple measures to validate and encourage participation, the low response rate may have been a consequence of limited availability on the part of the responding officers. Alternatively, the respondents may have had some concerns over providing information on behalf of their agency on issues of training and caseloads. Although only 370 responses are needed to generalize to a solicitation of 10,000 (Krejcie and Morgan 1970), the volunteer bias precludes strong conclusions and does limit overall generalizability. Given the paucity of research in this area (see Hinduja 2004; Senjo 2004; Stambaugh et al. 2001), however, this sample provided a needed exploratory investigation into the capacity of state and local agencies to deal with computer crime.

Findings

Respondents were asked a battery of questions concerning their agency, computer crime investigations, and perceptions of computer crime offenders and activity. The survey instrument utilized measures adapted from multiple

Table 9.1 Size and Geographic Location of Law Enforcement Agencies

Region	Less Than 20	20 to 100	101 to 200	201 to 500	501 to 1000	1001 to 5000	More Than 5000	Total
Midwest	48	39	6	4	1	4	0	102
South	36	51	11	12	2	6	0	118
Pacific	15	10	7	1	2	2	1	38
Northeast	27	20	7	9	1	4	3	71
Mountain	11	14	3	1	0	0	0	29
Total	137	134	34	27	6	16	4	358

studies related to computer crime awareness in police agencies (see Goodman 1997; Hinduja 2004; Senjo 2004) and the general public (Furnell 2002). Each item will be explored and discussed in detail, starting with basic descriptive characteristics of the sample.

Demographic Composition

Basic descriptive information about the agency the respondent worked for was collected in lieu of demographic information from the respondent to maintain anonymity. In terms of agency size, 75.7 percent of the agencies had one hundred or less police officers serving in their agency (see Table 9.1). This is in fact under-representing smaller agencies as 93.9 percent of agencies have ninety-nine officers or fewer (BJS 2007). Thus, our sample consists of a higher percentage of larger agencies, which are more likely to have computer crime units and address computer crime, than is found in American policing. The geographic location of agencies was also collected using five bounded regions: the Midwest, South, Pacific, Northeast, and Mountain. Of the agencies surveyed, 28.5 percent indicated being in the Midwest, 33 percent in the South, 10.6 percent in the Pacific, 19.8 percent in the Northeast, and 8.1 percent in the Mountain region (see Table 9.1).

Data on the number of individuals residing within the agency's geographic boundaries were also collected. Eleven percent of the agencies reported having one million or more individuals residing in their jurisdiction. Twenty-seven percent of the agencies had 5,001 to 20,000 citizens and twenty-two percent had five thousand or fewer individuals residing within their jurisdictional boundaries.

In order to understand the extent to which officers within departments handle computer-related crime issues, respondents were asked how many part-time officers or investigators they had within their agencies who were assigned to handle digital evidence. Results indicate that 76 percent of agencies had no part-time officers or investigators assigned to deal with digital evidence. Of those agencies with part-time personnel, the largest reported category (17.1 percent) was three to seven officers total. There were more agencies reporting full-time digital evidence handlers, as 44.7 percent had between one and four investigators. This is a significant improvement over previous research indicating that there have been some changes to increase law enforcement staffing for computer crime (see Goodman 1997; Hindjua 2004). It is important to note, however, that 23 percent of all agencies indicated that they had no part or full-time officers who could properly work with digital evidence. Thus, there are still some staffing issues concerning digital evidence at the state and local level.

Additionally, respondents were asked to assess the number of part-time and full-time officers assigned to the investigation of online crimes. This term was used in lieu of computer crime to assess any and all investigations that take place via the Internet. The overwhelming majority of departments (83.6%) had no part-time officers assigned to these investigations. This may be a function of the expense and manpower needed, making it more difficult to staff such roles with part-time investigators. Overall, 46 percent reported having between one to three full-time officers assigned to online crimes. At the same time, it is important to note that 38.7 percent of all responding agencies had no part or full-time officers trained to investigate online crime. This is a sizeable proportion, suggesting that there is still a need to increase the staff to support computer crime investigations in state and local agencies.

Respondents were also asked to estimate the percentage of officers within their agency that had received various training related to computer crime. Specifically, respondents were asked what percentage of their officers had been trained in handling digital evidence. Of those surveyed, 79.3 percent indicated that 20 percent or less of their officers had been trained in the handling of digital evidence (see Table 9.2). In terms of officers trained in investigating online crimes, the majority (88.1 percent) of agencies indicated that 20 percent or less of their officers had received such training. In terms of the percent of officers within each agency that had been trained in the handling of digital evidence, the Midwest had the greatest percentage, with nine agencies within this region indicating that 100 percent of their officers are trained in handling digital evidence. This finding is in keeping with previous research (e.g., Hinduja 2004) and suggests that there are slight improvements taking place to change the investigative power of state and local agencies to deal with computer crime.

Table 9.2 The Percentage of Officers Trained for
Digital Evidence and Computer Crime

Percentage of Officers	Digital Evidence (n-354)	Online Crime (n-345)
10	70.3	81.2
20	9.0	6.9
30–40	5.9	6.4
50–60	5.0	2.9
70–90	4.2	0.9
100	5.6	1.7

Investigations

Respondents were asked to indicate whether or not their agency actively investigated various forms of economic, sexual, and hacking-related computer crimes (see Table 9.3 for detail). The most common type of investigation conducted involved identity theft (79.2 percent), followed by fraud (71.9 percent) and online harassment (71.8 percent) (see Hinduja 2004 for similar finding on harassment). This is a distinct shift from previously identified investigative priorities, as sex offenses appeared to be the dominant crime reported to state and local agencies (Stambaugh et al. 2001). Such a change may be a reflection of the increasing use of the Internet for financial transactions and information, as well as improved awareness of this type of crime in the general population (see Burns et al. 2004; Holt and Lampke 2010). Child pornography

Table 9.3 Types of Computer Crimes Investigated by
State and Local Agencies

	Yes	No
Identity theft (n=355)	79.2	20.8
Fraud (n=356)	71.9	28.1
Harassment (n=358)	71.8	28.2
Child porn (n=358)	61.7	38.3
Solicitation of children (n=358)	51.7	48.3
Sex crimes (n=357)	42.0	58.0
Hacking/intrusion (n=353)	32.0	68.0

Table 9.4 Number of Active Cases Involving
Digital Evidence or Computer Crime

Number of Cases	Digital Evidence		Online Crime	
	N	Percentage	N	Percentage
0 cases	67	18.7	96	27.9
1–2 cases	54	15.0	53	15.4
3–5 cases	67	18.7	48	13.9
6–19 cases	63	17.6	62	18.0
20–99 cases	49	13.7	58	16.9
100–800 cases	40	11.2	23	6.7
1000 or more cases	18	5.0	4	1.2
Total	358	100	344	100

and the solicitation of minors were also somewhat common as more than half of the responding agencies conduct such investigations. The least examined form of computer crime were hacking and computer intrusion cases. This results from both the difficulty in investigating these crimes as well as the cross-state and international dynamics of computer hacking, as offenders can reside anywhere in the country or world and victimize multiple machines in any location (see Brenner 2008; McQuade 2006; Taylor et al. 2010; Wall 2007). The jurisdictional issues that can arise make hacking investigations more likely to fall under federal law enforcement agency purview.

Respondents were also asked to identify how many cases their agency had dealt with in the last twelve months involving online crime and digital evidence to give some insight into the prevalence of these issues in state and local agencies (see Table 9.4). With regard to digital evidence, 70 percent of the agencies had nineteen or fewer cases involving digital evidence within the last twelve months. 18.7 percent had no cases within the prior year that had digital evidence. Thus, there are relatively few cases being investigated with digital evidence by these agencies among first responders in keeping with previous research. Respondents were also asked how many digital evidence cases were cleared by arrest in the past twelve months (results not shown). Of the agencies involved, 33.5 percent indicated zero arrests, while 25.9 percent said that there were one or two cases that resulted in an arrest. Only 5 percent of agencies indicated that they had made one hundred or more arrests from cases involving the handling of digital evidence. Thus, despite the use of digital forensic techniques, there appears to be a relatively small number of cases cleared by arrest at the local level.

Similar patterns were identified concerning cases involving some form of computer crime, such as computer hacking or sex offenses (see Table 9.4).

Specifically, 75.2 percent reported they had nineteen or fewer online crime cases within the previous year, more than half of the agencies (57.2 percent) had five or fewer cases, and 27.9 percent stated they had zero. The number of computer crime cases cleared by arrest was much smaller than in the digital evidence category. Most agencies (65 percent) had less than two cases cleared by arrest, which is sensible given the relative anonymity the Internet provides for offenders (see McQuade 2006; Wall 2007).

Attitudes toward Computer Crime

Respondents were also asked to indicate their level of agreement with various statements related to computer crime, including offender behaviors, victim impacts, and citizen awareness of this problem (see Table 9.5). One of the most significant points of agreement (98.1 percent) was in support of the statement, "Computer crime is a serious problem in American society." This suggests that officers recognize the seriousness of computer crime. Clearly, a part of this is due to the fact that most of them (92.8 percent) agreed with the following statement, "Computers allow individuals to feel less responsible for their actions, increasing the likelihood of crime." In addition, 82.1 percent believed that attacks on computer systems pose a threat equal to or greater than physical attacks. This indicates that law enforcement agencies are aware of the danger posed by acts of cyberterror, particularly in the post 9/11 world.

Most respondents, however, felt that individuals in their community did not recognize the risk that they face from these offenses. Only 15.1 percent agreed that, "Citizens in our community understand the risk of computer crime." This is surprising in light of the significant recognition of cybercrime as a problem among law enforcement agencies. Thus, there may be a disconnect between law enforcement and citizens' perceptions of the severity of computer crime.

A majority of the respondents (89.4 percent) also believed that budget constraints limited their ability to investigate computer crimes (see Hinduja 2004; Stambaugh et al. 2001). Coupled with their beliefs that computer crime is a serious problem, this implied that these officers believed that more funding would lead to better investigations of computer crime. Almost half of the respondents (47.9 percent), however, responded that computer crimes detract officers' attention from street crimes, possibly implying that this issue has not improved since earlier studies and commentaries (Goodman 1997; Hinduja 2004; Stambaugh et al. 2001). Thus, budget constraints might be a strong factor in why local law enforcement does not focus more on computer crimes. Also, state and local law enforcement agencies' interest in investigating these crimes may not be as strong as their belief that it is a serious problem.

Table 9.5 Officers' Reported Attitudes Toward Computer Crimes

Statement	Agree	Disagree
Computer crime is a serious problem in American society.	98.1	1.9
Computers allow individuals to feel less responsible for their actions increasing the likelihood of crime.	92.8	7.2
Budget constraints limit our ability to investigate computer crimes.	89.4	10.6
Attacks on computer systems pose a threat equal to or greater than physical attacks.	82.1	17.9
Computer crimes have a greater impact in corporate settings rather than in home settings.	69.9	30.1
The majority of computer crimes are perpetrated by individuals in their teens and twenties.	48.5	51.5
Computer crimes detract officers' attention from street crimes.	47.9	52.1
Computer criminals often reside in foreign countries rather than the US.	45.9	54.1
Computer crime occurs more frequently in businesses rather than among home users.	41.5	58.5
Convicted hackers should be allowed to work in computing jobs.	18.1	81.9
Citizens in our community understand the risk of computer crime.	15.1	84.9
Convicted hackers should be allowed to have a computer at home.	13.2	86.8

There were, however, some disagreements among the respondents as to the types of offenders who engage in computer crimes and who is more likely to be victimized. A little less than half of the respondents (45.9 percent) agreed that computer criminals often reside in foreign countries, indicating that half of the respondents believed that most of our computer crime problem is home-grown. Half of the respondents (48.5 percent) agreed that most computer criminals are in their teens and twenties. This is a shift from previous studies, which found greater support for the contention that computer criminals are older individuals (Furnell 2002; Senjo 2004). The research literature is mixed concerning these issues, as computer hackers are largely younger males (Brenner 2008; Jordan and Taylor 1998; Holt 2007), while there are few metrics on the demographic composition of pedophiles and online sex offenders (see Quayle and Taylor 2002). The relative split noted in this data may be a reflection of increasing awareness of the variation in offender characteristics. In addition, only 41.5 percent believed that businesses were more likely to be the victims of computer crime relative to home users. At the same time, almost 70 percent agreed that computer crime had a greater impact in corporate settings. Thus, the respondents believed that individuals were more likely to be victimized, but the consequences were greater for corporations (see also Furnell 2002).

Furthermore, the majority of the sample did not support the notion that convicted computer hackers should be allowed to work in computing jobs (81.9 percent) or have a computer in their homes (86.8 percent). This finding is similar to research on the general population's attitudes toward computer crime offending (see Furnell 2002). It is important to note, however, that reformed hackers play important roles in the computer security community, and can assist in the investigation of computer crimes (see Furnell 2002; Holt 2007; Taylor et al. 2010). These individuals could also facilitate training and assist state and local law enforcement in light of the dearth of officers and resources to investigate these crimes. Thus, local law enforcement agencies desire to restrict hackers' access to technology may actually be problematic given their capacity to assist policing agencies.

Perceptions of Computer Crime Offending

In order to assess how law enforcement agencies perceive computer crimes relative to terrestrial crimes, respondents were asked to rank the severity of a variety of offenses on a five-point scale from least serious (1) to most serious (5). The mean scores for each form of crime are presented in Table 9.6 and provide an interesting perspective on the perceived impact of both computer and real world crimes and the relationships between these offenses (see also Senjo 2004).

The respondents considered stealing something worth less than five dollars to be the least serious crime of the crimes examined. In fact, they considered five different types of theft—stealing something worth less than five dollars; using someone else's Internet connection; media and software piracy; and stealing something more than fifty dollars—to be the least serious crimes overall. Thus, less serious forms of crime and relatively equal, regardless of whether they based in the physical or virtual world. Purposely damaging property was considered slightly more severe than the minor forms of theft, with harassment via the Internet considered the next severe. The respondents indicated that threats, although virtual with possibly no physical contact ever between victim and offender, are still considered more serious than real world property damage.

A similar clustering of severity was noted for breaking into a vehicle or building to steal something, viewing electronic data without permission, and hitting someone without any reason. The relationship between burglary and hacking has been proposed by a variety of scholars, and the appearance of this relationship suggests law enforcement agencies may share this point of view (see Wall 2001). In addition, it appears that the respondents equated serious forms of privacy violation (e.g., having electronic data viewed and having something stolen from a vehicle or building) to be equivalent of minor forms of violence. Malicious software infections, such as the spread of viruses, however, were ranked higher than these offenses. This is sensible given that malware can be used as an attack platform for various types of hacking and theft (Bossler and Holt 2009; Brenner 2008; Taylor et al. 2010), as well as damage computer systems and networks. This finding suggests state and local law enforcement agencies recognize the severity of more significant hacker-related computer crimes.

The mean scores for electronic theft of money and the sale of hard drugs were also relatively similar. Both offenses have a significant impact, though for very different reasons. The financial impact of electronic theft for victims can be quite substantial, and are complex offenses for law enforcement agencies to investigate and clear by arrest (see Internet Crime Complaint Center 2010; Newman and Clarke 2003). Drug sales, however, have significant negative consequences for drug abusers and the larger community, including increased rates of disorder, theft, prostitution, and lethal violence (see Harocopos and Hough 2005). These issues may drive the similar perceived impact of these offenses.

Finally, officers reported the following crime types as the most severe: child pornography and sexual solicitation and physical and cyber terrorist attacks. Though there are clear and significant threats posed by virtual and real world acts of terror, it is surprising that child offenses are perceived as having greater severity than terror attacks. The significant social stigma associated with child sex offenses (see Durkin 1997; Durkin and Bryant 1999; Holt et al. 2010) may, however, account of this ranking. Specifically, child victims can be easily taken advantage of, and coerced into acts due to their innocence and naiveté (Durkin 1997; Durkin and Bryant 1999). Regardless, these findings suggest that local law enforcement agencies perceive there to be significant overlap between virtual and terrestrial crimes.

In addition, the respondents were asked to indicate the frequency with which certain computer crimes take place, ranging from never (1) to very frequently (6). The mean scores for the frequency of each offense are presented in Table 9.7. The high mean scores suggest that local agencies feel computer crimes occur with some regularity, with acts of cyber-terror performed least often (4.58). Electronic theft and viewing data without permission are also perceived to occur with some frequency, which may be a reflection of the increasing investigation of these offenses at the state and local level (see Burns et al. 2004). The perceived prevalence of harassment and malware infections may be a con-

Table 9.6 Perceived Severity of Computer Crimes

Offense Type	Mean Severity	N
Stealing something worth less than $5 dollars	2.09	357
Using someone else's wireless connection	2.92	355
Unauthorized copying of media	2.97	358
Stealing something worth more than $50	3.19	357
Unauthorized copying of software	3.26	358
Purposely damaging or destroying property	3.50	358
Harassment over the Internet	3.68	358
Breaking into a vehicle or building to steal something	3.82	357
Viewing someone else's electronic data without permission	3.85	358
Hitting someone without any reason	3.88	358
Viruses and malicious software infection	4.20	358
Electronic theft of money from accounts	4.46	357
Selling hard drugs such as heroin, cocaine, or meth	4.49	358
Terrorist attacks against electronic targets (cyberterror)	4.59	359
Terrorist attacks against physical targets	4.84	356
Child pornography and sexual solicitation	4.86	358

sequence of increasing media and research coverage which suggest these offenses are increasing yearly (see Bossler and Holt 2010; Finn 2004; Holt and Bossler 2009; Taylor et al. 2010).

Respondents ranked the most common forms of computer crime to be software and media piracy. Empirical research on digital piracy suggests this is a prevalent offense that cuts across race, age, and economic conditions (see Higgins 2005; Higgins, Fell, and Wilson 2007; Hinduja 2001, 2003; McQuade 2006; Wall 2007). Thus, state and local agencies appear to have a perspective on computer crime that conforms to the broader research literature on computer offending generally.

Respondents were also asked to assess the threat of cyberterror attacks posed by various countries on a scale from least serious (1) to most serious (5) (see Table 9.8). The countries selected for this inventory were based in part on reports from various media and research on national participation in computer crime and attacks against military and private targets (see Brenner 2008; Holt,

Table 9.7 Perceived Frequency of Computer Crimes

Offense Type	Mean Frequency	N
Terrorist attacks against electronic targets (cyber-terror)	4.58	359
Viewing someone else's electronic data without permission	4.83	359
Electronic theft of money from accounts	4.96	358
Harassment over the Internet	5.10	358
Viruses and malicious software infection	5.11	359
Child pornography and sexual solicitation	5.35	359
Unauthorized copying of software	5.38	359
Unauthorized copying of media	5.54	359

Soles, and Leslie 2008; Taylor et al. 2010). Additionally, a number of Middle Eastern nations were included as controls since they have limited participation in actual cyber-attacks, but heavy participation in e-jihad as a means of recruitment and information sharing for terror groups (see Brenner 2008; Taylor et al. 2010).

Brazil was ranked the least threatening nation overall by respondents. This could be a reflection of a lack of knowledge about the hacking landscape in Brazil, or a more general consequence of the fact that Brazilian hackers regularly target South American financial institutions and customers rather than those in other nations (Taylor et al. 2010). Egypt, Afghanistan, Romania, Japan, and Iraq were all considered moderate threats. It appears that some of the countries in this group might be viewed as threats more because of the war on terrorism and law enforcement perceptions that these countries desire to attack the United States rather than their actual ability to strike critical infrastructure.

Russia was ranked as a high threat, but placed below Iran. Russian hackers have engaged in a variety of attacks against US financial institutions and critical infrastructure (see Holt et al. 2008; Honeynet Research Alliance 2003) as well as cyber-attacks against neighboring nations, such as Estonia and Georgia (Brenner 2008; Jaffe 2006; Landler and Markoff 2008). Few, if any, attacks have been attributed to Iran. Thus, this threat ranking appears to stem from regular reports about the nuclear threat posed by Iran and its posturing toward other nations around the world. Finally, China was ranked as the highest overall threat in keeping with multiple media reports of high level intrusions by Chinese hackers into sensitive networks in governments around the world

Table 9.8 Perceived Threat of Cyberterror Attacks from Multiple Nations

Country	Mean Frequency	N
Brazil	2.91	357
Egypt	3.22	353
Afghanistan	3.33	355
Romania	3.33	357
Japan	3.36	356
Iraq	3.45	356
Russia	3.74	356
Iran	3.92	356
China	4.32	359

(Holt et al. 2008; Taylor et al. 2010). Thus, local and state law enforcement agencies appear to share some perspectives on the broader landscape of cyberthreats, but also appear to assign too high of threats to countries based more on the desire to attack the United States than their ability to complete such an intrusion.

Awareness of Technology

To gain some perspective on state and local officers' knowledge of computer technology and offending, respondents were presented with various technology-specific terms and asked to identify whether they were familiar with the term, unsure of its meaning, or had never heard it before (see Table 9.9). The findings indicate that most respondents felt that they knew the meanings of many essential terms needed to understand both basic computing software and computer crimes. A majority of the officers reported knowledge of the terms spam, firewall, spyware, and cookies. This is sensible given that these terms are commonly used with regard to the Internet and computer security as a whole (Taylor et al. 2010; Wall 2007). There was, however, less recognition for the terms Adware and podcast. Thus, state and local agencies have a grasp of the basic terms that support web browsers and Internet use.

Respondents also appeared to be familiar with most terms related to either a type of computer crime or an attack tool. For example, identity theft, virus, and cyberstalking were identified by most respondents. The reported knowledge of identity theft and cyberstalking may be related to the prevalence of investigations at the local level and in media accounts. Phishing, where criminals attempt to obtain financial information from unwitting victims via email (James

Table 9.9 Knowledge of Terms Related to Computer
Technology and Computer Crime

Term	I have a good idea what this term means	Not really sure what this term means	I have never heard this term
Identity theft	98.6	1.1	0.3
Viruses	97.7	2.3	0.0
Spam	96.6	3.4	0.0
Firewall	95.5	4.5	0.0
Spyware	93.8	5.9	0.3
Cookies	89.8	8.8	1.4
Cyberstalking	85.2	13.7	1.1
Phishing	79.3	13.1	7.7
Adware	78.3	17.7	3.9
Podcasts	65.4	28.6	5.9
Carding	18.9	44.5	36.6

2005), was identified by fewer officers (79 percent). The one item most respondents did not know was "carding," where individuals buy and sell stolen personal information for the purposes of fraud and theft (Holt and Lampke 2010; Honeynet Research Alliance 2003). This may be a consequence of the relatively recent emergence of this crime and that it is mostly investigated by federal agencies due to the international scope of these offenses. Regardless, these findings suggest that local policing officers have a strong awareness of computer crime terms and that their knowledge has increased over the last decade (Goodman 1997).

In addition, respondents appeared to have some recognition of terms related to cyber-terrorism (see Table 9.10). Many of the respondents knew the term "critical infrastructure," which is a positive finding given the prominence of this phrase in recent years related to physical terror attacks (see Taylor et al. 2010). Most respondents had also heard of the People's Liberation Army and the term "e-jihad." This is encouraging since these phrases are related to two distinct groups involvement in cyberterror. The People's Liberation Army, the name of the Chinese military, is responsible for several serious computer intrusions against Department of Defense computer networks, power grids, and other systems (Brenner 2008). E-jihad is a phrase related to the development of terror groups' usage of the internet for various activities, from recruitment

Table 9.10 Knowledge of Terms Related to Computer
Technology and Computer Crime

Term	I have a good idea what this term means	Not really sure what this term means	I have never heard this term
People's Liberation Army	78.5	17.8	3.7
Critical Infrastructure	77.3	15.3	7.4
E-jihad	70.5	20.2	9.4
Information Warfare	47.6	40.8	11.5
Firesale	34.7	43.8	21.5

to misinformation to attacks against different targets (see Brenner 2008; Taylor et al. 2010).

Knowledge of the term "information warfare" was much lower, with less than half of all respondents recognizing this word. The phrase "information warfare" is primarily used in the military community to represent any behavior involving the use of or gathering of information to gain advantage over another party (see Taylor et al. 2010). This can include acts of cyberterrorism or data theft, and comprises a significant potential overlap between law enforcement practices and military activity. The relative concentration of this term among military actors may, however, account for the lack of awareness in state and local law enforcement agencies. Finally, the term "firesale" was included as a control because it is not a phrase used in the academic or policing communities. Instead, this term is used in popular media to describe a cataclysmic series of cyberattacks. Since only 34.7 percent of respondents knew this term, it appears that the respondents have not been significantly swayed by media accounts of cyberterror attacks. Taken as a whole, the respondents appear to have some sound understanding of key phrases related to cyberterror as well as computer crime generally.

Discussion and Conclusions

Despite the increasing body of research on computer crime offending and victimization, few studies have considered the capacity of local law enforcement agencies to investigate and combat these crimes (see Burns et al. 2004; Hinduja 2004; McQuade 2006; Senjo 2004; Stambaugh et al. 2001; Taylor et al. 2010). This study attempted to address this issue through an examination of 437 state and local law enforcement agents and officers to understand their investigative capabilities and perspectives on computer crime. As a whole, the findings suggest that law enforcement agencies have shifted their investigative resources to become more actively involved in financial offenses than in the past (see Burns et al. 2004; Hinduja 2004; Senjo 2004; Stambaugh et al. 2001). While local agencies are still investigating sex offenses, there were more agencies suggesting they investigate economic-driven computer crimes. Such a finding is a positive indicator, given the tremendous economic impact of computer-based fraud for businesses and individuals alike (Internet Crime Complaint Center 2010; Newman and Clarke 2003; Wall 2007).

At the same time, the lack of agencies investigating computer hacking and intrusions is in keeping with previous research on policing (see Hinduja 2004; Stambaugh et al. 2001). This may, however, be a function of limited resources and jurisdictional issues that complicate reporting and proper exploration (Brenner 2008; Taylor et al. 2010; Wall 2007). Additionally, the relative paucity of cleared and active cases involving both computer crimes and digital evidence indicate that these offenses are relatively underexamined at the local level (see Hinduja 2004). This exploratory finding, however, demands greater research, and emphasizes the need for improved statistical reporting to better comprehend the problem of computer crime (Brenner 2008; Hinduja 2004; Holt 2003; Wall 2007).

The attitudinal results suggest that state and local law enforcement may have improved their situational awareness and preparation to deal with computer crime cases. Specifically, local agencies have an increased overall recognition of the serious threat computer crimes pose. Additionally, the mixed agreement surrounding victim impact indicates that police officers may understand that certain offenses, such as hacking or fraud, may have a greater impact for businesses, while stalking could impact individuals more heavily. Finally, the respondents' significant agreement with the need for increased funding to support the investigation suggests that there is a need for greater resource allocation to improve the local response to computer crimes (Hinduja 2004; Stambaugh et al. 2001).

The perceived severity of computer offending relative to street crimes also gives some valuable insights into the nature of computer crime investigation. The relatively low significance of minor theft and piracy suggests that these offenses may have minimal priority among law enforcement agencies. This could be a function of the lack of victims or the underreporting of these offenses, particularly piracy where there is no distinct or immediate individual affected (see Hinduja 2001). The relatively high severity of malware is also a positive finding, as malware can be used in a variety of ways by computer hackers and attackers to engage in different forms of crime (see Bossler and Holt 2009; Brenner 2008; Taylor et al. 2010). Additionally, the noted severity of both physical and computer-based terror attacks suggests that state and local agencies understand the need to reorient some of their priorities in order to act as first responders to serious incidents, particularly in the wake of the 9/11 attacks (see Brenner 2008). Finally, the extremely high placement of child pornography is in keeping with previous research (see Senjo 2004) and reflects the social concerns surrounding this type of offense (see Holt et al. 2010).

Additionally, the noted variation in knowledge of various computer technology and crime terms indicates that law enforcement officers have some awareness of the resources that undergird the Internet and web browsers. In addition, the recognition of the more prominent forms of computer crime, including spam, phishing, and cyberstalking, provides some support for an improved response to computer crime at the local level. The fact that most officers ranked Russia and China as the greatest threats toward US critical infrastructure is also instructive, as this idea has been promulgated in both research and popular media (see Brenner 2008; Denning 2001; Holt et al. 2008; McQuade 2006; Taylor et al. 2010; Wall 2007). Thus, local agencies appear to have some grounding in the threats and problems operating in virtual environments today.

Taken as a whole, this study indicates an improvement in state and local law enforcement responses and training to deal with various computer crimes. In the years following the recommendations made by the National Institute of Justice report (Stambaugh et al. 2001), it appears that there is greater recognition of the problem of computer crime among first responders. The preliminary and exploratory nature of these findings, due to the response rate, however, clearly requires replication to be verified and validated. We caution others not to make strong conclusions from our findings, but rather examine the trends found. In addition to increasing the size and representativeness of the sample, future researchers will want to compare and contrast line officers with little to no training in digital forensics and computer crime investigation with officers who have more extensive training. Finally, sampling managers within law enforcement agencies is needed to consider the acceptance and knowledge of individuals who control the economic and procedural dynamics within state and local agencies. Such research can provide critical information on the greater landscape of law enforcement and their ability to adapt and respond to the growing problem of computer crime in modern society.

References

Aeilts, Tony. 2005. Defending against cybercrime and terrorism. *FBI Law Enforcement Bulletin* 74: 14–20.

Berson, Ilene R. 2003. Grooming cybervictims: The psychosocial effects of online exploitation of youth. *Journal of School Violence* 2: 5–18.

Bossler, Adam M., and Thomas J. Holt. 2009. On-line activities, guardianship, and malware infection: An examination of routine activities theory. *International Journal of Cyber Criminology* 3: 400–420.

Brenner, Susan W. 2008. *Cyberthreats: The Emerging Fault Lines of the Nation State.* New York: Oxford University Press.

Bureau of Justice Statistics. 2007. *Census of State and Local Law Enforcement Agencies, 2004.* Washington, DC: Government Printing Office.

Burns, Ronald G., Keith H. Whitworth, and Carol Y. Thompson. (2004). Accessing law enforcement preparedness to address Internet fraud. *Journal of Criminal Justice* 32: 477–493.

Computer Security Institute. 2008. Computer Crime and Security Survey. (June 3, 2009) http://www.cybercrime.gov/FBI2008.pdf.

Denning, Dorothy E. 2001. Activism, hacktivism, and cyberterrorism: The Internet as a tool for influencing foreign policy. In *Networks and Netwars: The Future of Terror, Crime, and Militancy*, eds. John Arquilla and David F. Ronfeldt, 239–288. Santa Monica, CA: Rand.

Durkin, Keith F. 1997. Misuse of the Internet by pedophiles: Implications for law enforcement and probation practice. *Federal Probation* 61: 14–18.

Durkin, Keith F., and Clifton D. Bryant. 1999. Propagandizing pederasty: A thematic analysis of the on-line exculpatory accounts of unrepentant pedophiles. *Deviant Behavior* 20: 103–127.

Finn, Jerry. 2004. A survey of online harassment at a university campus. *Journal of Interpersonal Violence* 19: 468–483.

Furnell, Steven. 2002. *Cybercrime: Vandalizing the Information Society.* Boston: Addison-Wesley.

Goodman, Marc D. 1997. Why the police don't care about computer crime. *Harvard Journal of Law and Technology* 10: 465–494.

Harocopos, Alex, and Mike Hough. 2005. Drug dealing in open-air markets. *Problem-Oriented Guides for Police* No. 31. Washington D.C.: U.S. Department of Justice Office of Community Oriented Policing Services.

Higgins, George E. 2005. Can low self-control help with the understanding of the software piracy problem? *Deviant Behavior* 26: 1–24.

Higgins, George E., Brian D. Fell, and Abby L. Wilson. 2007. Low self-control and social learning in understanding students' intentions to pirate movies in the United States. *Social Science Computer Review* 25: 339–357.

Hinduja, Sameer. 2001. Correlates of Internet software piracy. *Journal of Contemporary Criminal Justice* 17: 369–382.

Hinduja, Sameer. 2003. Trends and patterns among software pirates. *Ethics and Information Technology* 5: 49–61.

Hinduja, Sameer 2004. Perceptions of local and state law enforcement concerning the role of computer crime investigative teams. *Policing: An International Journal of Police Strategies & Management* 27: 341–357.

Holt, Thomas J. 2003. Examining a transnational problem: An analysis of computer crime victimization in eight countries from 1999 to 2001. *International Journal of Comparative and Applied Criminal Justice* 27: 199–220.

Holt, Thomas J. 2007. Subcultural evolution? Examining the influence of on- and off-line experiences on deviant subcultures. *Deviant Behavior* 28: 171–198.

Holt, Thomas J., and Kristie R. Blevins. 2007. Examining sex work from the client's perspective: Assessing johns using online data. *Deviant Behavior* 28: 333–354.

Holt, Thomas J., Kristie R. Blevins, and Natasha Burkert. 2010. Considering the pedophile subculture on-line. *Sexual Abuse: Journal of Research and Treatment* 22: 3–24.

Holt, Thomas J., and Adam M. Bossler. 2009. Examining the applicability of lifestyle-routine activities theory for cybercrime victimization. *Deviant Behavior* 30: 1–25.

Holt, Thomas J. and Danielle C. Graves. 2007. A qualitative analysis of advanced fee fraud schemes. *The International Journal of Cyber-Criminology* 1: 137–154.

Holt, Thomas J. and Eric Lampke. 2010. Exploring stolen data markets on-line: Products and market forces. *Criminal Justice Studies* 23: 33–50.

Holt, Thomas J., Joshua B. Soles, and Lyudmila Leslie. 2008. Characterizing malware writers and computer attackers in their own words. Proceedings of the 2008 International Conference on Information Warfare and Security, Peter Kiewit Institute, University of Nebraska Omaha.

Honeynet Research Alliance. 2003. Profile: Automated Credit Card Fraud. *Know Your Enemy Paper* series. (July 20, 2008), http://www.honeynet.org/papers/profiles/cc-fraud.pdf.

Internet Crime Complaint Center. 2010. IC3 2009 Internet Crime Report. (March 24, 2010), http://www.ic3.gov/media/annualreport/2009_IC3Report.pdf.

Jaffe, Greg. 2006. Gates Urges NATO Ministers To Defend Against Cyber Attacks. *The Wall Street Journal On-line*. (June 15, 2006), http://online.wsj.com/article/SB118190166163536578.html?mod=googlenews_wsj.

James, Lance. 2005. *Phishing Exposed*. Rockland: Syngress.

Jewkes, Yvvonne, and Keith Sharp. 2003. Crime, deviance and the disembodied self: transcending the dangers of corporeality. In *Dot.cons: Crime, deviance and identity on the* Internet, ed. Yvvone Jewkes, 1–14. Portland, OR: Willan Publishing.

Jordan, Tim, and Paul Taylor. 1998. A Sociology of Hackers. *The Sociological Review* 46: 757–80.

Krejcie, Robert V. and Daryle W. Morgan. 1970. Determining sample size for research activities. *Educational and Psychological Measurement*, 30: 607–610.

Landler, Mark and John Markoff. 2008. "Digital Fears Emerge After Data Siege in Estonia," *The New York Times*, (May 24, 2007), www.nytimes.com/2007/05/29/technology/29estonia.html.

Mann, David, and Mike Sutton. 1998. Netcrime: More change in the organization of thieving. *British Journal of Criminology* 38: 201–229.

McQuade, Sam. 2006. Technology-enabled crime, policing and security. *Journal of Technology Studies* 32: 32–42.

Motion Picture Association of America. 2007. *2005 Piracy fact sheet*. (December 12, 2007). http://www.mpaa.org/researchStatistics.asp.

Newman, Grame, and Ronald Clarke. 2003. *Superhighway robbery: Preventing e-commerce crime*. Cullompton: Willan Press.

Quayle, Ethel, and Max Taylor. 2002. Child pornography and the Internet: Perpetuating a cycle of abuse. *Deviant Behavior* 23: 331–361.

Quinn, James F., and Craig J. Forsyth. 2005. Describing sexual behavior in the era of the internet: A typology for empirical research.*Deviant Behavior* 26: 191–207.

Senjo, Scott R. 2004. An analysis of computer-related crime: Comparing police officer perceptions with empirical data. *Security Journal* 17: 55–71.

Sharp, Keith, and Sarah Earle. 2003. "Cyberpunters and cyberwhores: prostitution on the Internet." In *Dot Cons. Crime, Deviance and Identity on the Internet*, ed. Yvonne Jewkes, 36–52. Portland, OR: Willan Publishing.

Soothhill, Keith, and Teela Sanders. 2005. The geographical mobility, preferences and pleasures of prolific punters: A demonstration study of the activities of prostitutes' clients. *Sociological Research On-Line* 10. (October 10, 2005). http://www.socresonline.org.uk/10/1/soothill.html.

Speer, David L. 2000. Redefining borders: The challenges of cybercrime. *Crime, Law, and Social Change* 34: 259–273.

Stambaugh, Hollis, David S. Beaupre, David J. Icove, Richard Baker, Wayne Cassady, and Wayne P. Williams. 2001. *Electronic crime needs assessment for state and local law enforcement.* Washington, DC: National Institute of Justice. NCJ 186276.

Taylor, Robert W., Eric J. Fritsch, John Liederbach, and Thomas J. Holt. 2010. *Digital Crime and Digital Terrorism, 2nd edition.* Upper Saddle River, NJ: Pearson Prentice Hall.

Wall, D. S. 2001. Cybercrimes and the Internet. pp. 1–17 in *Crime and the Internet,* edited by D. S. Wall. New York: Routledge.

Wall, David S. 2007. *Cybercrime: The transformation of crime in the information age.* Cambridge: Polity Press.

Contributors

Jessica Aldridge has an M.A. in Sociology from Western Kentucky University and is pursuing her Ph.D. in Environmental Sociology at Oklahoma State University. Her primary research interests include environmental attitudes and natural resource management.

Dr. Keith Andrew is the Director of the Cyber Defense Laboratory and a Professor and Department Head of Physics and Astronomy at Western Kentucky University.

Dr. Adam M. Bossler is an Assistant Professor of Justice Studies at Georgia Southern University. He received his Ph.D. in criminology and criminal justice from the University of Missouri—St. Louis. His research interests include testing criminological theories that have received little empirical testing, examining the application of traditional criminological theories to cybercrime offending and victimization, exploring law enforcement readiness for cybercrime, and evaluating policies and programs aimed at reducing youth violence.

Dr. Marjie T. Britz is a Professor of Criminal Justice at Clemson University. She holds a Bachelor's of Science in Forensic Science and Police Administration from Jacksonville State University, a Master's of Science and a Doctorate of Philosophy in Criminal Justice from Michigan State University. She has published in the areas of computer crime, organized crime, and the police subculture. She has acted as a consultant to a variety of organizations, and provided training to an assortment of law enforcement agencies. In addition, she has served on editorial and supervisory boards in both academic and practitioner venues. Her latest work on computer crime includes the second edition of *Computer Forensics and Cybercrime: An Introduction.* She is currently completing her latest manuscript on Italian organized crime in the United States, and continuing her research on street gangs, cybergangs, terrorism, and transnational organized crime.

Ms. Andrea Brockman is currently a doctoral candidate of Clinical Psychology with a concentration in Forensics at Nova Southeastern University. She received a dual bachelor's degree in psychology and criminal justice and a master's degree in criminal justice all of which were from Valdosta State University. Her early training began at Valdosta State Prison as a correctional counselor. Currently, she is receiving clinical training at an adolescent drug abuse and treatment program. Ms. Brockman's research interests include correctional officer stress, cybercrime, police psychology, and hostage negotiations.

Scott Cunningham is an Assistant Professor in the Department of Economics at Baylor University. His research focuses on the economics of crime and vice, specifically drug abuse, prison growth, sex and STD health outcomes, and crime.

Dr. Holli Drummond is an Assistant Professor of Sociology at Western Kentucky University. Her research interests are in the area of criminology, with emphasis on juvenile delinquency, gender and crime, and communities and crime. Her current work is focused on explaining variation by gender and race/ethnicity in the social psychological processes leading to delinquency, and how these processes are shaped by community, school, and family contexts. Dr. Drummond's research cuts across a number of disciplines (e.g., criminology, social psychology, social inequality, gender) and considers causal processes that operate on different levels of explanation.

Sarah Fitzgerald is a Masters student in the School of Criminal Justice at Michigan State University. Her research interests include terrorism, qualitative research, and on-line crime.

Dr. Thomas J. Holt (Editor) is an Assistant Professor in the School of Criminal Justice at Michigan State University specializing in computer crime, cybercrime, and technology. His research focuses on computer hacking, malware, and the role that technology and the Internet play in facilitating all manner of crime and deviance. Dr. Holt has been published in a variety of academic journals, including *Crime and Delinquency*, *Deviant Behavior* and the *Journal of Criminal Justice*, and is a coauthor of the book *Digital Crime and Digital Terror*. He is the project lead for the Spartan Devils Honeynet Project, a joint project of Michigan State University, Arizona State University, and private industry, and a member of the editorial board of the International Journal of Cyber Criminology.

Lindsay Hopper is the Research and Development Manager at Western Kentucky University's Cyber Defense Laboratory. At WKU, she has worked on numerous research projects, including active RFID tracking, non-destructive elemental analysis, network security, autonomous sensor networks, and social research of online groups. She is also a Certified Ethical Hacker. Mrs. Hopper's current research focus is on the analysis and development of network intrusion detection tools and the integration of the social sciences into WKU's network security research.

Ronald Hopper is the Operations Manager at Western Kentucky University's Cyber Defense Laboratory and Assistant Facility Security Officer for Western Kentucky University. Mr. Hopper's research interests are interdisciplinary, reaching across the fields of computer network security, sociology, anthropology, and criminal justice. At WKU, he has worked on numerous research projects, including microcultural studies in research environments, surface analysis for trace elements using XRF, settlement patterning and strategies of extinct culture groups, analysis of team dynamics in online gaming, network security, and social research of online groups. His current research focus is as the project manager for the integration of the social sciences into WKU's network security research program and the development of quantitative testing metrics for the identification of network analysts.

Dr. Wilson Huang is Professor of Criminal Justice in the Department of Sociology, Anthropology, and Criminal Justice at Valdosta State University. He received his doctoral degree in criminal justice from the University of Maryland, College Park. Dr. Huang has published refereed articles in the areas of criminal violence, sentencing, hotel crime, and more recently in cybercrime. His teaching interests include policing, comparative criminal justice, crime and technology, and program evaluations.

Todd D. Kendall has a Ph.D. and M.A. in economics from the University of Chicago specializing in industrial organization, antitrust, and applied microeconomics. Prior to joining Compass Lexecon, he was Assistant Professor of Economics at Clemson University in South Carolina. He has published in academic journals and been frequently cited in the press. Since joining Compass Lexecon, he has worked on projects involving mining and securities exchanges.

Catherine D. Marcum is an assistant professor of Justice Studies in the Political Science Department at Georgia Southern University. She has recently been published (or has articles forthcoming) in the *Deviant Behavior, Criminal Justice Studies: A Critical Journal of Crime, Law, and Society, International Journal of Cyber Criminology,* and *Journal of Child Sexual Abuse.* Her research interests include cyber criminality, adolescent victimization, sexual offending and victimization, and corrections. Please address all correspondence to: Georgia Southern University, Department of Political Science, Campus Box 8101, Statesboro, GA 30460.

Dr. Marc Rogers is the director of the Cyber Forensics Program in the Dept. of Computer and Information Technology at Purdue University. He is a Professor, University Faculty Scholar and Fellow—Center for Education and Research in Information Assurance and Security (CERIAS). Dr. Rogers is the International Chair of the Law, Compliance and Investigation Domain of the Common Body of Knowledge (CBK) committee, Chair of the Ethics Committee for the Digital and Multimedia Sciences section of the American Academy of Forensic Sciences, and Chair of the Certification and Test Committee—Digital Forensics Certification Board. He is the Editor-in-Chief of the Journal of Digital Forensic Practice and sits on the editorial board for several other professional journals. He is also a member of other various national and international committees focusing on digital forensic science and digital evidence. Dr. Rogers is the author of books, book chapters, and journal publications in the field of digital forensics and applied psychological analysis. His research interests include applied cyber forensics, psychological digital crime scene analysis, and cyber terrorism. Cybercrime Scene Analysis, and Cyber-terrorism. He has authored several book chapters, and articles in the area of computer forensics and forensic psychology.

Kathryn C. Seigfried-Spellar, M.A. is a doctoral student in the Department of Computer and Information Technology at Purdue University. Her research interests include computer forensics, child pornography, pedophilia, and cybercrime profiling.

Dr. Paul Taylor is senior lecturer in the Institute of Communications Studies, University of Leeds, UK. His research interests include digital culture and themes of dis-empowerment; critical theories of mass media culture—in particular, the works of Theodor Adorno and Siegfried Kracauer, Leo Lowenthal, Jean Baudrillard; and psychoanalytically-influenced media theory—including the work of Friederich Kittler and Slavoj Zizek. He is the founder-editor of the peer-reviewed, *International Journal of Zizek Studies*. He has authored and co-authored numerous books and refereed articles on critical theory including *Critical Theories of Mass Media: Then and Now* and *Digital Matters: Theory and Culture of the Matrix*. Contact: p.a.taylor@leeds.ac.uk

Cassie Wade is a research associate at Western Kentucky University's Cyber Defense Laboratory. Ms. Wade's research interests are interdisciplinary, reaching across the fields of computer network security, sociology, and criminal justice. Her current research focus is on the development of quantitative testing metrics for the identification of network analysts.

Index